Reporting with Understanding

Reporting with

GARY ATKINS

Understanding

WILLIAM RIVERS

 The Iowa State University Press / Ames

GARY ATKINS is an Associate Professor of Journalism at Seattle University, Seattle, Washington. A former reporter for the *Press-Enterprise* of Riverside, California, he has published numerous freelance stories and magazine articles. Journalistic objectivity and values are his research interests.

WILLIAM RIVERS is the Paul C. Edwards Professor of Communication at Stanford University, Stanford, California. He is the author or co-author of more than thirty books, among them *Free-lancer and Staff Writer, News in Print, Responsibility in Mass Communication,* and *Free but Regulated* (Iowa State University Press).

©1987 The Iowa State University Press, Ames, Iowa 50010. All rights reserved

Roger Ricklefs, "Leaders Are A Sadder Group," which appears in Chapter 4, is reprinted by permission of *The Wall Street Journal,* ©Dow Jones and Company, Inc., 1983. All Rights Reserved.

Max Frankel's letter of 29 Oct. 1972 to David Thiemann, which appears in Chapter 5, has been reprinted by permission of the author.

The newspaper articles on pages 88–89 and 155–56 have been reprinted by permission of the *Riverside Press-Enterprise*.

Clark Mollenhoff and John Siegenthaler, "Check List for an Investigative Reporter," which appears in Chapter 6, has been reprinted by permission of the author.

Composed by the Iowa State University Press
Printed in the United States of America

FIRST EDITION, 1987

Library of Congress Cataloging-in-Publication Data

Atkins, Gary L., 1949–
    Reporting with understanding

    Includes index.
    1. Reporters and reporting.   I. Rivers, William L.
II. Title.
PN4781.A767   1987   070.4'3   86–22808
ISBN 0–8138–1517–7

Contents

IT IS EASY TO BELIEVE that teaching journalism students how to report was once much less difficult. Cultural eons ago—say, about the 1950s—the profession itself appeared much more homogenous. Journalistic objectivity in building sources and collecting information was not nearly as questioned, or as subject to sociological analysis, as it seems to be now. Spot news, rather than complicated economic processes, reigned supreme on the front pages. The key "beats" were politics, the courts, and the police. Period. Religion and business were off in a corner; women were ensconced on society pages; minorities were unheard of; environmental and energy concerns did not exist. The inverted pyramid style of writing, with its straightforward news summary lead, commanded an almost moral allegiance. Interviewing was *the* taken-for-granted method of collecting information. Certainly no one in the newsroom talked much about multiple regression analysis, or about tracking corporate chicanery through 10-K's.

Journalism students being educated today will carry the profession into the twenty-first century and into times when the historic mission of journalism—to inform and enlighten citizens, enabling more effective participation in their own governance—will assume a global nature. Increasingly the journalist's mission will include helping all of us to understand and accept our diversity. The challenge to students, and certainly to their teachers, will be to evolve both the correct *methods* and the proper *specialties* to succeed in this mission. Such a task is not simple, nor will it be quickly mastered. Through this book, we hope to make at least a small contribution to the process.

We do not here explore philosophical or sociological considerations about what methods or specialties might be appropriate to the profession of journalism as it moves toward its two-hundredth year of existence. Excellent work and criticism in this area has been offered in the past decade by such thinkers in the area of sociology of knowledge as Todd Gitlin, Herbert Gans, and Gaye Tuchman, as well as from Paulo Freire on the Third World viewpoint of the need for a more "thematic" journalism.

Preface

Certainly their perceptions will become part of the evolution of journalistic methods. So, too, will the reflections of such scholars as Michael Schudson, whose historical work on the rise of the notion of journalistic objectivity and the definition of news is invaluable for understanding how reporters traditionally have seen their world and their role.

This is a book about practice. We have relied upon the wisdom of practitioners of journalism, those who through experience are discovering methods of improving their work, and we have assembled what they have to say about the methods they use and the specialties being created. That is not to say that practice is cut off from reflection; indeed, the movement toward reporting methods such as precision journalism or analysis of paper trails, and the redefinition of specialties such as business or religion, are examples of practitioners responding to reflections — others' or their own. The real key to reporting with understanding is this blend of practice and reflection upon practice.

This book is organized in two major sections. The first looks at methods of gathering and presenting information that are common to all journalists. These include building sources, managing interviews, following paper trails, conducting observations and investigations, and using social science methods of surveying and analysis. The second section looks at various specialties, which are themselves the ways in which journalists "organize" the world in order to report upon it. Some of the specialties we consider are traditional ones such as politics and law enforcement. Some are longtime beats that have taken on new importance and have been redefined in the past decade, such as business and religion. Others, such as minority affairs and the environment, are relatively new to journalism, having evolved primarily in the past twenty years. Several other specialties could have been included, and perhaps they will be in the future.

For the assistance we have received from our colleagues in the preparation of this text, we are grateful.

Gathering

PART I

Information:
METHODS OF THE TRADE

1 *Cultivating Sources*

The first essence of journalism is to know what you want to know; the second is to find out who will tell you.

— JOHN GUNTHER

PEOPLE KNOW WHAT'S HAPPENING.

No other words better explain why journalists need, even crave, sources. No word quite describes the nakedness of a journalist who, story assignment in hand and deadline forty-eight hours away, arrives unannounced, maybe unwanted, and undeniably sourceless in an unfamiliar town.

People know what's happening.

The journalist's job is to find those people who can provide the most truthful account of what is happening. That may be one person; more likely it will be several, each with a particular perspective and each with a fragment of the whole picture. Without sources, journalists can be too easily limited to reporting whatever information happens to come their way courtesy of press releases, news conferences, and willing — but possibly deceptive — interviewees.

Like winning friends and influencing people, there is no surefire recipe for developing sources — whatever some may claim. The successful cultivation of sources is one-third mystery, one-third grace, and one-third hard work. The work is up to the individual reporter; the other two-thirds come as and when they will, and often the most the reporter can do is simply be alert enough to recognize that the drunk on the phone complaining about the mayor's latest trip may well be the city auditor.

Or he may be just a drunk.

It is easiest to write a recipe for discouraging sources. Be rude to people. Act as if only you know what is newsworthy. Ignore secretaries. Demean janitors. Hold conferences only with corporation presidents. Refuse phone calls. Protect your privacy by turning down bylines. Most importantly, work only nine to five.

Encouraging sources is harder. They must be cultivated and even nurtured, rather like gardens. Leave them to dry in a hot sun and they wilt. Norm Udevitz, a reporter on the *Denver Post,* puts it this way: "You have to establish a temporary, but wild, passionate relationship with your source. You've got to gain his confidence."

A "source" in this context, it should be remembered, is somewhat different from an "interviewee." Anyone can be an interviewee. The director of a government agency who is interviewed by a journalist is a source only in the broadest sense. The same director becomes a source in the sense most professional journalists use when he or she starts providing tips about where to look for interesting stories or begins relating "inside" information about the organization or its personnel. Paul Williams, in his book *Investigative Reporting and Editing,* even distinguishes between the source—an expert who has been carefully cultivated and who can usually be trusted to provide accurate information—and the tipster, who more resembles that phantom of Hollywood imagination, phoning at midnight to demand urgent rendezvous in smoke-stained bars.

The best way to develop sources is often to just begin writing—and be sure to get a byline.

> Writers seldom choose as friends those self-contained characters who are never in trouble, never unhappy or ill, never make mistakes, and always count their change when it is handed to them.
> —CATHERINE DRINKER BOWEN

Your first stories may have to be simple ones; you do not have sources yet. A reporter new on the energy beat might, for example, just pick up a copy of the local utility's annual report (on file with the federal government—see the chapter on "The Paper Trail") and write a story on "Who Owns Your Electricity Company." He might profile a director or two. Likely as not, the reporter will start getting phone calls. The important thing is that the story must carry your byline. That way, the potential sources who are familiar with the subject will know who to contact.

Just as importantly, the story should be fair and objective. Some reporters, especially beginning ones, figure on writing their Pulitzer Prize–winning piece the first time they leave the office. Some expect to write only Pulitzer pieces. Some want to write only investigative pieces. Some want always to ride the White Horse. But that does not work.

Especially when you are just beginning on a new beat or a new subject, you will not want to be perceived either as a mouthpiece or as an implacable foe. Cultivate sources on both sides of the fence, if you can.

Another tactic for developing sources, especially in large organizations, is to look for those people—janitors, secretaries, middle-level bureaucrats—who have a reason to be dissatisfied or who are idealistic about what their organization should be doing (and therefore probably a bit disappointed). "In every agency," Dick Cady of the *Indianapolis Star* once said, "there are people who are frustrated, angry, for whatever reasons. It could be because they didn't get promoted or because they're simply idealists. It could be strictly blatant politics. But they're there—lots of them."

Gerry O'Neill, who has worked on the *Boston Globe*'s investigative Spotlight team, also points out that "civil servants are very prone to flattery because they don't get much of it. They feel they have a thankless, underpaid job. If you're solicitous without being unctuous, I think that can work well. We send birthday cards, which is kind of obnoxious, but it works."

Obnoxious or not, birthday cards are an example of another important consideration in developing sources: treat people like people, not like objects. Every seemingly monolithic government agency or corporation is composed of human beings. Talk to them about their children. The latest election. The weekend football game. The wearying task of dealing with the public. Do it not just to manipulate them; they will see through that very easily. Do it because you really care. One of your responsibilities as a journalist in a democratic society is to help individuals have access to the media, not to prance as if you were a godlike professional. Do it because you are human and they are human.

After all, if you were not interested in human beings, you would not be in journalism in the first place.

Finding sources often requires initiative and a willingness to pound both the streets and the doors.

Let me tell you the secret that has led me to my goal. My strength lies solely in my tenacity.

—LOUIS PASTEUR

To cultivate sources, you have to get out of your office. It is hard to find new sources in a newsroom. Robert Jackson of the *Los Angeles*

Times notes, "We have a national editor whose favorite expression is 'goyakod.' The word is an acronym around our bureau for 'Go out, you all, and knock on doors.' The more you do that, the more you think you ought to throw away your telephone. There are many times when you say, 'Should I go see a guy'–maybe it's in another city–'should I just surprise him and go see him or should I take the easy way out and just call him on the phone.' And I think, without fail, every time that I have bestirred myself to go somewhere and see a guy, I have found the effort extremely worthwhile. You get much more out of somebody by seeing them in person. I kick myself every time I do it. I kick myself for the times I've given in out of weakness and simply called somebody on the phone."

Few newspapers have the resources of the *Los Angeles Times,* of course, and few reporters have the luxury of time to "goyakod" always. But the principle is good, nevertheless. Whenever possible, get out of the office; go in person. Your chances of turning an interviewee into a source or of finding an entirely new source–who may simply be inspired to call you because you walked by–will be immeasurably improved.

The principle applies to student reporters as well. Often students have to be prodded out of the safe haven of the campus newspaper office, with its refrigerator, rock posters, and stereo, to actually "goyakod."

The newsroom should not be totally overlooked, though. Most particularly, the older reporters should be tapped as potential in-house sources. Some of them may be able to help you understand formal organizational charts by telling you about the informal power structures behind those charts. When you drop cold into an unfamiliar town, state, or beat, sometimes nothing is more comforting than discovering an old-time reporter who has been diligently covering the Klickitat County Council for twenty-seven years.

It is also useful to decide where you need sources–in what office or in what area of expertise–and then to deliberately set out to cultivate the people who hold particular titles. Study those organizational charts. Try to learn the informal power structures, especially the "alliances" among certain government officials or certain businessmen. Start a note card file on individuals and see how many of them turn up to be members of the same club. Then join it yourself, or at least get to know the desk clerk.

When you need experts, check with trade associations or universities. Photocopy the list of associations from the Washington, D.C., phone book; you will find an association for almost every special interest you can think of. (Always be aware, of course, that they do have their *special interest.*)

In *Poison Penmanship,* muckraker Jessica Mitford tells of seeking out Dr. Sheldon Margen, chairman of the Department of Nutritional Sciences at the University of California, to help her decipher reports on medical experiments in that state's prisons. Margen not only helped her translate the reports, pointing out that the procedures followed by the state corrections department would never be allowed on student subjects, but he also kept exploding furiously, "God, that kills me!" "Wow!" He made good copy as well as provided an essential service.

"Rather than trying to unravel some tricky point of law yourself, ask a lawyer," Mitford writes. "If you need to understand corporate records, get an accountant to help. Technical literature in most fields is written (no doubt deliberately) so as to be unintelligible to the layman, and there is grave danger that in trying to decipher it without expert help, you will make some ghastly mistake upon which the professionals will gleefully leap once your piece is published."

University students have especially good opportunities to cultivate authoritative sources: their own professors. Do not graduate without getting to know that accounting instructor. Or the internationally known expert on government financing. Or the political science professor who knows about professional polling methods and can help you detect holes in Senator Hiram Bagpipe's latest survey. Or the chemist who can analyze water quality for stories about pollution or toxic waste.

To summarize:

- Write about the subject, fairly and objectively.
- Talk to more than just the people at the top.
- Treat humans like humans. Be pleasant and courteous and interested in them.
- Seek out dissidents and idealists.
- Get out of the office, but don't ignore the potential sources three desks away.
- Cultivate outside experts.
- Study those formal organizational charts and learn the informal power structures behind them, then target your energy to certain areas.
- Be aware when you are cultivating and when you are wasting time.
- Be careful in smoky bars. But go.

Always evaluate the information provided by sources very carefully, with an eye to the sources' motives.

> An open foe may prove a curse, but a
> pretended friend is worse.
>
> —JOHN GAY

Any reporter who relies on sources would do well to always remember the story of Dr. Josef Gregor and his cockroach pills.

Dr. Gregor, whose Ph.D. came from an unidentified South American university, formed a New York group called Metamorphosis in spring 1981, and, to quote the *Chicago Tribune,* soon had seventy persons "madly chowing down 'cockroach pills' " to help them get rid of acne, anemia, and even the misery of nuclear fallout. When Dr. Gregor called a press conference, United Press International covered it, quoted people who supposedly had been taking the pills for a year and moved the story over the wires. About 175 newspapers across the country printed the story, including respected ones such as the *Philadelphia Inquirer,* the *Washington Star,* and the *Dallas Times Herald.*

Dr. Gregor turned out to be a journalism teacher at New York's School of Visual Arts, who had been telling his students that the media could be easily duped. With his class's help, he staged an event to prove it. The whole story had been modeled after Franz Kafka's famous story in which Gregor Samsa awakens one morning to discover that he has become a giant cockroachlike creature.

How do you know that what you are being told is true? If a willing interviewee such as "Dr. Gregor" can dupe the press so easily, how much easier is it for the source, especially the unnamed source, to mislead you?

The only real answer is that a reporter is always taking a gamble. But, as the reporter and the writer, you can choose how you stack the odds. You can work as if you are sleepwalking, never bothering to verify people's credentials, never bothering to ask yourself how reasonable the information is, always putting the "facts" in through your ears and out through your fingers with a minimum of evaluation in between . . . *or* you can do your own homework. You can become familiar with the subject you are covering. You can check credentials. You can demand verification from your source. You can seek independent evaluations from contacts *not* provided by your source. (Dr. Gregor provided many, many students for reporters to talk to—all of them in on the trick.) You can be alert for inconsistencies. You can watch for clues. (Gregor—Metamorphosis—Cockroaches.)

A survey of members of the Investigative Reporters and Editors Association, asking how professionals evaluate information from sources, produced these guidelines:

- How reliable and accurate is the source over a period of time?
- What is the source's motive in disclosing the information?
- What is the status or position of the source?
- What is the appearance of the information on its face?

Naturally, a journalist will place more trust in a source who has been known for many years and who has never misled than in someone who arrives off the street. Similarly, a reporter will listen more attentively to a bank vice-president discussing a possible bank closure than to a janitor—unless, of course, that janitor can offer as verification some photocopied memos about the possible closure that were dropped in a trash can.

Asking—or guessing—the source's motive for releasing the information can be revealing. Some may act from selfishness; some may set a reporter on a different trail of questioning just to protect themselves; some may be entirely selfless. Dick Lyneis, who investigated organized crime for the *Riverside* (Calif.) *Press-Enterprise,* points out, for example, that he has gotten many tips from federal investigators who simply do not have the time to track down every lead about corruption they come across. Some are happy to share with reporters.

But, Lyneis also notes, others can be self-interested. "If they're talking to me, there's something in it for them as well as for me. I try to say as little and hear as much as I can."

Just because your information may come from a self-interested source is no reason to disregard it, though. Most reporters try to judge the information on its own merits—and on its own reasonableness—rather than on the motives of the person who is giving it to them.

Most important, you should never forget that your own motive is to convey a truthful account.

*Be aware of the different types of sources
you will use. Always protect those to whom
you promise confidentiality, but do not
promise lightly.*

> Government differs from other ships in
> leaking most at the top.
> —ARTHUR SCHLESINGER, JR.

Sources fall into three categories: those that can be named, those that could be named but really do not need to be, and those that must not be named. Dr. Margen, to whom Jessica Mitford turned for help on her prison story, is an example of the first kind. Margen not only translated the medical gibberish for Mitford but also did not mind being quoted. Had he not been as colorful to quote, he might well have been the second kind of source, one who *could* be named but does not play an essential enough role that he *has* to be named. Mitford could simply have attributed her translation of the medical jargon to a University of California professor.

Had Margen provided the translation but insisted upon not being identified (say he was a medical doctor working for the California prison system rather than a university professor), then he would have been the third kind of source: the confidential one. That would have been especially true had he been a medical doctor on the inside of the prison system who was slipping records to Mitford. His identity would have to be protected, perhaps all the way to the jailhouse door—and through it, too.

As of now, journalists have no absolute legal right to keep the names of their sources confidential. In 1972, the U.S. Supreme Court ruled against journalists' arguments that the First Amendment protection of a free press includes within it a right to gather information and, thus, a right to protect the confidential sources who provide vital information. The 1972 cases (*Branzburg v. Hayes,* together with *In re Pappas* and *United States v. Caldwell*) focused on the question of whether reporters could be required to reveal the names of confidential sources before grand juries investigating crimes. In his opinion for the Court, Justice Byron White wrote:

> . . . The great weight of authority is that newsmen are not exempt
> from the normal duty of appearing before a grand jury and answering
> questions relevant to a criminal investigation. . . . We cannot seriously
> entertain the notion that the First Amendment protects a newsman's
> agreement to conceal the criminal conduct of his source, or evidence
> thereof, on the theory that it is better to write about crime than to do
> something about it.

In the same opinion, though, White as much as invited the legislatures and Congress to pass "shield laws" giving newsmen the right to protect their sources. He even invited state courts to find within state constitutions such protection:

> At the federal level, Congress has freedom to determine whether a statutory newsman's privilege is necessary and desirable. . . . There is also merit in leaving state legislatures free, within First Amendment limits, to fashion their own standards in light of the conditions and problems with respect to the relations between law enforcement officers and press in their own areas. It goes without saying, of course, that we are powerless to bar state courts from responding in their own way and construing their own constitutions so as to recognize a newsman's privilege, either qualified or absolute.

Justice Potter Stewart, in a dissenting opinion in the same case, set forth a three-pronged test that has often been used to determine whether journalists should reveal their sources. Stewart proposed that the government should have to demonstrate in court that (1) there is probable cause to believe that the journalist has information clearly relevant to a criminal case; (2) alternative means of getting the information in ways that would be less destructive of the First Amendment do not exist; and (3) there is a "compelling and overriding interest" in having the information. Despite being a dissent, Stewart's test has often been used in federal and state courts that recognize a limited privilege allowing reporters to withhold the names of their sources.

In addition, a number of states have passed shield laws. However, such laws can be ignored by courts when they conflict with the *constitutional* rights of defendants in criminal cases. For example, after a series of articles in the *New York Times* led to a murder indictment against a physician, the doctor's attorneys subpoenaed reporter Myron Farber and his notes on interviews. Though Farber was covered by a New Jersey shield law, the court ruled that the physician had the constitutional right to have compulsory process for obtaining witnesses, and so the shield law had to yield.

The shield laws also vary from state to state, providing different degrees of protection. A reporter is well-advised to be familiar with the law of the state in which he or she is practicing.

Good reporters have always clarified – beforehand – the amount of protection sources expect in exchange for the information they have to give. The old rules of thumb still hold:

Off the record: The information is to be held in complete confidence and is not to be printed in any form. Nor is it to be passed along to other reporters. Some reporters also interpret it to mean that the reporter cannot use the information in any way at all, such as in phrasing a question to be put to another person. That is why many journalists will not agree to hear any information that is "off the record," since it does them absolutely no good to hear it. It may satisfy their curiosity, but it does not help the journalist's readers at all.

Not for attribution: The information is not to be attributed to a specific source but can be attributed to one identified generally, say as a "White House source" or "City Hall source." From time to time, great debates rage among journalists about whether such "not for attribution" information should be used. Those on the pro side argue that much essential information would not be published otherwise, and those on the con side contend that too often the practice allows sources to manipulate the media. Sometimes, beginning reporters—and even experienced reporters who feel they cannot be "stars" unless they, too, have their mysterious unnamed sources—do abuse the "not-for-attribution" protection, either by failing to name sources who could be named or by failing to try to persuade a reluctant source to allow his or her identity to be published. The best guideline: always identify your source when you can.

Background only: The information can be used only by the writer on his or her own authority and not attributed at all, not even to a "reliable source." Instead, the journalist must present the information as if it had been gathered from original research.

(Reporters should note that often the sources will not automatically understand the differences in these categories, so if a source offers to say something "off the record," the reporter is well advised to immediately clarify what the person means. The source may only mean that the information is not to be attributed to him by name.)

To these long-standing rules of thumb, a few new wrinkles have been added in past years, largely thanks to aggressive libel attorneys and local judges who have no particular interest in defending the First Amendment. Does the source mind if his name is revealed to the editors? Do the editors demand to know the name—or at least the identity—of the source? Can the name or identity be revealed if demanded by a grand jury or a judge? Is the name to be kept confidential even if the reporter has to go to jail? What if someone comes forward, says she is your source and a judge orders you to confirm it? In these days when more and more county prosecutors are happy to let reporters do their investigative legwork—and then subpoena them—it is in reporters' own interests to be absolutely clear about what level of confidentiality has to be maintained—and for how long. (Are you free to reveal the source's name if he or she dies?) The days of casually agreeing to assure confidentiality—if they ever existed—are certainly over.

Some newspapers, such as the *Bergen Record* in New Jersey, have had their anonymous sources in sensitive stories swear out written statements that are signed before a notary public (who, presumably, also agrees to maintain the confidential agreement). In the statements, the anonymous source (say, a state-employed maintenance man who has been spending his working time improving a supervisor's residence) gives his information and agrees to a critical qualification on confidentiality:

"I understand that the information I have given to reporter——may be used in a news story in the *Record* and that my name will not be used in that story. However, both——and the *Record* have my permission to disclose my name as a source if court action develops after publication of the story, such as a libel suit or criminal proceedings. I am also willing to testify as to my first-hand observations."

Such a written agreement emphasizes the degree of seriousness with which the granting of confidentiality and the giving of confidential information or sensitive information is to be approached.

If you are going to use unnamed sources, remember to keep them unnamed—not only in the story but around the office, at home, and at the restaurant, too. You create a dangerous charade if you keep your source's name from your readers but spread it all over your own office.

During the Arizona Project, in which journalists from newspapers across the country joined together to ferret out corruption in Arizona, maintenance of confidentiality was a top priority. Jack Driscoll, a member of the team, recalls, "We numbered each source in our memos [to each other] so that we never used the name of a confidential source. For instance, if Norm [Udevitz, another team member] had five sources, he might use "U" (for his last name)—1. And he would know who "U-1" is. And Bob Greene [the team leader] knew the name of the sources, so that only two persons knew. I could read memos and not know—even though I was in the operation—who they were talking about."

The Arizona Project reporters were careful off-duty too. Team member Dick Lyneis said, "One of the things that made us all really paranoid . . . was the number of beautiful girls around the cocktail lounge. They were really friendly. I'm sure it wasn't because any of us were particularly attractive. They were trying to monitor what we were doing."

Few reporters will be involved in investigations quite so cloak-and-dagger, but even on the smallest weekly or daily, be it in Lewiston, Idaho, or Brawley, California, confidential is confidential. Unnamed is unnamed.

If you want sources to keep talking and to keep telling you what is happening, you will remember that.

EXERCISES

1. One way a reporter new to a beat or a story builds sources is by discovering who performs—or is supposed to perform—certain types of work. Practice by

dissecting the bureaucracy closest to you: your own university. First, create a formal organizational chart showing all key officials from the board of directors down to the deans and department heads, along with the key decision-making committees. Next, add in the names of the middle-level bureaucrats: the assistant admissions officers and assistant coaches and grant writers. You should to able to get most of the information from a campus telephone directory; if the university is a particularly large one, you many want to limit the scope of your study to just the top layers of administration. Finally, add in the names of key secretaries.

If you do not understand the function of any of the university branches, conduct a quick telephone interview with the head of the office or her secretary.

Once you have the chart, put it to use on actual stories for the student newspaper. You should now be able to seek information from more than just the obvious source. For example:

a. Who might you contact to find out about the effects of a new academic grievance policy that lets students appeal grades?
b. Who might you call to find out about the discussions in the last board of directors meeting?
c. Who might slip you the minutes from that directors' meeting?
d. Who might tell you why certain business executives were appointed to the board of regents?
e. Who could tell you how much the university president spent on travel last year? And where he or she went?
f. Who might tell you which faculty members have tenure and which do not?
g. Who would know early whether tuition is going to increase next year? (Don't look just to the top university officials; how about the people who have to send next year's catalog to the printer several months in advance? At one university, that is how the student reporters discovered what the raises were going to be.)
h. Who would know whether your school has been lowering its admission standards? Who knows what the average test scores of entering students are?
i. Who can tell you how well the school's portfolio of stocks is doing? And what stocks the university has?
j. Who will offer insights about how well respected in the community your university's law school or business school really is?
k. Who will be able to signal a shift in the fine arts department's role on campus, from training professional artists to servicing humanities students with history-of-art courses?
l. Who might confirm for you that the newest building on campus, named for Harvey Philanthropist and built by Harvey Philanthropist's son, was shoddily constructed? (Think about the janitors who clean the building and the campus clean-up crew that responds whenever it leaks.)

2. Take apart your local city or county government and/or your local business community in the same fashion as exercise 1. Consider adding a chart on any "informal power networks" that you find among city officials and business executives. Which people belong to the same clubs? Eat lunch at the same downtown restaurant? Contribute to each other's campaigns? Sit on the same university board of regents (yours?)?

Limit your work and consider doing it as a weeklong class project. Then put together a story about "Who Runs Pleasantville's Government," "Who Runs Pleasantville's Business," or even "Who Runs Pleasantville." The results should be enlightening—and should tell you much about who has access to different types of information.

3. Clip three newspaper stories in which the reporter has used unnamed sources. Were the sources left anonymous out of convenience or necessity? If necessity, why do you think the source asked for confidentiality? Would you have granted confidentiality for the type or quality of information given? Would the story seem more believable if names and identities were included? If you were the reporter, and a judge ordered you to reveal the name of the source, would you go to jail to protect this source? In a class discussion or a short paper, explain your answers.

4. A U.S. attorney calls to tip you off to a series of federal drug raids that are about to occur and provides you with some fragmentary information about the raids and the suspects. He also insists that the information be "for background use only."

Once the defendants get to trial, they demand to know where you got your information, which concerned their past criminal records and their associations with each other. They contend that the information, which you included in your story about the raids, helped create an atmosphere in which they would be found guilty. To show that the government intentionally leaked the information to help its prosecution case, they subpoena several reporters, including you, asking for the names of those who gave the confidential information.

You refuse to disclose your source. Are you justified in doing so? Why? Why not?

After two days of adamantly refusing to disclose your source, the U.S. attorney is called to the stand. He admits he was the source. You are recalled to confirm his statement. Should you confirm it? (Suppose a person who was *not* your source said she was. Would you confirm or deny that?)

Write a short paper explaining why you would or would not confirm that the U.S. attorney is the source.

5. You write a story about a district court judge, quoting sources who say the judge has used her office to benefit herself and certain lawyers. The story sparks an investigation by the state judicial ethics commission, which interviews sixty people, including you. The commission agrees to let the judge question ten of the witnesses, including you. You answer questions about your own observations in the courtroom and about the conversations you reported in your story, but you refuse to reveal your confidential sources. You do concede that all of them are on the commission's list of sixty witnesses.

A state Supreme Court justice orders you to reveal their names. Do you? Write a short paper explaining your decision.

6. The local police chief reports that he was handcuffed by two assailants outside the home of a local resident and then shot. You publish several articles about the incident, including one saying that the state police department has dropped its investigation because the police chief flunked parts of a lie detector test about the assault. Confidential sources have told you that.

The police chief then sues for libel, claiming he did not fail the test, and he demands that you provide the names of your confidential sources. You refuse but offer to prove that the information is true. The trial court refuses your offer and orders you to reveal the sources.

Write a short paper explaining why you will or will not.

2 Managing Interviews and Observations

> Nobody holds a good opinion of a
> man who has a low opinion of himself.
>
> —ANTHONY TROLLOPE

IF YOU HAD PRACTICED JOURNALISM three centuries ago in England, you would have been a regular visitor to the coffeehouses that served as a public information network. Public coffeehouses were places where even lower-middle-class citizens could mingle with the "higher ups" and express their opinions. Articles printed in periodicals such as *The Tatler, The Spectator,* and *The Guardian* often grew from discussions initiated among those who gathered at the coffeehouses. Journalists who were there to ask questions and record the answers in their notebooks left a coffeehouse with something called interviews.

Although today's interviews are different from those of three centuries ago, most advanced students and practiced journalists agree on certain principles.

Prepare for the interview by researching the subject, formulating questions, and readying yourself psychologically.

> In plucking the fruit of memory,
> one runs the risk of spoiling its bloom.
>
> —JOSEPH CONRAD

Journalists who plan to conduct an interview for a profile or for general information should learn as much as they can before the interview—especially if they suspect that the subject will give evasive answers. Some prize-winning reporters make it a practice to list all their questions before the interview; any veteran reporter will have at least two

16

or three questions noted down. Preparation extends even to your own mental readiness. Decribing how he primes himself before an interview, Richard Meryman writes:

> I keep telling myself that the perfect interview is a perfect set of questions. I don't touch any alcohol at all for about three days before an interview. I try to get a great deal of sleep. I don't eat starch or sugar. I spend the whole day or at least half the day before in bed. I eat steak for breakfast. Basically, I'm clearing my mind, getting my reflexes and attention as high as I can get them.

Careful preparation will make the job of recording answers easier. Whether you bring pencil and notebook or a tape recorder to the interview, your ability to fit responses into their larger context, to structure the interview with selected questions, and to quickly comprehend new or subtle directions in the subject's answers will help you remember (and later recreate) the events of the interview.

Maintain a professional demeanor in both your physical appearance and the way that you ask questions and respond to the answers.

The temptation of advising politicians
plays powerfully on a writer's ego.
                    —SANDY GRADY

All journalists know they must be prompt, courteous, and careful about good grooming. When phrasing your questions, be both pleasant and professional; never adopt an apologetic tone. Good reporters are careful not to respond strongly to answers, whether they feel surprise or shock, boredom, or disapproval. By remaining calm and objective, you will avoid distortions in both the interviewee's subsequent responses and your own reporting of the conversation.

In particular, reporters know they must not give advice to their subjects. Public officials faced with knotty questions may look to the journalists for subtle cues as to which way they should go. Your attitude should be, in essence: "This is your question; my task is to report."

Ask simple questions using positive words and conversational tactics that encourage discussion.

> He who, when called upon to speak a disagreeable truth, tells it boldly and has done is both bolder and milder than he who nibbles in a low voice and never ceases nibbling.
>
> —JOHANN KASPAR LAVATER

Reporters gain advantages in an interview when they speak distinctly and ask questions that require one answer. Using positive rather than negative wording will lend an aggressive directness to your questions. For instance, the question "You wouldn't know who did that, would you?" is much more demanding when rephrased as "You probably know who did that, don't you?"

It never hurts to repeat a question when you are not certain of the answer. For example, a journalist might say, "Let me be sure of this answer; I want to know. . . ." Reporters often get clearer or more complete answers when they respond to an answer with the simple question, "Why?" This tactic usually ensures a detailed response of more than a few words.

Always welcome interruptions in interviews; they give you time to review the subject's answers and to crystallize your remaining questions. To accommodate such natural digressions, try to conduct interviews that are halfway between a monologue and a dialogue. If the subject dominates the interview with a long, unfocused speech, all the necessary points are unlikely to be covered. On the other hand, interviewers who intrude too often, acting as equal partners, will come across as showing off and risk offending the interviewees. By asking complete questions and commenting appropriately—and briefly—on the answers, reporters can show that they are knowledgeable while stimulating the interviewee to give more information.

Wait until near the end of the interview to ask questions that your subject would prefer not to answer.

> And Mr. Turnbull had predicted evil consequences . . . and now doing the best in his power to bring about the verification of his own prophecies.
> —ANTHONY TROLLOPE

This is simple common sense: if the interviewee is likely to become angry or to grow sufficiently hostile to end the interview, let this occur after you have gathered most of the information you need. Although some occasions may arise where you will want to make it clear at the beginning that this conversation is to be a businesslike exchange, not a delicate exercise in diplomacy, these exceptions do not negate the general rule: tough questions last.

Be aware of the inherent limitations of the interview.

> It is amazing how complete is the delusion that beauty is goodness.
> —LEO TOLSTOY

Advanced students should realize that an accurate picture can be elusive, especially when interviewing for profiles. Psychologists David Weiss and Rene Dawis have written that "it is indefensible to assume the validity of purportedly factual data obtained by interviews." A journalist has capsulized the conflicting goals of interviewer and subject by declaring: "*I* want the truth; *they* want to be beautiful."

Irving Wallace, who has written many magazine articles and several best-selling novels based on interviewing, has observed how far a reporter's profile can diverge from the truth:

> Some friends and I were discussing this subject recently, and all of us having known certain famous people—authors, entertainers, politicians—were amazed at how different these celebrities were (based on our fairly intimate knowledge) from what we read of them in magazines. We happened to know especially well three very celebrated personalities in different fields who were being written about in magazines. When we read about the three, we read that they were strong, assured, aggressive, dedicated talents. Yet, as we knew them in private, all three were

as stable as mounds of Jello; they were nervous, sick, unsure, and one was a charlatan. But they knew how to pull on their public masks when they were being interviewed and analyzed by journalists. They wanted to convey a certain image of themselves, and they succeeded, and few people knew the truth of their frailties.

If the interview is so error-prone, why use it? The title of a monograph by two social psychologists, Eugene J. Webb and Jerry R. Salancik, suggests one answer: *The Interview; or, The Only Wheel in Town.* The title comes from an anecdote familiar to gamblers:

FIRST GAMBLER, *arriving in town:* Any action around?
SECOND GAMBLER: Roulette.
FIRST GAMBLER: You play?
SECOND GAMBLER: Yes.
FIRST GAMBLER: Is the wheel straight?
SECOND GAMBLER: No.
FIRST GAMBLER: Why do you play?
SECOND GAMBLER: It's the only wheel in town.

Avoid basing a profile on the results of a single interview.

> Secret and self-contained, and solitary as an oyster.
> —CHARLES DICKENS

The primary culprit in a distorted account is obvious to most veteran interviewers: the single interview. No other practice is so self-defeating. Interviewing the same subject again and again is helpful for the same reason that a lengthy interview is usually better than a short one. Answers to even simple questions are likely to have several dimensions, especially if they touch on the subject's innermost thoughts or motives. A single interview or a short one doesn't give the reporter time to return to a question or to probe for a deeper response.

A journalist tells of interviewing a young American race-car driver who sought the world's land speed record, then held by a European driver. When the journalist asked him early in the interview why he was in such a dangerous occupation, the young man spoke grandly of the challenge of speed and the need to bring the world's record home to the United States. Much later, when they had covered many other subjects and were less formal with each other, the journalist asked him again why he drove for a world record. The driver then admitted that, as someone with little education and a taste for splendor, he saw no other path for himself.

If possible, you should also avoid limiting your interviews to the one person who is the focus of your profile. Reporters who expect to reach the truth about someone by simply asking that person questions will find themselves imprisoned in their subject's perspective. Wallace points up the need for interviewing the subject's friends, enemies, and acquaintances: "You wouldn't really know what goes on in my head and heart because I wouldn't tell you, even if *I* understood. We all have protective devices out of necessity because a living man must possess a private self."

In many cases, the subject's friends and/or enemies can throw a light on the private self. As Joseph and Stewart Alsop suggest: "The reporter has to talk to enough people so that he can reduce the degree to which he may be misled."

Develop sophistication in preparing questions and pursuing answers.

> Oh what a tangled web we weave, When
> first we practise to deceive!
> —WALTER SCOTT

Richard Reeves, a former reporter for the *New York Times* who is now a syndicated columnist, was asked about how he interviewed politicians. He emphasized preparation and technique:

> It is my perception that no public figure—I don't care whether it's an actor or politician—tells the truth, the whole truth, on first outing. You've got to develop a whole series of techniques to deal with that. Preparation is obviously one of them. You're really in trouble if you go to someone who's experienced in dealing with the press without knowing at least as much as he knows about the areas you're most interested in. And it's a very old saying but it's true that you should not ask a question unless you know the answer to it. I can't stress that too strongly. In dealing with people whom you have reason to believe will deceive you—and I would take that to be every politician—you should look very carefully into what they've said on subjects in the past and, without letting them know you know they've answered this question before, ask them the same question and see how the answer differs. I think it's very important, in dealing with politicians particularly, to establish the pattern of untruth that they're telling you. In what direction are they deceiving you? Then you learn an awful lot about what they are doing at a given time.
>
> The other facet is that the people we interview get increasingly sophisticated. I think they are getting more and more sophisticated. We have an awful lot to learn from legal techniques, especially courtroom techniques. In this area, I think we are a little simple-minded. We think that we are clever because we have a good question. But if you watch

good courtroom attorneys work, their questions are often in a long series. The answers to the first five questions may do nothing but box the
person in, or they may even be meaningless. I think all reporters should
be much more sophisticated about questioning techniques.

When interviewing public figures, prepare yourself to handle intimidation or well-oiled responses.

> Immodest words admit of no defense,
> for want of decency is want of sense.
> —WENTWORTH DILLON

Journalists can encounter particular difficulties when interviewing
many leaders—in politics, civic organizations, management, labor, and
the like. Tom Wicker, a columnist for the *New York Times,* has recounted
the first time he called on President Johnson at the White House:

> It was about a week after he succeeded John Kennedy, one evening
> in the imposing Oval Office, and he was seated in the middle of the room,
> under a barber's sheet, while someone unobtrusively cut his hair. Men
> seem defenseless and little-boyish in that familiar pose, but not Lyndon
> Johnson, not that night. I had known him for years, but only as reporters
> know officials—and already, that soon, the unmistakable aura of power
> and of the unique loneliness of the Presidency hung about him. I mut-
> tered something embarrassing about the country's good fortune in hav-
> ing such an experienced man to pick up the pieces, but he didn't answer,
> he merely looked at me, studying me, gauging me. I stood uncomforta-
> bly, trying to meet his eyes squarely, trying futilely to measure up; and I
> remember thinking: *This is somebody. This is really somebody.* And it was
> only when those narrow and demanding eyes had beaten me down, and I
> had looked away (turning red, I suppose, and beginning to sweat a little)
> that he relaxed, told me to sit down, and ordered an "orange drink" for
> us both.

Even when the obvious mantle of power is absent, an antagonistic
subject can challenge the interviewer. When Dan Rather, the CBS news
anchorman, who is kindly but a tough interviewer, first faced President
Nixon's two top aides, John Ehrlichman and H. R. Haldeman, Ehrlichman
charged that Rather was wrong in his reporting 90 percent of the time.
Rather responded, "Then you have nothing to worry about; any reporter
who's wrong 90 percent of the time can't last."

Haldeman complained, "What concerns me is that you are sometimes wrong, but your style is very positive. You sound like you know what you're talking about; people believe you."

Ehrlichman added, "Yeah, people believe you, and they shouldn't."

Rather responded, "I hope they do, and maybe now we are getting down to the root of it. You have trouble getting people to believe you."

You can often prompt a less rehearsed answer by rephrasing the expected question. When Vice President Spiro Agnew began his attacks on the media, Rather posed this reverse-twist question at Nixon's next press conference: "Mr. President, is there anything that the vice president has said about the media with which you do *not* agree?" The traditional question in such circumstances is so obvious—"Do you agree with the vice president's speech on the media?"—that the other reporters laughed. Nixon, who had been responding smoothly to other questions, opened his mouth—and for a moment nothing would come out.

Journalists who go into the interview with a good grasp of the topic to be discussed and an arsenal of ready facts will have greater success in pinning down policymakers. In an hour-long television interview with Nixon, which CBS assigned to Rather over protests from the White House, Rather used numerous statistics to effectively challenge the president:

> RATHER: Public opinion polls—the Harris Poll was the last one, the Gallup Polls before—indicated that the American people, in overwhelming majority, gave you high marks for decisiveness, for willingness to change. But in the case of the Harris Poll, about 50 percent said that you had failed to inspire confidence and faith and lacked personal warmth and compassion. Why do you suppose that is?

> PRESIDENT NIXON: Well, it's because people tell the pollsters that, of course. So that's what the people must believe. But on the other hand, without trying to psychoanalyze myself, because that's your job, I would simply answer the question that my strong point is not rhetoric, it isn't showmanship, it isn't big promises, those things that breed the glamour and excitement that people call charisma and warmth. My strong point is performance. I always do more than I said. . . .

> RATHER: But the same Harris Poll indicated that only a third of the people thought that you had kept your campaign promises. So if you would explain, obviously as briefly as possible but as fully as you think necessary, in 1968 you said, "I pledge to redress the present economic imbalance without increasing unemployment"—direct quotation. Now, unemployment was, I believe, 3.6 percent when you came in; it's at or near 6 percent for the last several months.

> PRESIDENT NIXON: Let's take that one first.

> RATHER: Yes, please.

PRESIDENT NIXON: Unemployment was 3.6 when I came in, at a cost of 300 casualties a week in Vietnam. Since I've come in, we have got 400,000 people home from Vietnam. There's two million people who have been let out of defense plants and out of the armed services as a result of our winding up—winding *down*—the war in Vietnam, and if those people were still in the defense plants and still in Vietnam, unemployment would still be 3.6. That's too high a cost.

RATHER: But wasn't that foreseeable, Mr. President?

PRESIDENT NIXON, *beginning to stumble:* That was foreseeable, but my point is—my point is that we were—what I was saying was. . . .

These and further questions that elicited so many stumbling responses outraged Nixon's supporters as well as others who thought reporters should approach whoever occupies the presidential office gingerly, if not obsequiously. The interviewer's first loyalty, however, should be to the facts.

Control the interview by finding a happy medium between aggressive iconoclasm and respectful subservience.

> Fling the bold banner of untruth on high,
> And sing the full, free candour of the lie!
> —EDMUND VANCE COOKE

The lesson to be learned from encounters between reporters and officials is that the journalist should manage the interview. On the one hand, you should avoid assuming the attitude of superiority displayed by the reporter who once abruptly ended an interview with a high public official by exclaiming, "You have just wasted a half hour of my time!" On the other hand, be wary of the tactics of the extremely bland interviewer who serves up batting-practice questions and meekly accepts the answers.

To balance between being the sole authority and playing the obedient servant is difficult, but when an interviewer asks questions confidently and has the air of one who knows that these questions should be answered, nine times out of ten the interview will succeed. Remember what Maurice Zolotow, a widely known free-lance writer, has said: "A good interview is really a good conversation. Don't just pretend, but listen with every faculty at your command. If you do this, and act like you're listening, people will tell you anything. They even tell you things they shouldn't. People like to talk about themselves—it's the most interesting subject in the world."

Capitalize on your knowledge about your subject to inspire confidence and to pose penetrating questions.

The humblest citizen of all the land, when clad in the armor of a righteous cause, is stronger than all the hosts of Error.
—WILLIAM JENNINGS BRYAN

The interviewee in the following transcript is Lou Cannon, who once worked for the *San Jose Mercury* and now works for the *Washington Post.* The interviewer introduced himself to Cannon as a former newspaper reporter who is now a free-lance writer. The interviewer's first question then reassured Cannon that he was talking to a knowledgeable journalist. If the interviewer had begun with a more naive question ("How do you like reporting in Washington?"), Cannon would have been justifiably more guarded in his replies.

Although few journalists are happy to be interviewed, observe the length of Cannon's answers. He answered only one question in two short sentences, devoting many long sentences to the rest. This reflects the acuity of the interviewer's questions, a natural outgrowth of his knowledge of the subject.

QUESTION: Earlier, you worked for the *San Jose Mercury;* now you work for the *Washington Post.* What's the difference? Are you much more informal with the editor or the city editor in San Jose than you are with the *Washington Post*?

CANNON: Not really. In the case of the San Jose paper, I was an editor there, before I was a reporter from '61 to '65, so when I went to Sacramento I knew all of the editors. I knew all the people that I was dealing with. Essentially I would say that I had probably a little less direction, but that was because I was working out of the office. I was working away. Now when you are working away from the *Post* you have less direction.

I would say that there are fewer differences. There are very few differences from the day-to-day relationships. The differences are more determined by the personality on the desk than by the differences in the papers. Where there is a difference, there is more thought, advanced thought, to stories at the *Post.* You would be more likely to sit down and discuss a dramatic story, or a story idea, with the editor. But once you are out of the story, the relationships fall pretty much in the same pattern with most newspapers where I have been.

QUESTION: Is it also evident that the people on the *Post* are better than anyone else that you have worked with?

CANNON: The analogy that comes to mind is one of sports analogy, so beloved by our last presidents, it seems. I would say that there are very good reporters working on every newspaper that I have ever worked for. Reporters that are of the same craft and class as the reporters working for the *Washington Post* and the *L.A. Times,* the *New York Times.*

When I worked in San Jose, for instance, there are several reporters who worked there who have gone on. Bob Lindsley is now the west coast reporter for the *New York Times* and worked in New York for a number of years. Frank Jenson became an outstanding foreign correspondent for the Associated Press. These people had the same skills and gifts in San Jose that they had afterward. The differences in the overall quality, that's where the sports come in. It's like, if you go into a double A or a triple A baseball league, you'll see a few players that are as good, maybe even better than the run of the mill players in the majors. But the overall quality tends to be higher at the *Post.* The national staff, which I am most familiar with, most of the reporters are mature reporters who have served their apprenticeship either on the paper's metro staff or on other newspapers. It's a highly competitive paper. There's emphasis on production at that newspaper, so the overall quality tends to be high.

QUESTION: Do you also tend to be freer in writing than fifteen years ago, wherever you were? In commenting, or perhaps using your opinions?

CANNON: Well, I feel freer. But that may be because I've developed a greater skill expressing myself. You know, commentary, interpretation, opinion (or whatever those words are). Journalism is an art form, as well as a number of other things, I always insist. There are acceptable ways that you can get interpretation into a newspaper and unacceptable ways. I suspect that I have become more skilled, without being particularly conscious of it, knowing what those ways are. I think that is generally true. Once having said that, reporters, if they are good reporters, not simply a guy who wants to get his political kicks off in a newsroom, have more latitude. In addition to those things, I have probably moved from situations which are more free.

The reporter at San Jose, at least while I was there, had much more freedom in Sacramento than in San Jose. The reporter in the Washington Bureau, where I worked afterward, had even more latitude. The *Washington Post,* with all of the drawbacks and criticisms and imperfections it may have, is really the freest newspaper where I have ever worked. I do not feel that I have had at any time to express a regimented or corporate opinion. There are stories that I do not believe we cover as well as we do other kinds of stories, that it is hard to get in the paper with. But that is not because of lack of freedom. Like any newspaper, we are attuned to some things and not attuned to others. But in the actual reporting of the story . . . to tell you truthfully, one of the trepidations I had about coming to work at the *Post* was that I might have to express a particular kind of party line. The editor who hired me, Richard Harwood, assured me that was not the case. And it isn't the case. I have never felt that any story that I have done at the *Post* has had to represent a particular point of view.

QUESTION: Or did they initiate your coming there? Or did you initiate it?

CANNON: Yes. They asked me to come.

QUESTION: Is that regular? With the other people too?

CANNON: Well, I think that is the best way to come to the *Post*. A number of reporters, I don't know what the percentage is, there have been several instances where the *Post* has gone out to get reporters that they thought had been doing a good job at other papers and asked them to come aboard. I am sure that there have been many more where people have applied. I think in my book, I say that the applications every year are in the thousands. And you know they hire a handful of people. So I would assume that most of the reporters on the metro staff, the younger reporters, are a great percentage of those who apply. I think that there may be more reporters on the national staff who have been asked. But to tell you the truth, I don't really know what the relationships are. I know there are a number in both categories. I am sure if you put that question to a *Post* editor, to Harwood, he would be able to tell you.

QUESTION: How often have you had a story killed because it did not measure up to today's news, or something like that, or perhaps they felt that this was bad for some reason or other? Is it often that you attempt to get in, as they do in the *New York Times,* and quite often don't get in? Is that necessarily so?

CANNON: I have very rarely had a story that I wrote that didn't get in. Again, I'm not sure how typical that is or isn't. For one thing, most of the time I have been writing stories that we either have a commitment to cover regularly, like we cover the White House regularly, or a high degree of interest, like political stories. The other thing is I usually make it a practice to discuss with the editor what I am doing, so you get some early indication of interest in the story. The only times that I have had any problem with stories have been when I have done a story in an area where we just don't get excited about. Let me give you an example: Theoretically, I am now doing intergovernmental stories. I did a story about White House people under Carter. Jack Watson met with the representatives of city and county and state people there and promised a new era of governmental relations that was taken with a certain degree of salt. It was an interesting story, I felt, but it just got on the "in type" list. That is what we call our stories that aren't published. I don't think it ever got into the paper, but I had been away for weeks, and it might have got in.

There are certain types of stories that we say we are interested in, that I think we are really not. I think that for certain types of environmental stories that is true. So it seems to me that most reporters are going to learn that it is a lot of competition to get into the paper. They quickly learn what stories are going to get and which are not. It's a problem. That limits the range of stories. But I don't have the problem of stories being killed for any reason . . . the editor doesn't agree or anything else. . . . [That] is a very rare occurrence at that newspaper. It is just that you do have an awful lot of stories. When I left, the "in type" list was two pages long so there is a competition for an interesting story. I guess that I should say that we have had different editors, and different editors are interested in different things. Some editors have been terribly interested in FBI stories, other editors were interested in politics, so to some degree it is determined by who's on the desk, who's in charge at the moment.

QUESTION: Tell me about the competitiveness. How does this manifest itself; that is, is it very competitive there?

CANNON: Well, there are different manifestations. There are a number of reporters who are assigned rather specific beats, and then there are reporters who have more general assignments, or who are general-assignment reporters doing a different variety of things. You will get in some cases a crowding. You will get a reporter who will get into someone else's area because he thinks that he can get into the paper that way. I think that the paper encourages a little bit of that. I've never heard it spelled out as a "codified theory" but I think that the idea of creative tension permeates the aspects of that newspaper, so that they have reporters that are competitive with one another.

Now in my own view, a certain amount of that is O.K. because you can get people that are−*lazy* is the word that I would use. You can get people who stop doing the things that made them good reporters in the first place, and yet if you get too much of that, as in any organization, it becomes counterproductive and people get to feeling bad and worrying about their places. Most reporters have fairly well-developed egos anyway and I have seen occasions where the competition can get out of hand, or worry a reporter because he is not getting into the paper. He can feel troubled. You have a fairly high degree of anxiety. I think in big newspapers (that is one of the reasons that I did not want to come to the *Post*) during the period that I have been there, I have had a feeling of kind of a great adventure at the *Post*. There is a certain sense of excitement. There is consciousness, I think, that is widely shared (people use the expression that it is a zoo or madhouse), but also that it is really an important place to be, and it is a very good paper. Just speaking for myself, I get a great deal of satisfaction out of that. I do think that it is the best paper. Sure.

QUESTION: Dave Broder. I'm going to spin out in some detail the fact that he is *the* most respected correspondent, because, although he is a columnist at the same time, he also reports. This seems to be just what he needs to write a column. That is, rather than sitting down and sucking his thumb and writing about whatever he thinks, instead, he is probably always on the telephone, always talking to people, etc. Does that seem . . . ?

CANNON: David is a great man. A wonderful colleague and a very good friend. I entirely agree with your notion. I think that Dave is a strong columnist because he does do the reporting. But Dave has been extremely influential on that newspaper. The thing that he really never gets any outside credit for, nor seeks credit for either, is, unlike a lot of reporters that are the political stars of the newspaper, Dave tries to get everybody who is working on that paper in his area into the offense. I've really been able to come in there and do all kinds of important and political stories, which I know that I wouldn't have been able to do on the other newspapers. On other newspapers, the star of the show preempted those for himself. That has not been the case on the *Washington Post*. People like myself and Jules Witcover have been able to come in and get significant pieces of the action.

Dave actively seeks to do that. He is particularly good with young reporters. You know in every campaign we have reporters that are assigned to us from cityside who work on campaigns. Dave goes out of his way to make people who are part of a reporting team feel at home and see that they have an important role to contribute. I think that he is really kind of the renaissance man of political reporting. He is a person. . .what's the saying: "How do I become a better writer? Become a better man," is the advice. And David practices a very high degree of conduct—personal conduct—relationships with his colleagues. I think that it all comes together. I think that the product at the *Post* in this area has in many ways been shaped by him. And I don't mean just his own personal product. He is a very important contributing force there.

I think one of the reasons that I have had such a good piece of the action at that paper is because of his attitude. You see very little elbowing among the political reporters. Most of us try to emulate Dave's own example when we have other reporters working with us.

QUESTION: One thing that baffles me is that he is not a visual writer. That is, he never makes phrases, or hardly ever makes phrases. It doesn't seem to me that he was in the forefront of Watergate, for example. He wasn't there.

CANNON: Practically nobody was. There were thirteen reporters who were there out of three thousand.

QUESTION: It is puzzling to some observers that he is rated by people in other papers as the best political correspondent. How do you explain this by the product itself?

CANNON: Dave's insights into the political process seem to me to have been superior to nearly all of his colleagues. He understands a great deal about process. I am interested in concepts of federalism and intergovernmental relationships and things that do not make many readers' hearts go pit-a-pat. Dave is too. I think that the range of his interest is very great. He can understand different types of political stories. I would contend that he understands, I hope I do, that in a republic almost every kind of story is essentially political. Because the solutions to things which really are technological stories or sociological stories are political solutions. The energy thing being a good example.

So Dave has something to say about a great many things, and he's thoughtful. He's fair-minded. There are many issues that we may not personally agree upon. I can't think of an issue that he wouldn't be open to discourse or thought about. He values thoughtful people in the cross-ideological spectrum. These things that I'm saying are unusual things. Frankly, I also think that Dave is a good writer, but I think that these things rate higher than ability to formulate a phrase. To remember after we are gone.

QUESTION: Is his interest rooted in that he once worked for the *Congressional Quarterly, Washington Star* staff, *New York Times?*

CANNON: You would have to ask him that, but I think that is the effect and not the cause. Those of us who are interested in political reporting do things that reflect that interest, rather than the other way around. I think that it is advantageous to work for different kinds of publications, but I don't think that it is a key that Dave worked for the *Congressional Quarterly,* even though I would recommend that as training for anyone.

Phrase questions in a noncommittal way to lead the interviewee as little as possible.

> A newspaperman is one whose job is to chronicle daily events and to place the facts before the public in some reasonable perspective. Events and facts have a life of their own. They are independent of the dreams and desires of men.
> —GEORGE REEDY

Some veteran journalists are beginning to adopt the interviewing techniques of social scientists. Diana Tillinghast, a professor of communication who teaches reporting and precision journalism, which involves numbers and statistics, gives the following interviewing instructions to her students:

1. Read all of the questions, explanations, and transitions *in the exact order* that they are presented in the questionnaire.
2. Read all of the questions *exactly* as they are worded on the questionnaire. Changes in the wording (and the order of questions) can change the meaning of the question.
3. Repeat any questions that you feel have *not* been understood. However, in doing so, do not suggest any answers or give your interpretation to the question.

Slight variations in a question can elicit very different answers, as

Stanley L. Peyne illustrates in *The Art of Asking Questions*. Peyne describes a study in which people were asked similar questions:

"Do you think anything *should* be done to make it easier for people to pay doctor or hospital bills?"

"Do you think anything *could* be done to make it easier for people to pay doctor or hospital bills?"

"Do you think anything *might* be done to make it easier for people to pay hospital bills?"

The difference in responses is instructive: 82 percent said something *should* be done; 77 percent said something *could* be done; and 63 percent said something *might* be done.

For a complete picture, flesh out research and interviewing with observations.

> The secret of success in life is known only
> to those who have not succeeded.
> —JOHN CHURTON COLLINS

Critics of the universities are correct in contending that too many students and professors base their work primarily on reading and thinking, divorced from the actualities of the world. Like students, instead of weaving arabesques of thought around quotations from books and articles, journalists should use their reading as a foundation, then consult "real life" authorities: other people as interviewees and themselves as observers. Interviewing and observing will not guarantee perfect accuracy, of course, but reading, thinking, interviewing, and observing together will push the writers closer to the truth about what goes on in the world.

Often they will discover a new dimension to previously unexamined reality. An extraordinary observer, Annie Dillard, described in an article in *Harper's* the surprise of flushing blackbirds from an apparently empty tree:

> For nature does reveal as well as concealing, now-you-don't-see-it, now-you-do. For a week this September migrating red-winged blackbirds were feeding heavily down by Tinker Creek at the back of the house. One day I went out to investigate the racket; I walked up to a tree, an Osage orange, and a hundred birds flew away. They simply materialized out of the tree. I saw a tree, then a whisk of color, then a tree again. I walked closer and another hundred blackbirds took flight. Not a branch, not a twig budged: the birds were apparently weightless as well as invisible. Or, it was as if the leaves of the Osage orange had

been freed from a spell in the form of red-winged blackbirds; they flew from the tree, caught my eye in the sky, and vanished. When I looked again at the tree, the leaves had reassembled as if nothing had happened. Finally I walked directly to the trunk of the tree and a final hundred, the real diehards, appeared, spread, and vanished. How could so many hide in the tree without my seeing them?

Reporters will also learn how much preconceptions can affect what they see. Walter Lippmann made the point in a famous essay that explains how stereotypes shape our view of the world: "For the most part we do not see first, then define; we define first and then see. In the great blooming, buzzing confusion of the outer world we pick out what our culture has already defined for us, and we tend to perceive that which we have picked out in the form stereotyped."

Only when people have been instructed to "observe—*really* observe," do they shut out the many competing details in favor of concentrating on a particular subject—for instance, a certain professor. This description of Antony Raubitschek, a professor of classics, uses imaginative language to bring a distinctive character to life:

> For an hour suspended in time Cicero and Ovid and Plato and Socrates, with a multitude of other spirits, are sitting at the elbows of the students.
>
> Antony Raubitschek refers to them in the present tense: ". . . but Cicero doesn't see it that way. He feels the. . . ." One might expect to turn and see the Roman orator, complete with a wart on the end of his nose, the wart which gave him his name.
>
> In the graduate seminars held by Raubitschek, participants obliterate the centuries in the same natural way. They continue arguments which were started before the time of Christ, buttressing their beliefs with quotations from the ancient masters, as if they had buttonholed them on the way to class.
>
> All the while Raubitschek is encouraging them with a virtuoso display of reactions which include deep-chested guffaws that affect every part of his body, a wagging of his thick fingers to indicate a wrong assumption, the dropping of his voice to a sibilant confidential whisper.
>
> To mark a major point, he raises his voice several octaves so that the key word of his sentences bursts out like a cartoon balloon. When he is caught up in the momentum of his exposition it seems the most natural thing in the world when he switches to the language of the immortals. Then the words come softly and reverently to the hushed audience, rapt in an ancient spell.
>
> The venerable figure seems to be orchestrated to some music which cannot be heard until the observer feels the tide of Raubitschek's sweeping enthusiasm.
>
> His range of performance is so wide that students who are asked how they would describe their professor come up with a diverse spectrum of images:

"Santa Claus!"

"The lovable old Viennese doctor in a schmaltzy movie epic." (This is near the mark, since Raubitschek was raised in Vienna and speaks with a Viennese accent so thick that one can almost taste Linzertorte.)

"A cross between a teddy bear and the Wizard of Oz."

Use all five senses—plus intuition—when observing.

> Heights were made to be looked at, not looked from.
> —GILBERT KEITH CHESTERTON

When students in a college journalism class were asked how they observe, they responded as though the question were bizarre: "By seeing, of course. How else could you observe anybody or anything?" One student thought a minute, then added, "Also by hearing what a person speaks like." That covers only two of the senses. What else should the students have added?

Smell: The scent of freshly mown grass, mothballs, a breeze off the ocean, hot asphalt, baking bread are all powerfully evocative cues to a scene.

Taste: Many conversations and encounters take place over shared meals or a casual drink; remembering what food and beverages taste like will add another dimension to your recollection of the event.

Touch: When you're examining a new product—whether a nubbly wool sweater or the smooth keyboard of a computer terminal—you'll use your sense of touch to amplify what you see.

All five senses are parts of observing. Too often, though, we take into account only sight, recording details such as height, distance, and color. The primary avenue of sensory input to our brains is our eyes: 20 percent of the cortex of our brains is devoted to vision alone. Sound is second only to sight in our values. Even though smell, taste, and touch are always operating, they are silent partners.

You should not forget the sixth sense that forms another part of observing: intuition. When you interview someone, you can usually tell whether or not you should continue a particular line of questioning. For example, a student reported the following experience when interviewing a bachelor of forty:

> When I was interviewing Bill, I could tell that he warmed up to questions about travel and his experiences overseas. But because he was tired and seemed somewhat tense about his job at Larkin, he got slightly

uneasy when I asked him how he enjoyed being a Resident Fellow. He explained the situation and then guided his answers away from the topic. He also tensed up when I asked him whether he traveled alone. He is not married, and from what I've heard, he has no interest in becoming married. From his reactions, I knew it was a delicate subject, so I did not pursue it further.

Depending on how aggressive you are—or how important you consider the questions your subject is evading—you can choose to pursue that line of questioning or let it go in the interest of reassuring your subject. In any case, remember the importance of intuition.

When you're observing people, places, and objects, think of the six kinds of observing. Even in an interview, where you naturally would concentrate on what you see and hear from your subject, don't forget that you have met this person in a particular place; use your senses of smell, taste, and touch in describing that place. Finally, keep in mind that the success of your interview could depend on your intuition.

EXERCISES

1. Select one student who has done something of note or has interesting qualities to be the subject of an interview. Then select a group of two or three students to act as interviewers. The remainder of the class will be the audience. Conduct the interview. When the interview is completed, each student in the audience should write an evaluation by addressing these questions:
a. Did the interviewers ask the right questions?
b. What questions would you have asked that they did not ask?
c. Did the interviewee's personality reveal itself in the process of the interview?
d. How might you have conducted the interview differently? For example: Were the interviewers too bland or too tough? Did they or did they not follow up questions with other related questions that required a more complete answer?

2. After reading the following summary of Walter Cronkite's career, list fifteen questions that you would ask him:

> Walter Cronkite is the former managing editor and television newscaster for CBS from New York City. Born in St. Joseph, Missouri, in 1916, he was a student at the University of Texas from 1933 to 1935. He first joined the Scripps-Howard Newspapers, then worked for ten years for United Press.
> Cronkite joined CBS in 1950 and became a Washington news correspondent for four years. He was transferred to CBS in New York as a television news analyst. When the CBS news operation was transformed, Cronkite was made the managing editor. In 1965, CBS became the first of the networks to change the early-evening news program from fifteen minutes to thirty minutes. Throughout Cronkite's tenure as managing editor, the CBS news operation was a leader in reporting.

3. Choose another classmate to interview. Begin by asking whether the high school curriculum prepared him or her for college. Have the answer to that

question dictate your next question and continue the interview in this way until you think you have covered the subject adequately. Write a question-and-answer story of at least 800 words based on this interview, then read your interview story and compare it with another interview story written by a classmate. Note the different questions that your fellow student asked his or her subject. List the questions you asked and the questions asked by your classmate. Which are better?

4. Ask a classmate to attend with you an event such as a football game, a rock concert, or a political rally. Then, separately, each of you should write a story of at least 600 words about the event. Compare the two stories. Which is better? Why?

5. Study a photograph of an event for thirty seconds, then take fifteen minutes to describe the event in writing. Each student should read his or her description and let the class discuss how well the description fits the picture. While considering each description, ask these and other questions:
   a. Are there mistakes?
   b. Have important elements been omitted?
   c. Have unimportant elements been included?
   d. Have unimportant elements been overemphasized?

6. Beginning writers often fail to describe a person they have interviewed. Here is a sample description of a professor:

> Whimsical stories give the only indication of age. Everything else about the man emits ambiguous signals. A youthful, springy step moves him about the room as muscular forearms trace pictures in the air of a myriad carefully choreographed, unspoken expressions.
>
> A corduroy shirt and sporty slacks are his uniform. It used to be coat and tie, "but I don't have to look old anymore."
>
> His strong forehead juts out to mirror an equally impressive jaw. Heavy silver eyebrows set off a glowing tan that sheets his wrinkling skin.
>
> Bleached white hair with flashes of silver is combed straight back and slightly rightward from a part on the left. The hair is thick and full—mussed on the sides, but impeccably drawn back in front.
>
> His speaking ability is a tell-tale sign of experience. Forceful shouts from drawn lips startle students to attention and near whispers draw them silently forward out of their seats. The voice, addictive in its tone, seems to come from so low that tangled shoelaces would be tantamount to a tongue twister.
>
> Every serious phrase is followed by a smile. Subtle facial expressions speak louder than echoing words.
>
> But each day is new, every gesture appears original.

Write a 150-word description of one of your instructors without giving height, weight, or color of eyes and hair.

3 *Following the Paper Trail*

What is research, but a blind date with
knowledge.

—WILL HENRY

IMAGINE THAT YOU ARE the star public affairs reporter for the *Puyallup
Press*—or, perhaps, the aspiring star reporter. Your editor, a gargantuan
man with a bald head and small eyes, wanders past your desk as you
finish page 257 of the novel you are writing on company time and drops a
list of questions he wants you to answer by the end of the day, which is
only a few hours away.

  • Joan Didion will be appearing at a Puyallup bookstore tomorrow.
The story about her needs some paragraphs about the books she has
written and about what critics have said.
  • The political reporter wants to know what real estate a Puyallup
city council member owns and how much it is assessed at. The reporter
also wants to know how much the council member pays in taxes on the
property.
  • The Endangered Species Act is up for review in Congress. The
wire editor needs some additional paragraphs about when it was originally passed and what it says.
  • The environmental reporter wants you to find out how much a
federal Bureau of Land Management official recently spent on a business
trip to a Hawaii conference. Where did the official stay? How much did
the official spend on meals?
  • Someone else wants to know who the first women executed in the
electric chair was. That same someone also wants to know who invented
the first ice cream cone for a story about competition between two ice
cream shops.
  • The business reporter needs statistics and information about a
large corporation that is about to open a factory in town. What are its
assets? Who are its directors? What are its subsidiaries? How profitable

has it been in recent years? What are its interlocks with other major corporations?

• Two union-busting consultants are in town to give speeches to several local businessmen. The labor reporter wants some facts about their backgrounds that are not being provided by the public relations officers of local corporations.

• A plant manager at a local factory insists that workers there enjoy better pension and health benefits than those elsewhere. Is it true?

You could, of course, rely on the journalist's chief method of collecting information to find out many of the answers; you could interview. However, in many cases, you could actually find the information more quickly if you knew which *documents* to turn to. Although the interview is – and is likely to remain – the reporter's primary tool of gathering information, in recent years journalists have begun to speak more and more of another method, that of knowing how to follow a *paper trail.*

Perhaps one of the reasons that paper trails have become so important in recent years is that the kinds of stories that journalists report have gotten so much more complicated. To conduct a good interview, a reporter will often need to have conducted a substantial amount of paper research. To understand the complexities of bureaucracies and corporations, a reporter will have to have studied the laws that affect those organizations and the regulations they have promulgated. Certainly, to track corruption or wrongdoing, the reporter will have to turn to documents as solid evidence.

Too often, beginning reporters fail to look for the paper that can help them to develop ideas for new and important stories, or to flesh out a story so that it will mean more to readers, or to get started on investigations.

"People will go out," Jim Long, a reporter for the *Oregon Journal,* once said, "and they'll try to cover an agriculture department, or some other department in the state, and they'll never even read the statutes that tell what the department is supposed to be doing, or the regulations promulgated by the department. It requires a tremendous capacity for tedium and self-boredom, but once you get into it, it'll be just like reading *Fanny Hill.* You'll find all kinds of things to get going on."

*Paper trails have many paths—through the
libraries, the government offices, the boxes
of private papers individuals are willing to
share.*

> You'll feel like an ass when you read some of
> these documents and you'll say, "Hey, I
> didn't know that," and you'll be onto a story.
>   —JIM LONG

The paper trail, broadly defined, includes all the normal reference sources you might find in a library, such as encyclopedias, books, newspaper clippings, magazines, trade reference books, and so forth, as well as public records filed with various government agencies and private records stashed almost anywhere and everywhere. Documents come in three legal categories: those that are totally public (such as the library reference works); those that are public as defined by federal and state freedom of information acts (such as campaign expenditure reports); and those that are defined as private (but that still may be accessible through friendly sources or even direct requests to the person likely to be holding them). If a reporter plans a very thorough research job, all three are likely to be sought: a reporter conducting a nursing home investigation might well examine federal regulations on file at the library, state licensing records of investigations at a state social services department, and private audit records from a friendly accountant.

Consider these three examples of the value of knowing how to pursue a paper trail:

- In 1982, Loretta Tofani, a suburban courthouse reporter for the *Washington Post,* started work on a story about rapes occurring in the county jail. Her first problem was to find jail guards and prisoners who would be willing to talk. Using both the interview and paper trail routes, she contacted sheriff's deputies who could give her the names of friendly guards and examined court records on lawsuits that had been filed against the county jail. The court records gave her the names, telephone numbers, and home addresses of several jail guards not listed in the telephone book. She also used the court records on convictions for jail rapes to gather a list of prisoners and—since many had been transferred to other jails or released—to track them down.

Alternating between information flowing from the interviews and that flowing from records, she was eventually able to interview guards who confirmed that rapes were happening about a dozen times a week, to talk to jail medical workers who gave her records describing the evidence of rape for many specific victims, and to gather details from twenty-four jail rapists, only two of whom had actually been prosecuted for the crime. The series eventually prompted a grand jury and FBI investigation.

• At the *Providence* (R.I.) *Journal-Bulletin,* reporters Bruce DeSilva and Bob Stewart became interested in the way in which a public housing authority was using federal grant money to enrich a number of individuals. To discover who was getting approval to build projects for the state Housing and Mortgage Finance Corporation (HMFC), the two first went to the state branch of the federal Housing and Urban Development Department (HUD). After some delay, HUD provided a list of who was getting the federal money channeled through the HMFC, but the reporters, by comparing the developers' names on the signs that were erected at the projects with the HUD list, discovered that the list seemed to be wrong. They then began trying to find out who was behind the names contained on the HUD list; by using the New Jersey state "limited partnership" records, they were eventually able to list nearly 1,000 individual names that made up some 300 different firms. The newspaper computer staff designed a program that would absorb all the names and then generate an alphabetized listing of individuals showing all of their project and partnership interests; that in turn gave the reporters an indication of patterns in the way in which the HMFC was directing its money to the benefit of certain individuals.

• In Grand Rapids, Michigan, Mark Lagerkvist of WZZM-TV uncovered a story about how a large development corporation, through the use of a dummy company, was able to bilk the Medicaid program of hundreds of thousands of dollars. The federal tax money was being used to finance what Lagerkvist considered a luxurious playground for the businessmen in Appleton, Michigan. Lagerkvist worked largely through the inspection and licensing records that the Michigan Department of Public Health maintained, as well as through state records on business ownership, to show that the dummy company that operated several Michigan nursing homes was controlled by the development corporation. The mother company was charging the nursing homes exorbitant management and rental fees, which were then being passed along to the federal government through Medicaid reimbursements.

Not all use of records leads to such glamorous stories, of course; in fact, most use does not. Indeed, it should not. Following a paper trail is not just an investigative technique meant to expose someone or something, but rather a fundamental reporting method meant to produce more thorough information.

Think about the paper you need first. Sometimes the problem lies in locating the right document; sometimes the greater concern is to avoid being buried in tons of irrelevant paper.

> Government is the only institution that can take a valuable commodity like paper and make it worthless by applying ink.
> —LUDWIG VAN MOSES

No book can tell a beginning reporter about all the kinds of paper that exist; any that did would be immediately out of date anyway because new records and even new record-keeping methods are being constantly developed. (For example, nowadays reporters need to think not only about the kinds of records that are on library and government shelves, but about those stored in computers as well.) In the next sections of this chapter, a number of commonly used records will be mentioned, but before getting to specifics, a journalist in pursuit of a record will do well to reflect on a way of approaching the mass of paper that exists. Here are some suggestions for doing so; although they may appear to be very commonsensical steps to take, under deadline pressure they can be easily forgotten:

First, recognize the concept of a paper trail. This sounds basic and it is, but many journalists are so used to gathering information strictly by interview or direct observation that they forget to take time to check paper sources. They set off for an interview with an author without checking *Book Review Digest,* even though they may never have heard of the author and even though the *Digest* may be sitting on their own company's library shelves. They write news stories about legislative acts or Supreme Court decisions without ever reading the texts. They write stories about universities without bothering to read the charters or the policies about which they might be reporting.

The first step, then, is to simply remember that there very likely is a paper trail that is going to make your story more thorough than if you rely on interviews alone. If you want or need a record, there probably is one — somewhere. What is entailed in locating the record is a process of *thinking* and *problem-solving.* When reporter Loretta Tofani could not find the telephone numbers of the jail guards listed in the most obvious place, the phone book, she discovered a second source, the court records. When a journalism student, Bill McClement, needed to talk to jurors after a fairly routine murder trial, attorneys told him the names and home telephone numbers were not for public release. Undaunted, he found a complete listing on another record in the court clerk's office.

That kind of problem-solving leads to the second step. To find a record that may not be waiting for you on library shelves, *look for those points at which private matters intersect with public concerns.* A family quarrel over money becomes a public concern when it turns into a lawsuit or a bankruptcy filing. Information you could only get otherwise by pilfering from Internal Revenue Service files (not recommended, by the way) may be waiting for you at a local family law or bankruptcy court. An indication of how much money a physician is making from poor patients may be on file through Medicare or Medicaid records. Information on corporate ownership will be available from the federal Securities and Exchange Commission if the company tries to sell stock to the public.

Thirdly, once you start obtaining records, remember that they do not stand by themselves. *The paper trail must always be supplemented with interviews and with logic.* Some reporters become so entranced by what at first glance can appear to be a treasure trove of information that they forget that the records themselves may be misleading, outdated, or incomplete. Those that are filed with government agencies are usually filed for some specific purpose; in using information gained from them for other purposes, reporters need to question whether such a transfer is really fair and accurate. Further, many records require the kind of interpretation that can come only through an interview.

Records also need to be compared and contrasted with others, either on file with the same agency or with a different agency. Often comparing records will turn up contradictions that will need to be resolved through interviews—or that will become part of the story itself. (For example, corporations may report a much rosier picture than exists in their annual publications for stockholders, while acknowledging financial difficulties in their reports to the Securities and Exchange Commission.)

Dovetailing records can help build a more complete picture. Especially in a story requiring thorough research, most of the information a journalist wants will not necessarily be available from a single record, or even a single agency. Be prepared to seek out several sources, to compare records or reference books, and then to fit them together to form a more complete story. In the WZZM-TV case cited earlier, for example, the reporter did the work that clerks in separate government agencies had not done (and seldom have time to do): he dovetailed state licensing records on nursing homes with state records on business ownership to reveal a fraud involving federal money.

Finally, remember that if you hit a dead end in trying to get a record from one agency, in all probability some other agency has the same record. Journalists can actually take heart from all the usual jokes and complaints about bureaucracy and about having to fill out forms in triplicate. Triplicate forms usually go to different offices; although one refuses you, the other might not. Bureaucracy often does not know what its various parts are doing, opening the way for reporters to play one agency or even one branch of the same agency against another for information. Denied information from a regional office of one federal agency, journalists often have been able to get either the same or similar information from another regional office of the same federal agency—and then have sometimes been able to use that to force the original regional office to open up. *When you hit a brick wall, think about what other agency or individual might have the record you want.*

Sometimes you can just go back on a different day, to a different clerk, and get what you want.

The paper trail begins at that institution reporters so often neglect—the library.

My mind is made up.
Don't confuse me with facts.
                              —SIGN ON A DESK

Odd as it may seem, some journalists—perhaps those haunted by deadlines and memories of interminable English term papers—overlook the handiest and most accessible source on the paper trail: the public or academic research library. Here, little-known reference sources abound with background information that can make the difference between a sloppy, superficial story and a really informative one. It is worth recalling that the excellent investigative reporter I. F. Stone did much of his work with the very same congressional reports and official transcripts that show up each day at libraries across the nation.

In addition to the most obvious reference guides to newspapers, magazines, and specialty journals in the social sciences, indices to business worth (see the chapter on reporting business and economics for more information about these), and directories for many major professions, many libraries now provide computer searches, which enable you to track information through countless sources.

Here are a few of the reference materials that may prove handiest:

For biographical information: Any of the relevant vanity publications and "Who's Who"s will help in this area—and there are many. They usually provide basic background about an individual's place of birth, education, family, and awards. In addition, *Biography Index* references material found in more than 1,500 periodicals. *Current Biography* contains thoroughly researched articles about prominent individuals in a variety of fields. And, of course, if you are interested in a prominent person who has died, the *New York Times Obituaries Index* can lead you to articles that not only contain the usual biographical material but may also hold the kinds of colorful or revealing anecdotes you need to make a story more interesting. One or several of these publications would be the stopping place for finding the answer to that first question raised at the beginning of the chapter: who is Joan Didion?

For book information: No journalist can keep abreast of all the books that are written, but any that has a sudden interview with an author that everyone else appears to have heard of can still succeed by turning to a source such as *Book Review Digest.* The digest not only tells you what the book is about, but what critics have said about it. The *Book Review Index* can lead you to various publications in which you can find the actual reviews. An hour spent with these can give you enough background to prepare an article that will appeal both to those who have read the book and to those who have not.

For miscellaneous information: One of the standbys for miscellaneous trivia is, of course, *The Guinness Book of World Records.* But others come in handy, too. For example, *Famous First Facts* can answer those questions about who was the first woman executed in the electric chair (for a story on women and capital punishment?) or who invented the ice cream cone. Another source, the *Gallup Poll Digest,* carries reports from Gallup Polls for the previous decades. If you are researching a story on sexual attitudes now and in previous decades, for example, this can be just the book for you.

For government information: If you are trying to decipher the workings of the federal government or track down the intentions of legislators who passed the Endangered Species Act, then you need to know how to work with the large number of federal reference sources—which are often paralleled by similar reference sources for states. The *United States Government Manual* can explain the role of an agency you have never heard of, and it can also lead you to different agencies and individuals who may be concerned with a particular problem. The Congressional Information Service (CIS) provides a compilation, organized by date, of the laws passed by Congress as well as a copy of the legislative report that accompanied the passage. The report can give you background on why the law was passed. If someone refers to Public Law 54-380, CIS is the place to look it up. The *United States Code* then compiles all of the laws into categories (such as laws affecting natural resource management, civil rights, education, etc.) and renumbers them. Regulations that the various federal agencies write to enforce the laws are published daily in the *Federal Register* and then compiled in the *Code of Federal Regulations.*

A reporter researching the Endangered Species Act, then, might pursue it through CIS, to the *United States Code,* to the *Code of Federal Regulations.* That would give the journalist a thorough handle on the public rationale for passing the law and on how it is supposed to be enforced. Naturally, the reporter might want to look at the various federal court decisions affecting the act, too.

For census information: Some of the most revealing, most accessible, and most overlooked publications are those from the U.S. Census Bureau; these can be found at almost every major library. The well-known population census is conducted every ten years and can provide an excellent picture of a community and its various racial, ethnic, and occupation groups. The housing census, conducted at the same time, portrays the state of home ownership, kinds of homes, and so forth. Such information is always useful when writing about proposed shopping centers in particular neighborhoods, education patterns, the "gentrification" of certain areas (the change of low-income neighborhoods into middle-class or upper-class ones), and so forth. In addition to these two censuses, the federal bureau also conducts others, including one of agriculture and one of business. These are issued during the interims between the major population counts and can provide statistics about the number of farms in an area, the size of businesses, ownership patterns, and so forth. Reporters can use the data to show whether large corporations are taking over the small family farms in their area, for example, or whether farmland is being converted to suburban housing developments.

In addition to the census books that can be found on library shelves, the bureau issues data on computer discs; while the books cover large regions (such as states or counties), the discs contain statistics at the census block level (about the size of a city block), allowing much more precise study.

For information on information: Countless other reference works exist, including reference works listing other reference books. You might consider checking such guides as Bell and Swidan's *Reference Books: A Brief Guide,* Wyner's *American Reference Books Annual,* and William Rivers's *Finding Facts.*

*Thinking about the paper trail you have
left in your life can be helpful in finding
documents about other individuals.*

Twice he cursed the government; but then
he reckoned the Lord forgave him for the
first and justified the second.
                                                —EDWIN JOHN PRATT

Beyond the libraries, there are vast collections of records in every
government, corporate, and institutional office. If you think about the
paper trail in your own life—the number of documents signed, the forms
filled out, the reports made, the bills paid—you will readily recognize how
extensive those records are, and how much information you can collect
about another individual, even if that person does not want to grant you
an interview. This is particularly true of anyone who has been in the
limelight for any reason. The trail left by an individual extends from birth
to death.

An important note is in order about pursuing any personal paper trail.
At all times the ethics of obtaining and publishing the information should
be uppermost in a journalist's mind. Sometimes the thrill of the search
and the excitement of finding out information about someone can obscure
all reason.

Legal considerations have to be kept in mind, too. Privacy law in the
United States has its roots in the late 1800s, when jurists began to believe
that individuals subjected to the exploits of the sensationalistic press
ought to have some recourse. For many decades there was very little
development in or expansion of privacy law, but in the late 1960s and
early 1970s the courts and legislatures developed new interest in declaring that individuals have a "right to privacy." The Supreme Court has
ruled that whatever is on the public record can be reported with impu-
nity—so long as it is reported accurately—but errors that create false
impressions are likely to subject journalists to "false light" privacy suits,
and reports based on records that are not public are likely to draw inva-
sion-of-privacy suits. The courts do recognize that "newsworthiness" is a
defense against such suits, but—significantly—at least one federal circuit
court of appeals has ruled that it is up to courts and juries, not just
editors, to determine in the end what is "newsworthy" and "of legitimate
public concern."

When you obtain records not legally defined as public, then, and
especially when those records reveal "private personal information" (such
as about sexual habits, past criminal behavior, medical histories, financial

status, etc.), be sure to temper your reportorial prowess with ethical and legal knowledge.

Birth certificates: These usually list the place of birth, the hospital, the ages of the parents, perhaps the father's occupation, the name of the attending physician, a notation about any birth defects, and sometimes information on the number of brothers and sisters. Technically these are not public records; you cannot simply ask for another person's birth certificate and be given it. However, you might find copies filed away in other public records and you may be able to obtain a copy from a friendly source.

School records: Yearbooks and such are usually available publicly and can provide information about an individual's classmates, teachers, and clubs and activities. Grade and attendance records, while not technically public, might also be available.

Marriage records: These, of course, tell whom an individual married and, just as important, who the witnesses were.

Property records: Located at various county offices (usually the assessor's, the recorder's, and the treasurer's), these can reveal what real property an individual owns, what it is assessed at, how much taxes are paid on it, who holds the mortgage, etc. All manner of financial transactions can be reported officially through a county recorder's office.

Business records: These will list the fictitious business names that an individual may have adopted, identify those who run state-chartered corporations, and document business partnerships. Remember that every business has contact with government at some point; even flower vendors usually have to get a city license. Others, such as professionals, may have to pass licensing tests administered by the state.

City directories: These are various guides that may give information about an individual's occupation, spouse, and civic activities and, in the case of "social registers" of the elite, provide information about schooling, membership in exclusive clubs, etc.

Expense accounts: Those of public officials are public record, and should be routinely examined by the appropriate beat reporters. Where did the presiding county court judge stay when he attended a judicial conference in Waikiki—at the best hotel or at a moderate one? Did he dine moderately? Did he take his spouse? Corporate workers have to file expense accounts, too, of course; these are not public documents but an enterprising journalist may be able to obtain them from a friendly company auditor or accountant.

Credit records: Technically these are private, but media outlets are businesses that have the capability to tap into any number of credit reporting services. These records provide information about an individual's bills, record in paying those bills, indebtedness, etc.

Driver's records: Usually available from the state divisions of motor vehicles, or from friendly police sources willing to run a check, these records cover auto registration (how many and what kind of automobiles does a person own) and driver's licenses. You can also track license plate numbers back to their owners.

Military records: Such documents contain information about commissions, military serial numbers, dates and places of birth, inductions, discharges, and so forth; for active servicemen, they can be obtained from the Pentagon; for former military personnel, turn to the Veterans Administration offices.

Newspaper libraries: If the individual has ever been newsworthy, the clippings libraries at local newspapers can be invaluable, since they often contain anecdotes about the person, connections with other individuals or businesses, and important activities. Sometimes public libraries clip the local papers and maintain files. If not, try the newspapers themselves. The bigger ones tend to turn the public away, but it is easy enough to find a reporter on the inside who will either pull the clips for you or clear the way so you can. Smaller newspapers are often thrilled to see you, but they may have a lousy and sporadically maintained library.

Income tax records: These, of course, are not public documents, but the Internal Revenue Service will respond to inquiries about whether a person has filed an income tax return for a certain year. Also, if the individual you are interested in is an officer of a nonprofit corporation, such corporate tax reports *are* public and you may be able to at least discover salary and fringe benefit payments. By the way, other government agencies as well as congressional committees can get access to private income tax records, usually for statistical or investigative purposes; those sometimes get leaked. Even IRS agents sometimes will leak information. President Nixon's tax reports, for example, were leaked to reporters.

Medical and psychological records: Again, these are technically private but sometimes available. In her investigation of jail rapes, for example, Loretta Tofani was able to convince medical workers at the jail to give her access to medical reports on individuals who had been assaulted. Sometimes these records also will be entered into legal proceedings, as parts of affidavits or as exhibits. At that point they become public records. While working on a story about two parents charged with murdering one of their daughters, for example, a reporter for the *Riverside Press-Enterprise* was able to obtain psychological studies of the father that had been entered into the court record.

Business records: If an individual is a prominent officer or executive of a publicly held corporation, labor union, insurance company, or financial institution, information about salary, fringe benefits, and expense accounts my be available from various reports filed with the federal government or with various state agencies.

Criminal history: Technically information about a person's past crimes is not public except in the court records where convictions or dismissals have been noted. However, the public records are not nationally computerized, whereas those used by law enforcement agencies are. A reporter thus does well to cultivate a friendly law source who is willing to run background checks (at some personal career risk) or to provide information from checks already run for the agency. Check with everyone from the local police to the federal drug enforcement and organized crime strike forces for this kind of information. (Criminal histories used to be freely available, but in the wake of privacy legislation they have become increasingly difficult to obtain.)

Professional associations: If an individual is a lawyer, the bar association can tell a reporter something about his background – for example, where he went to school. The same is true of medical associations if the person is a doctor, and of other types of professional associations.

Court records: These are always an immediate stopping place, since they can be a mine for all types of information. The tax returns you have been hankering to see may well be on file at divorce court or at bankruptcy court. The medical and psychological reports may be in evidence in a criminal trial. Background on an individual's family history or family property holdings may be lodged somewhere in a civil case file. Inheritance details may be readily accessible through probate court. Always check to see whether an individual has been sued or has sued someone else. And do not just stop at the official record of the proceedings; remember to delve into the folders full of affidavits or depositions or exhibits. Sometimes the really important details will be there.

Death certificates: As the beginning of an individual's life is marked by a piece of paper, so is the end. Death certificates list the time, place, and cause of death. Also, you may find coroner's investigation reports, especially if any foul play is suspected. These go into greater depth about the circumstances of an individual's death, often describing the room, other witnesses, situation of the body, and so forth.

Practice in using the Freedom of Information Act is essential, if sometimes frustrating.

Free men set themselves free.
—JAMES OPPENHEIM

In 1967, Congress attempted to ensure maximum openness in government proceedings by passing the Freedom of Information (FOI) Act, requiring all federal agencies to establish procedures whereby citizens could obtain information. The act also directed the agencies to establish reasonable fees for photocopying requested material (fees can be waived if the information will primarily benefit the general public, as through news reports), and to make available all information except that specifically exempted in certain categories. The exempt categories include items that are to be kept secret because of national security; internal personnel rules and practices; trade secrets or commercial and financial information submitted to government agencies with the understanding that it will remain secret; personnel and medical files; agency memorandums that would not normally be available; law enforcement investigation records that might interfere with enforcement or with privacy if released; certain reports from financial institutions to government regulatory agencies; and certain geological and geophysical data.

Since 1967 (and since 1974, when the FOI Act was broadened by several amendments designed to make more government documents available), many states have passed parallel legislation requiring the opening of their government files.

Freedom of information laws generally require that agencies respond quickly to any request for information. At the federal level, a response within ten days is required, with the agency allowed a ten-day extension so long as it informs you. If the agency denies the request, the denial can be appealed to the head of the agency. After the second denial, a journalist seeking information at the federal level can turn to the U.S. district courts, which may require that the agency surrender the material to a judge so that the judge can make an independent determination about whether the material fits into one of the exempt categories. The agency has to prove why it can legally withhold the information; you do not have to establish a good reason for getting it. In fact, you are not required to state the reason you want the information.

Often reporters will be able to get public records without having to cite the FOI Act, but sometimes a gentle prod may be necessary to get a civil servant to respond. If gentle prods do not succeed, it may be necessary to demand that the bureaucrat tell you which section of the FOI Act justifies withholding the information.

Most requests can be handled orally, but sometimes agencies are sticky about wanting the request in writing. Here is a sample letter:

> Title
> Name of Agency
> Address of Agency
> City, State, Zip
>
> Dear _____:
>
> I am requesting access to [identify the records as clearly as you can; you need not have the exact name or number, though] under the provisions of the Freedom of Information Act, 5 U.S.C. Section 552.
> Should there be any fees for searching or copying the records, please waive them since the information will be used to benefit the general public. [Or: Please inform me of what the charges for photocopying will be.]
> If any part or all of this request is denied, please cite the specific exemptions justifying the denial.
> I look forward to your handling this request as quickly as possible.
>
> Sincerely,
>
> [your name
> and title]

EXERCISES

1. Use information that should be available in your university library to answer the first six of the eight questions at the start of this chapter. What sources could you turn to? (The last two questions require the use of documents on file with federal agencies. See the chapter on reporting business and economics news for more information about such documents.)

2. Select a local politician and determine, solely through the use of public records, the following information:
a. What real estate does he or she own in your county (or in neighboring counties)?
b. What is that real estate assessed at? What taxes are paid on it? (You might want to take this a step further and see what the neighbors' properties are assessed at and how much they are paying in taxes. If you notice any large discrepancies in property that seems roughly similar, you may be on to a story.)
c. Has he or she ever sued anyone or been sued? (You may need to limit this to the last five-year period.)
d. Is he or she in a business partnership with anyone?

e. How much did he or she collect in contributions during the last campaign, and how much was spent? (This information will come from campaign financial reports, filed with the city, county, or state.) From whom did the contributions come?

You may want to stop here and simply treat this as an exercise in finding documents, or you may choose to go ahead, conduct interviews, and prepare a profile on the politician. The class could treat it as a project that will eventually produce a series of articles about the members of the city council.

3. Using the latest U.S. Census reports, prepare a statistical profile of a small city, county, or neighborhood. What is the racial and ethnic background of the people living there? What is the median income? What is the state of the housing? What is the value of the housing? How many occupants are renters and how many are owners? What is the average education of the occupants? If you want, compare current census information with that from previous decades for a story about the way in which the community surrounding your university has changed. By fleshing out the statistics with interviews, you should be able to develop a story about the changing face of the university neighborhood and, perhaps, the role the university has had in changing it.

4. Use the agricultural census to prepare a statistical picture of the way in which a neighboring rural county has been affected by urbanization or by changing economics. How much land has gone out of farming? Have the farm products changed significantly? Has the pattern of farm ownership shifted from owners who live and work the farm to corporations? Has the size of the average farm increased?

5. Prepare a study—or a story—on the kinds of paper trails that a single institution generates; for example, a local hospital or your own university. Focus only on the kinds of paper that have to be filed with public agencies; ignore, for example, the student registration forms that a university generates for internal use and instead discover what kinds of reports the university has to file with federal agencies, state agencies, and local zoning or planning boards. For the purpose of this exercise, you might assume that the institution you are studying is hostile and so you have to obtain a particular document from another source. Where might you find your university's affirmative action plan, for example? Is there a report that might list the salaries of all the top executives of the university? What about a report on the university's pension plan? How about a study of whether the university has complied with requirements for ending discrimination against women athletes? If the university (or hospital) generates radioactive wastes in its physics or medical laboratories, what kinds of inspection reports must it file on the disposal of that waste and on precautions to ensure that no employees are contaminated? Are there any reports on file with the federal Occupational Safety and Health Administration regarding working conditions for employees? Do any university executives or directors sit on political boards and have to file financial disclosure statements?

Remember: you are looking only for records that are public.

4 *Making Sense with Numbers and Statistics*

What is written without effort
is in general read without pleasure.

—SAMUEL JOHNSON

JARGON—that weedy cultural growth characterized by unintelligibility—seems to thrive on dense clusters of numbers, statistics, and percentages. Every reporter whose job it is to turn out data for mass consumption has a doubly hard row to hoe: before the story can be shaped for a public wont to avoid all things numerical, the reporter must be steeled to cut through the tangle. For example, one former *Wall Street Journal* reporter remembers that paper as one of the leading newspapers in the United States, but he quit his job to escape writing so many stories full of numbers of dollars that affected businesses. "The *Journal* is a great newspaper. I know. But I knew I'd have to work for several years to graduate to writing non-number stories." The escape failed, however. He went to work for *Fortune* magazine, and, like any medium, it carries many numbers.

No matter where anyone works these days, the need exists to cope with numbers, statistics, and percentages. It is almost inevitable that any journalist who writes or edits any story will have to deal with numbers in some form. Whether or not you are one who trembles at the sight of a single six-digit figure, read on.

52

Learn and work by the numbers and you have most of your tools for running a business. A reporter must report numbers; that also involves learning and knowing how to report them.

Men are like numbers: they acquire their importance from their position.
— NAPOLEON

Although you may be one of the millions of people who think of arithmetic as complicated, boring, or both, almost inevitably you will be seeing numbers every day. For example, consider the address of your home, many of the streets you travel, your telephone — all of these are or contain numbers. No one can avoid numbers, not even by living an isolated life. If you had lived more than 200 years ago as a humble farmer, you could not have escaped numbers. Consider this interview conducted by a Frenchman, J. Hector St. John de Crevecour, with a frontier farmer in 1774:

Well, Friend, how do you do now; I am come fifty odd miles on purpose to see you; how do you go on with your new cutting and slashing?

Very well, good sir; we learn to use of the axe bravely, we shall make it out; we have a belly full of victuals every day; our cows run about and come home full of milk; our hogs get fat of themselves in the woods. Oh, this is a good country! God bless the King and William Penn; we shall do very well by and by, if we keep our health.

What did you give for your land?

Thirty-five shillings per acre, payable in seven years.

How many acres have you got?

A hundred and fifty. . . .

Like those of that other day, we have numbers that are a language. Consider food costs. Even winos who do not work know the costs of food — and probably wince when they think of the astronomical amount of money needed to buy a half pound of cheese or a loaf of bread. Some ordinary and extraordinary people have experienced job losses, thus gaining firsthand knowledge of unemployment figures. To most adults, tax rates are immediately recognizable as challenges. Those who live in homes must think of property tax increases, which almost automatically will increase the cost of living for both renters and homeowners. No matter who you are, you must think of numbers.

Every day the news media carry stories that quote numbers, statistics, or percentages. This is the stuff of precision journalism: cost-of-living increases; budget figures of the federal government, state government, county government, municipal government; election results; polls taken by newspapers, magazines, electronic media, or polling organizations; tax reports; census statistics; automobile sales; crime rates; and the number of serious accidents on the highways—all of these stories and many others begin as numbers.

A 716-page report ("Report on American Habits") from the Department of Health and Human Services during the first year of the Reagan presidency pointed the way to change in the living habits of many Americans. The trouble was, however, that this mammoth report was almost unreadable. The task of the reporters was to make its contents comprehensible so that Americans could determine what they must do. And, of course, the report contained many numbers.

As a reporter, you must learn to translate number-filled jargon into understandable English. Because most of your audience will not read reporting if you include number after number, write your stories so that those who are interested will read them. Here are a few rules of thumb:

1. *The information must be condensed.* Almost inevitably, those who prepare reports will attempt to state almost everything they think is useful. Much of it is not.

2. *Report significant aspects.* Ask yourself: how will readers be affected in their everyday lives?

3. *Place action in context.* Think of the past and the future. How would it have affected people earlier, and how will it affect your children and grandchildren?

4. *Always use simple language.* Do not think of yourself as one who is writing for a special audience, such as a reviewer of books, theater, and movies. Think of your audience as made up of interested readers who will not wade through jargon but will read simple English.

5. *Space out numbers.* In writing, think of your readers as though they hate numbers. Although you must include numbers, count them after writing the first draft. On the average, are there two or three numbers for each sentence? If so, you must space them out by eliminating a few or by writing additional number-free sentences between the number-filled ones.

Here is a story that follows the rules of thumb almost exactly:

COMMENTS	STORY
The reporter received many reports, all of which were longer than this story. He knew he had to condense the information.	Special-interest groups raised a record $189 million in the last election, betting more heavily than ever on incumbents and continuing to

He uses only one number in the first sentence. The reporter knows that many people hate numbers.

Note especially how the reporter spaces the numbers out. First, "23 months," then, ten words later, then two sentences, and so on.

favor Democrats, according to preliminary figures.

The Federal Election Commission said the total, raised by political-action committees in the nearly 23 months ended in late November, topped the amount raised in the 1979–1980 election period by $60 million, or 49 percent.

Most of the money goes to cover overhead costs, such as expensive direct-mail operations, or is given to state election campaigns. However, the commission said that through mid-October the special-interest groups had given $70.4 million to Senate and House campaigns, an increase of 39 percent from the period two years earlier, and more than double the amount of four years before.

He does not use all the numbers he has. Instead, he translates numbers into percentages.

Remember that the reporter must use simple language. Almost anyone who is in the tenth grade could read this story and understand it.

Through mid-October, incumbents received 69 percent of special-interest gifts, up from 62 percent in the previous election and 58 percent in the one before that, the figures show.

This is a difficult paragraph to write, but he managed it by using only percentages.

Democrats got 54 percent of the special-interest money, including 94 percent of labor-union donations from corporation-sponsored groups. Democrats got 54 percent of the political-action gifts in the comparable period in the 1980 elections, and 56 percent in 1978.

Those who are especially interested can read the statistics in the last section of the story.

These are the first 10 political-action committees in order of their donations to Congressional campaigns in the 21½ months ended October 13. . . .

The following lead sentences, however, present a special case:

Forty thousand Florida realtors are selling three million homesites so rapidly to the seven million tourists who visit the state each year, to the three thousand new residents who arrive each week, and to the hundreds of mail-in ten-dollar checks every day that Florida is hard put to hold onto all this business: one development is technically in Alabama. This is the little island of Pineda, a few miles west of the Florida border in Mobile Bay, which will soon be sliced into 2,148 waterfront lots. It is distinctly Floridian, however, for three Fort Lauderdale men are putting a million dollars into it, and a sizable portion of the money will be spent to raise eight hundred acres safely above high tide.

When analyzing the first sentence according to rules, it seems atrocious. This sentence piles figures atop one another: forty thousand, three million, seven million, three thousand, hundreds, ten-dollar—all in a breathless sixty-word sentence. Is that not atrocious? Not at all. The writer set out to write a pell-mell sentence, thinking, "How can I emphasize the immense Florida boom? How can I give it force? The thing I must do is to assault the readers with figures." The result is a creative impact that sets the tone for an article that does indeed emphasize the immensity of the boom. This technique should be used very sparingly.

Good statistical sampling is an exacting science, some say an art. Learn the science well enough to spot faulty techniques.

> First, get your facts, then you can distort them as much as you like.
> —MARK TWAIN

When people want to know what the general public believes about a particular topic, they know it is impossible to question individually the more than 230 million Americans. Instead, they employ a method social scientists have developed, termed *sampling*. If some people want to know how a large vat of lemonade tastes, they know drinking the entire vat would be silly. They also know that tasting a cup of that lemonade will tell them whether the entire vat tastes good, bad, or indifferent. Social scientists know that asking questions of 1,600 of 230 million people is rough sampling, but that it will be accurate within a limited range of error.

How do social scientists choose their samples? Say they want to survey people over the age of twenty-one in the United States. The interviewers are *not* given the right to interview just anyone over twenty-one. Instead, the planners of this survey work out *probability* sampling: each person in the United States then has a known probability of being in the sample.

How do they choose *national* samples? First, the survey organization decides how many will be interviewed. Second, the number of interviews that will be assigned to each section of the nation is determined by the percentage of the population living in each section. If 20 percent of the population lives in the Southeast, 20 percent of the interviews will be assigned to the Southeast. Because the planners must designate interview areas in each region, let's say Atlanta, one of the dozen largest metropolitan areas, will be one of the interview areas. Smaller cities and rural areas are chosen by chance; the Augusta, Georgia, area may fall in one sample along with a farm area in northern Florida. All city blocks in Augusta may be listed and a random sample of them chosen. Interviews are to be taken on, say, the 300 block of Elm Avenue and on the 1100 block of Alvarado Street in Augusta. To cut transportation costs, several interviews are *clustered* on the same block. All interviewers are told at which houses to interview, and which apartments in an apartment building. In the third dwelling unit, the interviewer may be told to interview the second oldest female. In the following unit, the interviewer may be told to interview the second oldest male. In selecting the interviewee, the interviewer cannot select just anyone. If the person to be interviewed is not at home, the interviewer would be directed to return there two or three more times. If the interviewee is never at home, he or she would be dropped. The interviewer can *never* talk to just anyone.

Sampling error is used by survey organizations to identify how close actual values are to those reported in a survey group. Sampling error does not include error that comes from having poor questions or incompetent interviewers. Also, 1,600 interviews cannot be expected to give precise estimates of attitudes of millions of people. For a sample of 1,600, the sampling error is plus or minus 2.5 percent. If an organization finds that 45.5 percent of the sample favors a proposal for limiting nuclear arms, the true population proportion is likely to be between 43 percent and 48 percent 95 percent of the time.

The sampling error in our example can be reduced by 50 percent if the survey organization quadruples the size of the sample to 6,400. However, the additional 4,800 interviews would also quadruple the cost to the organization. If a survey organization should be limited by money to 400 interviews, the sampling error would be doubled to plus or minus 5 percent. Using numbers much smaller would make it almost impossible to generate an accurate report, for as sample size is decreased, the sampling error is increased—sometimes to a point that is unacceptable to serious researchers. If there are ten or fewer cases, no one who knows about samples would trust such a report.

The problems and opportunities in polling
interviews are strikingly similar to those of
a news reporter's. Learn to be precise.

The surest way to convey misinformation is
often to tell the strict truth.
                                     —MARK TWAIN

Although the above statements about the social scientists' practices
are true, it is instructive to see what happens to those who attempt to
become social scientists. Many of those who try it are baffled by the
fieldwork, work other than experiments in a laboratory. Leonard Sellers,
a graduate student at Stanford, describes fieldwork problems he and his
colleagues experienced in conducting a survey:

> We randomly pulled some 300 names from the mailing lists of the
> two local Sierra Club chapters. This was for a survey of "eco-activists"—
> defined as any members of a conservation group—to find where they got
> environment information.
>   First, we had to word the information carefully to convince people
> that we weren't selling something. This worked for most people, but we
> still had to spend time with some, assuring them that we were not selling
> magazines.
>   Second, the demographics of our population—high education and
> income—caused some problems. There was a high percentage of un-
> listed phone numbers and M.D.s with answering services. Additionally,
> because of high education, some respondents were very hip to what we
> were doing. We were asked astute questions about our sampling proce-
> dure, questionnaire construction, and intended method of data analysis.
> The range of "experts," from biologists to statisticians, was wide and a
> little unsettling. To have your questionnaire critiqued while in the proc-
> ess of administering it is unnerving.
>   Because of the mixture of demographics and the survey area, which
> included Palo Alto and Berkeley, we also had a strange but rare problem.
> Graduate students administering the survey would sometimes find
> themselves dealing with "academic giants." At least one student com-
> pletely blew a questionnaire because the respondent turned out to be the
> man who had written the main textbooks in his undergraduate major;
> the student was so rattled by personally talking to the man that his
> interview was worthless.

Although such a problem is rare, its variations could be cited by many
interviewers. To minimize such occurrences, social scientists long ago
developed a method called *pretesting*. Instead of going immediately into
the field to question interviewees, the interview schedule first will be
tried out on a few people. The value of pretesting is suggested by an
experience of Rae Goodell when she was a graduate student. In a large
research project that was designed to analyze mass media coverage of

environmental news, her part was to identify the environmental reporters. She also had to describe the reporters' standards for environmental reporting and their opinions of its quality. She spent several weeks developing one questionnaire for reporters and another for editors. She devised her own questions, then checked them with professors and other graduate students. Other project workers who had other assignments asked Goodell to include questions that would yield information useful to them. (This is a fairly common occurrence in professional research projects.) When she was ready to pretest, the questionnaire for editors ran four pages; that for reporters ran five. Goodell has written of the results of the pretest:

> 1. I had the dullest question first. The project director wanted a definition of *environmental reporting* to come out of all this, and I had the two questions about definition first. After one of the pretests, I wrote in the margin: "Hit with a grabber first. This is the dullest."
> 2. As a once and future newspaper reporter, I had written the questions for the newspaper people, overlooking the radio and TV respondents; e.g., one question asked if the reporter had a problem getting "enough space from editors" for environmental stories; it had to be changed to "space from editors or air time from directors."
> 3. Some of the questions were hard to read — it was difficult to figure where I wanted the answer put. I typed up the final version for photocopying myself, to make sure questions were arranged clearly.
> 4. On one question, the pretest interviewees pointed out that I would get the "ideal" answer, the answer everyone knew was "right," rather than what was really going on. The question asked, "How diverse an audience do you try to reach with environmental stories." Everyone checked, and guaranteed that all survey respondents would check, "all readers or listeners."

As a result, the questionnaire that Goodell ultimately used in the field was quite different from the pretest version in length, spacing, question order, and wording.

Be skeptical when reporting on polls. Despite the lesson of the Truman/Dewey debacle in 1948, the gaffes go on.

> With effervescing opinions, the quickest way to let them get flat is to let them get exposed to the air.
> —OLIVER WENDELL HOLMES

Survey organizations are certain that they are on the right track because they have refined their methods of surveying. Are they right?

If you have learned what some respected survey organizations did on the night of the California election on November 2, 1982, you probably look at their predictions with skepticism. Decision Making Information (DMI) was right in forecasting that George Deukmejian would win the governorship with 49.1 percent of the vote, while Tom Bradley, Deukmejian's opponent, would receive 48.5 percent. The actual returns were Deukmejian, 49.0 percent; Bradley, 48.3 percent. Most of the many other polling organizations were far off the mark. Hugh Schwartz, Bradley's pollster, showed Bradley running 11 points ahead of Deukmejian. Even pollster Mervin Field, who heads the best-known surveying organization in California, predicted Bradley would win going away. Moreover, Field said he had taken 6,000 interviews with the voters exiting the precincts, which means that the sampling error should be only 1.5 percent. He also remarked that Edmund G. Brown, Jr., was leading Pete Wilson for election to the U.S. Senate. The actual results showed Wilson winning by 51 percent to Brown's 45 percent. Over and over, most of the surveying organizations were wrong.

Why did the highly trained pollsters' predictions go awry?

First, nearly all the pollsters used *exit polls,* a device in which surveyors station interviewers near precincts to ask voters on election day how they voted. The surveyors knew that any predictions taken before the election would register whom the voters favored at that particular time. The exit polls seemed a good device.

Bud Lewis directed the *Los Angeles Times* survey, which forswore exit polls. "I think it is dangerous and foolhardy to make projections based on exit polls," Lewis said, describing them as "typically subject to very high refusal rates"—people refusing to be questioned. He added that election officials frequently make it difficult for poll takers to approach those leaving the polls at a reasonable distance from polling places, and that in some neighborhoods, particularly those populated by many elderly people and minorities, voters are leary of being accosted by strangers taking the polls. The result may be a twisted sample.

How did Decision Making Information predict so closely the votes for the governor (and for the U.S. Senate)?

Gary Lawrence, vice president of DMI, was working in DMI's main office on the eve of the election. Scanning a printout of the U.S. Senate race, Lawrence saw that Republican Wilson, as expected, had a 5 percent lead over Democrat Brown. Then he saw an astonishing set of figures in the Republican-Democrat race. Almost overnight, it seemed, Democrat Bradley's lead over Republican Deukmejian had evaporated.

On the blackboard where Lawrence had been writing the "rolling averages" during the past ten days, he began to develop a different scenario. Lawrence had to explain the information he was getting from a telephone calling center where seven teams of nine men and women had been at work calling voters randomly since 5 P.M.

"We are always dealing with various scenarios," Lawrence said, explaining that understanding nightly poll-tracking is more art than science. That election eve night, more than 1,000 voters were telephoned by the trained callers. Supervisors sat in a glassed-in cage, monitoring the callers as they asked whether respondents were registered to vote. If not, was anyone else in the respondent's household a voter? If the answer was no again, the interview was terminated.

Lawrence then placed a new question on the lists of the callers, testing the probability that a potential voter would go to the polls. This question was pivotal in predicting that Bradley might be in trouble on election night. Lawrence thought it was more important to know who would vote rather than how many.

Just after midnight, seven hours before the polls opened, Lawrence's mood was brightening. "Wilson looks solid," he said. The Bradley-Deukmejian race was a "squeaker—either way." A bit later Lawrence went back to the blackboard and adjusted Bradley's lead upward to 3.5 percent, just outside his 3.1 percent margin of error. It was "too close to call," he said.

Early on election day, however, Lawrence had completed his various scenarios and concluded that if the voter turnout was in the mid-sixties— it actually was 67.7 percent—Wilson would win, 52.2 percent to 45.2 percent. Also, Deukmejian would defeat Bradley by 49.1 percent to 48.5 percent. Lawrence was so close to the final election returns that his predictions are remarkable.

Polling goes deeper than predicting the outcome of a senate race.

> I always avoid prophesying beforehand
> because it is much better to prophesy after
> the event has already taken place.
> —WINSTON CHURCHILL

One problem of sampling includes *weighting* in some surveys. A few researchers decide to oversample a group within a population so that the group's attitudes can be measured with more accuracy. For example, they might double-sample women if they want to generate an even more accurate estimate of their opinions; say the sample might include 500 men and 1,000 women. Nonetheless, the extra interviews with women should not be included when describing overall attitudes of the entire population. To solve the problem, half the interviews with women could be dropped, but that would completely waste the information gathered in those interviews. Instead, the women are "half-weighted," with each female being counted half as much as a male. Or the males can be double-weighted. Research tables would be constructed so that they would show only 1,000 respondents. This device allows the weighted results to be used without worrying about weighting. Most of the time, the use of weights in analysis is invisible.

Many leading survey organizations prefer to report percentage distributions on single variables: what proportion of people favor nuclear weaponry and what proportion oppose it? Academic researchers are more interested in understanding popular attitudes. Of course, explanation of popular attitudes requires the use of more than one variable. Say someone is interested in explaining why some people vote Democrat and others Republican. The vote itself is the *dependent variable*. Other variables are the *independent variables;* they predict or explain the dependent variable.

For example, religion and race could be used to help explain or predict a person's vote. The dependent variable may be likened to an effect, and the independent variable may be likened to a cause. Time order often gives a clue as to which is the dependent variable: causes occur before effects. If you were investigating the relationship between education and vote, education would be the independent variable – schooling occurs before voting begins. Of course, a person's vote does not indicate how much education he or she would have had in younger years.

In publishing results of a survey, don't overburden readers with statistical jargon.

Every style that is not boring is a good one.
                                              —VOLTAIRE

On January 6, 1983, the *Wall Street Journal* published the following survey, a fine example of numerical craftsmanship:

COMMENTS	STORY
	By ROGER RICKLEFS
	Staff Reporter of The Wall Street Journal
The first two paragraphs of this story list no numbers (except the year 1983). Because the reporter knows that the Wall Street Journal uses many numbers and statistics, he uses them judiciously when he must.	American business leaders are a sadder but wiser bunch this year. They tend to think economic conditions will improve in 1983, but they are much more guarded in their optimism than they were a year ago.
	Compared with a year ago, fewer expect the economy to improve and more expect any improvement to be only moderate, a Gallup Organization survey of business leaders for The Wall Street Journal indicates. Small-business owners are considerably less optimistic than their bigger-company counterparts.
Although the third paragraph carries some percentages, note how the fourth paragraph quotes someone who uses plain English, no numbers.	Asked in telephone interviews last month how they thought 1983 would differ from 1982 for business generally, a large share—46% at the big companies, 33% at medium-sized concerns and 31% at small businesses—mentioned an end to the recession and or improvement in the economy. These figures compared with 56%, 39% and 36% in a similar poll in December 1981.
	"There will be some recovery, but it will be slow and gradual," says the chairman of a large coal company. The president of a medium-sized publishing concern expects "no significant difference. . . . Hope fades." But an oil executive thinks 1983 "should be better because '82 was so damn terrible."

Now that the readers are lured by the reporter's simple language, he uses a few percentages.

Some Optimism

The share of executives mentioning that they expect "only moderate improvement" in the economy this year increased to 29% in the big companies, 30% in the medium-sized and 20% in the small. A year earlier, the figures were only 5% or 6%.

But the news wasn't all bleak. Gallup finds only 5% of the big-company leaders mention that they think the recession will continue or worsen, down from 22% a year earlier. The figure also declines to 9% from 22% among medium-sized-company chiefs and to 9% from 19% among small-business owners.

Moreover, 13% of the big-company chiefs say they expect an improvement in the construction industry, compared with only 1% a year earlier. Medium-sized-company chiefs also mention this expectation more often, though small-business owners cite it a bit less frequently than they did in December 1981. . . .

When testing a poll for its accuracy, asking the right questions about it can reveal irregularities.

Truth is a fruit which should not be plucked until it is ripe.

— VOLTAIRE

The following questions should be used by journalists when they are assessing the validity of a poll. Nearly all of these were suggested by the American Association for Public Opinion.

1. *Who paid for the poll?* If someone has a vested interest in the results, that must be known and publicized.

2. *When was the poll taken?* Changes caused by events are so common that it is important to know exactly when the poll was taken.

3. *Who were the people interviewed?* For example, what broad group of people were interviewed?

4. *How were the interviews obtained?* By telephone, by mail, or by personal interviews?

5. *How were the questions worded?* Exactly what was asked is important. Minor differences in the wording of questions can produce different results.

6. *Who was interviewed?* It is important to know not only the area sampled but also the demographic breakdown of the sample.

7. *Who were the interviewers?* For example, if a candidate for mayor is the subject of polls taken by his or her supporters, the results may be biased.

8. *How were the people selected for interviews?* What was the sample design?

9. *How many people were interviewed?* The number of people interviewed is important in that it gives some idea of sampling error.

10. *What was the response rate?* What percentage of the people who were asked to be interviewed agreed to participate?

11. *What was the base of the data if it was based on part of total sample?* A survey organization questions 1,600 people and reports that among Catholic voters certain answers are seven times as popular as among Protestants. Some readers of the report are likely to believe that 1,600 Catholic voters were surveyed. In fact, a bit less than half those interviewed were Catholics.

Stephen Isaacs, formerly of the *Washington Post,* notes, "Many other points can be useful in evaluating a poll. These include whether interviewers had any discretion as to whom they interviewed; what time of day interviews were conducted; how the interviewers were supervised and whether their work was validated – checked to determine whether they actually did the interviews they reported and whether they reported the interviews truthfully; whether any 'weighting' was done to bring the actual interviewees into line with the demographic makeup of the electorate."

EXERCISES

1. Read again the story earlier in the chapter that begins, "Forty thousand Florida realtors are selling three million homes. . . ." Be prepared to answer this question in class: What do you think about this paragraph? Think about the paragraph and support your opinion with facts about reading.

2. Read the following story, and decide individually whether it uses too many numbers. Be prepared to vote and to explain why you think the story is good or bad:

Five percent of all hospital patients get infections from the hospital and about 20,000 of those die each year, the director of Bowman Hospital said last night.

About 2 million patients are infected from hospitals each year, accounting for 5 percent of all patients admitted to hospitals in the United States, Williams Boggs said.

"The estimated incidence may reach as high as 15 percent or more in some individual hospitals," Boggs said.

"The annual cost of hospital-associated infections is from about $1.5 billion to $1.8 billion nationwide," Boggs emphasized.

3. In October 1976, a nationwide vaccination program was mounted against swine flu. The shots were given to members of the groups most at risk: the elderly and the infirm. At the beginning, 24,000 people age sixty-five and over were given shots, and three of those died. Eight states suspended the vaccination program. If you were a statistician, what would you say?

4. Plan a schoolwide election; devise a survey attempting to predict election outcomes; and write follow-up stories on both the results of the survey and the actual election results:

a. Working as a group in class, develop a scenario for a student election at your school. Name the offices up for grabs, the candidates for each office, the parties or organizations they represent, if any, and the major issues of the election.

b. Work on your own to construct a hypothetical survey plan and questionnaire to predict the coming election. Record (1) the numbers of males and females running for office; (2) the actual numbers of students registered at your school, along with numbers and percentages of males and females; (3) the numbers of each sex you will interview in your sample; and (4) special considerations (if past voting records indicate strong turnouts by members of local Greek societies, for example, how will your sample take that into account?). Write out your survey questions and your method of conducting the survey.

c. Compile an imaginary set of results for your survey. Report them in the form of a news story in the student newspaper, incorporating statistics, quotations, and background information.

d. Assume the election has been held and decide the outcomes. Again in the form of a piece for the student paper, work the data into a comprehensive, comprehensible story.

e. In class, discuss the merits of plans and questionnaires devised by class members. Read aloud the survey stories and analyze successful uses of numerical material. Do the same for the election stories.

5 _Interpretive Stories_

> I do not believe you can do today's jobs with yesterday's methods, and be in business tomorrow.
>
> —NELSON JACKSON

CRITICS OF THE STRAIGHT NEWS STORY are right to confront those journalists who would use this single formula to report almost everything. One of the more thoughtful professors of communication, James Carey of the University of Illinois, argues for flexibility: "There must be a greater stylistic freedom among modern journalists and a more fluid definition of news, if only because the pace of social change continually presses the journalist into situations for which the conventional styles and conventional news definitions disable both perception and communication."

Actually, the demand for new approaches in news writing developed in the 1930s. At that time the average reporter generally wrote straight news stories by formula, beginning with the who, what, when, where, why, and how of an event and proceeding toward the end, with factual details in descending order of interest and importance. The reporter's job was to hold a mirror up to an event and to show its surface. Explaining why the event had occurred and what should be done about it was the task of columnists and editorial writers. Although a few reporters, primarily those in Washington and overseas, had license to interpret news and to explain complex events, almost everyone else conformed to straight news reporting.

With the coming of the New Deal in the 1930s, the old form became inadequate for reporting many events. Washington correspondents claim to fix the exact moment when the formula story proved too limited for certain events as the day in 1933 when the United States went off the gold standard. After journalists appealed to the White House for help in reporting that baffling change, a federal government economist was sent over to clarify the facts. The reporters, however, had limited success explaining what the economist had explained to them. Despite the initial failure, many correspondents committed themselves to explanatory journalism.

The increasing complexity of public affairs made this shift necessary. Relaying exactly what someone says is often misleading; unelaborated facts do not always add up to the truth. Therefore, the tradition of interpretive reporting established by Washington and foreign correspondents began to make its way back to the local newsrooms.

When writing interpretive stories, report the event and seek reactions as usual, but also add background information, an analysis of the less obvious meaning, and a projection of likely consequences.

> A writer's problem does not change; he himself changes and the world he lives in changes, but his problem remains the same. It is always how to write truly and, having found out what is true, to project it in such a way that it becomes part of the experience of the person who reads it.
> —ERNEST HEMINGWAY

Interpretive reporting is not an entirely satisfactory term. Some journalists argue that interpretation implies that the reporter is at liberty to slant the facts. Others prefer *news analysis* or *backgrounding,* which indicate more specific techniques. The following example should help us reach a definition of interpretive reporting.

Clay Whitehead, a former director of the White House Office of Telecommunications Policy, in a speech advised hundreds of local stations affiliated to networks to refrain from automatically broadcasting all the news and public affairs programs that the networks supplied. Dismissing much network programming as "ideological plugola," he stressed that each station is responsible for reviewing the network product. He also pointedly reminded station owners that they must renew their licenses every three years.

The first obligation of the news media was to report what Whitehead said. By most journalistic standards, that is the beginning and the end of the news story: an event occurs, and a reporter outlines it in direct quotations and paraphrase. If the event is important, and most journalists considered Whitehead's speech to be important, newspapers will publish photographs, television crews will film the speaker in action, and all media will report the event at some length.

Some reporters also sought reactions from those that the speech most directly affected: local broadcasters. A few journalists consider this additional reporting to be a natural part of the straight news story. Others sought reactions from a wide range of sources, including members of Congress and of the Federal Communications Commission as well as attorneys and professors with special knowledge of broadcasting.

But what about reporters who went still further? Some, for example, quoted other speeches by Whitehead and speeches on broadcasting by other administration officials in efforts to determine whether or not the speech fit a pattern that would give it additional significance. Nearly all of these journalists would agree that they had now moved from straight news into interpretation or news analysis.

Moreover, journalists who specialize in reporting on broadcasting went even further in subsequent stories. Drawing on years of experience following such events, they tried to explain the meaning of Whitehead's speech and its probable effects. This was clearly interpretive reporting. Reporters who had read the Communications Act or remembered its basic provisions pointed out that the act declares local stations responsible for everything they broadcast. Some who made this point left it at that, implying tacit support for Whitehead, while others emphasized that Whitehead's references to "ideological plugola" and "elitist gossip in the guise of news" turned his speech into a threatening political act. This suggests how differently reporters can interpret events. One reporter, noting that Whitehead not only denounced stations that broadcast everything the networks sent them but also suggested that he would support a policy to renew licenses every *five* years, interpreted that as a secret signal from Whitehead to local broadcasters: help us censor the networks, and we will change the law so that you can renew your licenses less frequently.

Clarify, explain, and analyze facts by focusing on "why."

Knowledge itself is power.
— FRANCIS BACON

Interpretive reporting moves a step beyond straight news. It usually concentrates its explanatory approach on a problem, issue, or controversy. Although verifiable fact should form the foundation of interpretive reporting, just as it does in straight-news reporting, the aim of the interpretive reporter is to go further than merely presenting facts. The focus is usually on *why*.

Two factors cause many critics to charge that interpretive reporting is opinion writing in disguise:

1. Because clarification requires that the reporter weigh and filter facts, the interpretive reporter enters the news process more personally than does the straight-news reporter. Although the interpretive reporter should *not* offer an opinion, he or she sometimes does so inadvertently.

2. An interpretive story does not depend on a formula; like a feature story, it may begin and end in any form the writer chooses. The latitude given the interpretive reporter may enable arrangement of facts in a way that suggests an opinion – again, inadvertently.

To test the objectivity of an interpretive story, you must decide whether the reporter has presented a full and fair account without revealing a personal stance.

Interpretation is actually quite different from opinion. Lester Markel, a late editor of the *New York Times,* put it this way:

> To report that the vice president attacks the press is news.
> To explain why the vice president makes the attack is interpretation.
> To assert that the vice president is a "radiclib" is opinion.
> Interpretation is an objective (as objective as human judgment can be) judgment based on knowledge and appraisal of a situation – good information and sound analysis; it reveals the deeper sense of the news, providing setting, sequence, above all significance. . . . Opinion, on the other hand, is a subjective judgment and should be confined to the editorial pages of newspapers.

Report contradictory accounts evenhandedly and identify falsehoods directly only when the evidence is unmistakable.

> The great enemy of clear language is insincerity. When there is a gap between one's real and one's declared aims, one turns, as it were, instinctively to long words and exhausted idioms, like a cuttlefish squirting out ink.
> —GEORGE ORWELL

One of the basic questions in journalism concerns how a reporter should handle falsehood or the suspicion that a statement is false. The situation is sometimes obvious: A public official responds to a reporter's question with the flat statement, "I do not use public funds on my vacation trips," and when confronted with official records that show he has, adds lamely, "I find that I was in error. I used public money because part of the trip was devoted to public business."

Relatively few instances are so obvious. For many years, reporters simply quoted falsehoods along with facts when the distinctions were not clear-cut; they left it to columnists and editorial writers to denounce those who lied. Unfortunately, columnists and editorial writers often have too little influence (or are not sufficiently informed) to counter the force of news stories. That is why Senator Joseph McCarthy, who knew how to manipulate the news media, became such a powerful demagogue in the early 1950s.

Interpretive reporting allows journalists to place conflicting evidence into a meaningful context, if only to emphasize that the truth of a matter remains unclear. Ordinarily, however, reporters identify a statement as "contrived" or "false" only in the unusual circumstances when they are able to lay out evidence supporting their conclusion so unmistakably that even partisans of different political persuasions would agree that it is justified.

Incorporate both analytic insight and fresh material into interpretive stories.

> The cleverly expressed opposite of any generally accepted idea is worth a fortune to somebody.
> —F. SCOTT FITZGERALD

All the great newspapers (the *New York Times,* the *Christian Science Monitor,* the *Washington Post,* the *Los Angeles Times,* and several others) and news-gathering agencies and magazines now boast stories that do not simply report the news but also interpret it.

Max Frankel, editorial page editor of the *New York Times,* explains how *Times* reporters and editors distinguish between news stories and interpretive stories (which they call news analyses):

> All good news stories should contain as much analytical insight as possible, and all good news analyses should bring fresh understanding, sometimes even fresh material, to the reader's attention. The essential difference is one of focus. The news story represents something that is happening, the dimensions of the event and its likely consequences, and some explanation for why it happened. But above all, its focus is *what* is

happening—an event, a trend, a revelation, an assertion. The news analysis, as we use it on the *Times,* differs only in that the principal focus of the story is to call attention to some analytical aspect of an event, a trend, etc. The President's announcement that he would visit China was clearly a news story. A simultaneous story pointing out the break with the past is analysis. Theoretically, there should be no reason why an analysis piece could not be incorporated in a news article, except that the length and focus of the news article might then run out of control.

Use historical perspectives, comparisons, light touches, even literary overtones to enhance interpretive stories.

> Reading is to the mind what exercise is to the body.
> —RICHARD STEELE

The *Christian Science Monitor,* which is ranked near the top on every list of great newspapers, incorporates analysis (or interpretation) into most of its news stories. Nearly every story in the *Monitor* has a strong interpretive framework, primarily because the paper is distributed to a widely scattered readership. As one observer points out:

> The *Monitor's* reliance on geographically diffuse subscribers . . . causes a time lag between the printing of the paper and its arrival in the mailbox. The *Monitor* is thus at a serious disadvantage in printing hot scoops.
> However, it would seem that the paper has made a virtue of necessity. . . . Instead of getting it on the front page first, the *Monitor* places emphasis on getting it into context. The value of the *Monitor* is not in the facts it prints, but in the understanding it offers.

Leads that provide historical perspectives are favorites with many *Monitor* correspondents. A deep background is apparent in this *Monitor* lead: "Black consciousness is sweeping South Africa as nothing has since Afrikaner nationalism caught fire here 30 years ago."

Monitor correspondents often provide new insight into an event by comparing it directly with another: "Leonid I. Brezhnev's visit to West Germany is just as dramatic, just as radical, just as freighted with long meanings, just as important to other peoples around the world as was the President's trip to Peking."

Like many other journalists who emphasize interpretation, *Monitor* editors and reporters realize that the interpretive approach can be excessively solemn and that they occasionally can sound a lighter note without fear of frivolity. A story on a royal wedding in London began: "It now seems certain that it will be in November when they bring the pumpkin from the palace stables, harness the mice, and send for the magic wand."

Some *Monitor* correspondents flavor their dispatches with literary touches, as in this story on a sex scandal among British high officials: "This capital is full of traffic and sunshine, green grass and gay flowers, and visitors laughing together in foreign tongues. But Westminster, at the heart of it, is a rather sad, silent, and reflective place. It weighs scandal in its hand and ponders the cost of it."

Metaphor turns up in some of the most serious *Monitor* stories, as in this one on Leonid Brezhnev's trip to West Germany and the slowly thawing relations between the United States and China, West Germany and Russia: "Those two hostilities were the solid rocks around which a world flowed for a generation. They seemed to be as inflexible as the laws of the Medes and Persians and as durable as the great religions."

These examples should make it obvious that the *Christian Science Monitor* has found a way not only to place news stories into an interpretive framework but to make the news interesting as well.

Acquire reporting experience and background knowledge in a news area, then rely on your analytic (and journalist's) instincts.

> I never desire to talk with a man who has written more than he has read.
> —SAMUEL JOHNSON

To know what is happening and why it is happening requires experience as well as intelligence. Time on the beat is nearly always necessary, but sometimes much more is called for. Max Frankel, who was then chief Washington correspondent of the *New York Times,* describes the elements that went into his reporting of President Richard Nixon's trip to China:

[BACKGROUND]

I had almost no experience of China, as such, although I had written for many years about China-U.S. relations and other aspects of the Chinese story—as Moscow correspondent for the *Times,* and as diplomatic correspondent for the *Times* in Washington. I had been among the first to write about the Sino-Soviet rift and had written extensively about U.S.

Asian policy during the 1960s. And while China was closed, with a fairly
thorough background in Communist affairs, I had also tried to follow
major domestic developments in China, from a distance.

[PREPARATION]

I have been the chief Washington correspondent and therefore the chief
Times correspondent on all the President's foreign travels, all the more
logically because of my thorough background in foreign affairs. I prepared for the trip with several months of extensive reading, including
two weeks of full-time reading – virtually everything available in English
on contemporary Chinese affairs and, above all, U.S.-China relations. I
interviewed several recent travelers to China, including colleagues on
the *Times* who preceded me there. I interviewed a half-dozen scholars
on Chinese affairs and an equal number of government officials. I asked
for special briefings on the President's plans and intentions from the
Secretary of State and obtained some of the briefing that members of his
party were given by CIA scholars. All of these sessions were extremely
helpful, though they necessarily involved different emphases and degrees of knowledge.
   I think the President's trip was the culmination of a major turn in
American policy toward China and in Chinese policy toward the rest of
the world. The president also had an important secondary reason of
wishing to push past the problem of Vietnam, of wishing to enhance his
chances of re-election, and in a very indirect way perhaps also contributing to a possible negotiated settlement in Vietnam. I did not, of course,
see much of China, only the U.S. party in China, and there is an important difference. The Chinese lived up to advance billing in their skill at
organizing such an extravaganza and in their stubborn but courteous
refusal to be prodded or interrogated farther than they intended. All in
all, the poverty of the country was possibly greater than I had imagined.

[COVERAGE]

A priori decisions on coverage can never fully satisfy history on the
"importance" of an event. All journalists can do is get a rough sense of
importance at that juncture *plus* a sense of the range and depth of reader
interest. I think on balance the editors of *Time* did very well. Judging by
the reader interest and reaction throughout, I do not think we provided
too much material. Some of the material, of course, was historical and
based on past events and news – but one function of an alert newspaper
is to recapitulate such material when the audience is prepared to absorb
it. Robert Semple has had general experience in foreign affairs, as our
White House correspondent, and accompanied the President on all his
other foreign travels. Tad Szulc has covered Chinese affairs on and off
for 20 years, dating to service in Hong Kong, Taiwan and Southeast Asia
and, in recent years, in his coverage of U.S. foreign policy.
   The traveling White House was wholly uncommunicative during
most of the China visit – until the final communique and briefing. We had

been forewarned of this, but the extent of their reticence was surprising—they would not even tell us the location of Mao's home nor would they comment on the many other small, but usually interesting and revealing details pertaining to physical arrangements, logistics, communications, etc. Chinese officials were no more helpful on the formal talks and they arranged only the well-known visits to farms, factories, etc. Moreover, conversation with individual Chinese was arduous: long probing was needed to gain any insight into their real feelings or problems, and this was only possible on a few, unplanned occasions. I wrote what I could learn, officially and unofficially. I do not think we overplayed the material.

The *Times* had no other representatives on the trip. John Burns of Toronto, one of the resident foreign correspondents whose dispatches often appear in the *Times,* was on hand for an occasional bit of advice. One or another edition of the *Times* was on deadline from about 6 A.M. to 1 P.M. Chinese time, which meant that I did most of my writing between midnight and 6 A.M., with only minor updatings and adaptations through the morning. I did not get much sleep, and missed going to bed altogether during three of our nights there. My schedule involved simply keeping busy and exposed with the available activities—including performances, banquets, etc., and squeezing independent walks, visits to diplomats, official guided tours in between the formal program. I determined the number of stories and their length each day. They were not significantly altered. I worked usually in the press rooms arranged by the Chinese at White House request, and filed my stories from there by telephone via satellite connections, which became available on between ten minutes' and one hour's notice.

The preparation, intelligence, experience, and twenty-hour days Frankel devoted to the China trip permitted the *Times* to publish column after column of long, clear news stories and incisive analyses. They won the Pulitzer Prize for Frankel.

Most readers prefer stories to analyses.

> The two most engaging powers of writers are to make new things familiar, familiar things new.
>
> —WILLIAM THACKERAY

Read the two opening paragraphs below; each begins a story written by a student interested in the housing shortage on campus. Decide which of the leads you prefer. Then read the rest of each excerpted story.

Story A

Roger Awad and his three roommates live off-campus. Every morning at 9 the four drive three and a half miles to school. They do not return home until about 4 P.M. They've adjusted well enough to daily commuting and the off-campus atmosphere, but they would still rather live on-campus.

Story B

Students choosing 1979–80 as their unguaranteed housing year became all too aware of the creeping housing shortage beyond the university this fall. Students desiring to live off campus found rentals farther away and more expensive than ever. Many of those opting for the waiting list faced homeless nights and ultimate disappointment.

Story A continued

But they have no choice. All four have unguaranteed housing this year and had lousy luck in the Housing Draw. There just isn't room for Roger and his roommates on campus.

The university has a housing shortage and everybody knows it. Students like Roger and his roommates, faculty, the administration and the city are all acutely aware of it, but what's being done to help?

There are about 12,000 students at the university but only about 8,000 living spaces on campus. Some 500–600 students are overseas or stopped out so that leaves over 3,000 who must find housing off-campus.

Faculty housing is no better off. According to Roger Whitney, assistant dean of student affairs and director of the housing center, prospective faculty are being "scared" away from the university due to problems in locating a house.

The problem has just begun. In addition, the city and the entire peninsula exhibit a great imbalance between the number of jobs and places to live. There are simply more people than places to live. Subsequently, it is quite difficult for 3,000 students to find room off-campus.

"We were really, really lucky," said Awad of his group's ability to find a house to rent.

Also, because of high demand and little supply, real estate and construction costs. . . .

Story B continued

"But that's nothing new," said Jean Kitaji, supervisor of the student housing office. "Sure there's a housing shortage on campus, but this year wasn't any worse than usual." The press played up the university's housing problem because of the area's shortage in general, according to Kitaji. This created louder protests this year about a problem that's been around for a while.

Figures show that there were about 5,100 spots available for about 6,100 undergraduates who originally wanted them this year. There were still 160 students on the waiting list the first week in October. On October 10, the remaining rooms were allocated on a first come, first served basis.

Kitaji asserts that these figures are a poor indicator of student housing trends. "People drop off the list without telling us. They can only wait so long before making a commitment elsewhere. There are also students who'd rather live on campus but don't bother to put their names on the waiting list.

"All we know is that according to our figures, it was no harder to get on campus from the waiting list than any other year. . . . Granted, we don't take surveys of the students and I'm sure they did have a tougher time finding off-campus housing, but what can we do?"

Ed Scoles, director of housing and food services management, asserted there were more students seeking campus lodging this year in an October 10 *Daily* interview. The crunch, which did not show up in Kitaji's figures, is "the worst in the past five years," according to Scoles. . . .

When thirty journalism students were asked which of the two leads they preferred, twenty-four voted for the lead in Story A. Why? Because most of them are interested in reading a *story*, not an *analysis*. Although Story A eventually becomes an analysis, readers are lured by its anecdotal beginning. Although after reading both stories many readers might prefer Story B, you should remember that the lead is crucial when you're attempting to interest the readers.

Examine your stories for signs of personal opinion. Unless your stances are those on which there is nearly universal agreement (opposition to pollution, crime, and so on) the story should be rewritten—not, however, in an effort to disguise your prejudices. The conclusions you reach should clearly evolve from objective analysis of the facts.

Those who write interpretively are also in danger of pontificating. In its worst form, this practice is called *thumbsucking,* a derisive term that many journalists apply to the work of those who no longer bother to interview or to undertake the legwork involved in seeking out the facts in a case before writing.

Read the following excerpt of a story (written by a student) and the comments, then continue to the first exercise.

Comments	Story
The lead invites attention, which is good.	"So from this time, every people and organization that goes against the Unification Church will gradually come down or drastically come down and die. Many people will die—those that go against our movement."
So far, this is fine. The writer has defined the subject.	So cries Reverend Sun Myung Moon, a Korean, self-ordained evangelist who has successfully campaigned throughout the United States, recruiting more than 30,000 youths to the Unification Church.
The vivid detail in this paragraph makes it interesting.	Many have left school, turned over their incomes and inheritances to Moon and his organization. They take

Here the writer has assumed that the readers know more than they do. All we know is that there is a person called "Moon" and he has some followers. These are called "Moonies"? What, exactly, do the deprogrammers deprogram? Who initiated these "carefully ingrained mental tapes"? What did they consist of?

Being "served" a conservatorship is sufficiently unfamiliar to merit a second brief explanation.

to the streets, smiling endlessly, grinning sheepishly, selling flowers and handing out brochures in the name of the Unification Church.

One of the most effective, yet controversial techniques used against the Moonies is deprogramming.

Ted Patrick began deprogramming years ago, removing students from the Children of God crusade, talking to them incessantly, breaking down the carefully ingrained mental tapes.

Patrick often made people stay awake long hours, without food or sleep, throttling them when necessary. He has been criticized often but was still flown around the country to deprogram members of various religious cults until February, when he was imprisoned on kidnaping convictions.

Kidnaping charges pressed by Moonies are a major problem for deprogrammers. Moonies spend most of their time in their communal homes, unreachable from outsiders. They must be lured from their camps with legal slyness or physical force.

Conservatorships, legal mandates that place youngsters under the guardianship of their parents for specific short duration, are often administered to place the child in custody of a group of deprogrammers.

The process can cost from $5,000 to $10,000, including legal fees, hotel rentals, food, telephone calls and possible payments for a rehabilitation center.

Leslie Maxwell, 21, a one-time Moonie, threw ashtrays, knocked over a table, and kicked the arresting officer when served her conservatorship. After seven days with deprogrammers in a locked hotel room, one month in a rehabilitation center, and one month traveling with an ex-Moonie companion, she became dedicated to anti-Moon efforts.

Neil Maxwell, Leslie's father, is warm, concerned, dedicated. He speaks kindly of the Moonie young-

The picture of Neil Maxwell is colored in very nicely. But what does he mean by giving back their "First Amendment rights"?

Now readers can understand what it is to become a Moonie. This seems to come too late. And you may still wonder what requires deprogramming.

Note, however, that this story generally is well written.

sters as "bright, loving, well-educated, ambitious...really fantastic kids. It's difficult to separate my anger for the Unification Church from dealing with these kids.

"We say reconditioning, not deprogramming," says Maxwell. He leans over, a pharmacist who has become fanatic, and pulls from his briefcase a black leather pouch Dyno-labeled "moonies."

"It is for their own good. We provide a cult member with enough information to enable him to make his own decision, giving him back his First Amendment rights," he says.

Since January, the Maxwells have counselled over 50 sets of parents, finding lawyers who will play the tricky business of conservatorships, contracting deprogrammers, arranging the nitty-gritty of their often paralegal operations.

Describing the Moonies' emotional lure, Maxwell says, "They don't use sex, they 'love bomb' you. You go into a room...and 15 people are around you saying how wonderful you are."

Newcomers feel wanted. Often leaving circumstances that were dry of feelings, distressed by lack of values, initiates are welcomed to a place where "nature is natural" and told that they must open their hearts to brotherly love and one-world brothership.

When asked if deprogramming is the same as the Moonies' "love bombing," Maxwell seems bewildered, angered.

He emphatically reminds me that deprogramming is not another form of brainwashing. He is a man who believes in ends justifying means. He "saved" his daughter that way. . . .

EXERCISES

1. Analyze the last story in this chapter by writing a paper in which you ask questions similar to these:
a. Does the writer reveal his opinions?

b. Does the writer clarify and analyze what the Moonies do?
c. The writer has written this story after hearing speeches and interviewing many people; does he use his research well?
Grade this story (A, excellent; B, good; C, average; D, acceptable; F, failure).

2. Read the interpretive or analytic stories in one edition of a small-city daily and in one edition of a large daily like the *New York Times* or the *Washington Post*. What percentage of each paper is made up of interpretive reporting?

3. Read an issue of the *Christian Science Monitor* and compare its stories with those in a more conventional newspaper. Which do you prefer? Why?

4. An interpretive story will require that you go far beyond the kind of surface facts you would derive from listening to a speech. Choose a subject that seems important on your campus and write an interpretive story of at least 700 words after you have researched the subject and interviewed at least three people.

6 Investigative Reporting

Everyone wishes to have truth on his side, but not everyone wishes to be on the side of truth.

—RICHARD WHATELY

BRIT HUME, a reporter who once worked for Washington columnist Jack Anderson, had an experience early in 1972 that illustrates the central problem of the news correspondent in Washington. Hume had acquired a two-page memorandum that he described as "the single most incriminating piece of paper I had ever seen." The memo, dated June 25, 1971, had been written by Dita Beard, a capitol lobbyist for the International Telephone and Telegraph Company (ITT), and was addressed to W. R. Merriam, head of the Washington office of ITT. In the memo Beard urged Merriam to use more discretion in discussing the company's pledge of $400,000 to underwrite the 1972 Republican national convention, which was then scheduled for San Diego. The memo also made it quite clear that the pledge was helping ITT, already one of the largest conglomerates in the world, negotiate new mergers that previously had been opposed by the federal government.

The Antitrust Division of the U.S. Department of Justice had brought three landmark suits against ITT to prevent the mergers. All three suits were settled in July 1971, a few weeks after Beard's memo. In line with the settlement, ITT was permitted the largest merger in corporate history. Soon after, Richard McLaren, chief of the Antitrust Division, was given a federal judgeship in Chicago. The coincidences certainly seemed suspect, and the Beard memo implicated both President Nixon and Attorney General John Mitchell.

When Brit Hume confronted Beard, she admitted writing the memo and even confessed that she herself had worked with Attorney General Mitchell in drafting the agreement by which ITT got most of what it wanted. But she denied the main point of her own memo: that the ITT pledge to underwrite the Republican convention helped the company win a favorable settlement from the Nixon administration. All the principals in the case, government officials as well as company executives, also denied that point. But as Hume and other reporters broadened their questioning to an everwidening circle of government officials and ITT executives, the contradictory statements became rampant and incriminating.

As an example of such contradictions, consider the role of Richard Kleindienst, the assistant attorney general, who became embroiled in the controversy when he was nominated to succeed Mitchell as attorney general. When the chairman of the Democratic National Committee became suspicious about the settlement of the ITT case in 1971 and inquired at the Department of Justice about it, Kleindienst wrote him a letter saying that the settlement was "handled and negotiated exclusively" by Richard McLaren and his Antitrust Division staff. But when Brit Hume had called Felix Rohatyn, a director of ITT, to ask about Dita Beard's memo, Rohatyn said that he had met with Kleindienst half a dozen times to handle "some of the negotiations and presentations" for the ITT settlement. Jack Anderson's column cited Hume's investigation in accusing Kleindienst of an "outright lie."

Hume and Anderson published column after column reporting their findings and accusing ITT and the Republican administration of striking a mutually beneficial deal. Testifying before the Senate Judiciary Committee, Kleindienst admitted meeting with Rohatyn but denied that he had "influenced the settlement of government antitrust litigation for partisan political reasons." For his part, Rohatyn told the Senate that he had not actually negotiated anything in his meetings with Kleindienst, that he was merely making an economic case for the mergers.

The Senate finally confirmed Kleindienst as attorney general by a vote of sixty-four to nineteen. President Richard Nixon eventually resigned in the midst of an even messier web of stalls and lies and obfuscations. But these historic events are less important to our thesis here than the basic questions that haunt anyone who investigates controversy: What and who should I believe? How should I evaluate the facts?

For example: There is no doubt that a memo from Dita Beard exists, but was the memo accurate in saying that the ITT pledge of money was helping with the company's antitrust merger cases? Or was this memo no more than an instance of self-aggrandizement by Beard in an effort to show that her work for the company was effective? Lobbyists often claim to do more than they have done. Was Beard being truthful in her subsequent denial of a connection between the pledge and the settlement?

There is no doubt that Kleindienst wrote a letter saying that he took no part in the ITT negotiations. But was Felix Rohatyn accurate in stating that he had handled "some of the negotiations" with Kleindienst, or did he misstate the nature of those meetings to persuade Brit Hume that *his* work for ITT was effective and that Beard's memo was inaccurate? Did Rohatyn's quite different testimony to the Senate committee accurately describe the meeting with Kleindienst?

Such questions can be multiplied, but even a hundred questions would not show how complicated the central problem really is. The true complexity is suggested by asking whether any reader should believe the account of the ITT case sketched in these pages. Some of the principals would surely argue that it is not accurate, or at least that it misleads, and that the account should have included other bits of evidence.

And what would be the effect on the reader if, instead of "Washington columnist Jack Anderson," the phrase used was "muckraking Washington columnist Jack Anderson?" What if this account had cast doubt on Anderson's credibility by pointing up one of his grievous errors, as when in 1972 he erroneously reported that Senator Thomas Eagleton, who was then the Democratic nominee for vice-president, had been arrested for drunken driving? Introducing such a fact would certainly cause at least a few readers to evaluate this case quite differently.

To evaluate all the relevant facts in the ITT case, one would first weigh the probable truth in the oral and written testimony of the principals, the government officials and ITT executives and lobbyists; then the probable truth in the accounts of that testimony published by Brit Hume and Jack Anderson; then the probable truth in the account published here; and finally and not least, the degree to which one's judgments of "probable truth" were themselves affected by one's *own* whims, idiosyncrasies, leanings, biases, and prejudices. Even if you have no political leanings or beliefs because you consider politics a dirty business, that attitude would certainly be pivotal in your judgments about the principals. If you consider politics a bore—not even worth your attention—then the opinions expressed by someone you respect are likely to shape your judgments. In short, evaluation of such issues is bound to be somewhat personal and subjective.

Nonetheless, Kleindienst was guilty. He was allowed to resign on April 30, 1973, during the Watergate mess. The next year, however, Kleindienst pleaded guilty to a misdemeanor charge that he had refused to testify "accurately and fully" before a congressional committee on the ITT antitrust settlement in the federal district court in Washington, D.C. He received a suspended sentence on June 7, 1974, on the ITT case.

Understand that investigative reporting, for all its glamour and hard work, varies mostly in degree with analytical reporting. It is a distillation of reportorial skills.

It is a great nuisance that knowledge can
only be acquired by hard work.
                                   —SOMERSET MAUGHAM

Investigative reporting sounds dramatic, exciting. It can be. But it also requires persistence, stubbornness, and even a special type of personality; it is difficult, time-consuming work.

The investigative story is a giant step away from the straight news story of the past. In this area, newspaper correspondents are leagues ahead of their colleagues in television (and probably always will be). Because the television correspondent must be on the air daily, or nearly so, days, weeks, or even months cannot be devoted to investigation, as they can by a print-media reporter. Tom Petit of NBC says he only goes ahead on a story after he knows he has the facts, "and that the facts can be filmed." His beginning probes, like those of almost all TV broadcasters, have to include the question of visuals: Is the story the kind that can be translated into moving film? Can it be made understandable within the framework of the medium? For the broadcast reporter, these kinds of questions often mean that the complex, abstract story, such as one on stock manipulations or real estate frauds, is never pursued. The daily byline is important to the newspaper correspondent as well, but good investigative reporting, on the other hand, can win prizes and high esteem.

Correspondents disagree about the definition of investigative reporting. For example, Max Frankel, the editorial page editor of the *New York Times,* once was the diplomatic correspondent on the *Times* Washington bureau staff headed by James "Scotty" Reston. They had different opinions about what kinds of news were worth digging for. At one point, Reston insisted that Frankel should invest sufficient time and energy to be able to report the identity of the new U.S. ambassador to Moscow three days before the appointment was to be officially announced. Frankel objected, arguing: "Scotty, I can find that out. It's easy. It's going to take me two days. In those two days I might learn something far more substantial, which we would never learn if I didn't invest the two days. But the ambassador to Moscow we will find out by the announcement."

Reflecting later on that disagreement, Frankel said, "Is it important? Reston regarded me as insufficiently zealous for feeling that it isn't. Al-

ways want to be first, he argued, because vigilance resides in that in-
stinct. He feels that if you get in the habit of waiting for government to
tell you *when* it wants to tell you, you're going to lapse on more serious
matters."

The eager-adversary approach that Reston promotes should guide
journalists in their daily work. Maintaining the sharp edge of vigilance is
pivotal to a good reporter and a reputable newspaper. But is a story that
unearths the name of the ambassador to Moscow investigative?

Perhaps, depending upon what editor or reporter you ask. One editor
proclaims, "All of our reporters are investigative reporters." This is facile,
of course, and misleading. Leonard Sellers, professor of journalism at San
Francisco State University, writes; "The investigative reporter is the one
who goes after information that is deliberately hidden because it involves
a legal or ethical wrong." Some investigative reporters who have been lost
in the semantic swamp of defining their work have responded to this
definition with, "That's it! That's it."

By Sellers's definition, investigative reporting is the practice of opening closed doors and closed mouths. Like analysis, investigative reporting
focuses on problems, issues, and controversies. In most cases, however,
an analytical reporter has little trouble because he is usually explaining
public events and can find many sources who are happy to help him. In
fact, one of the chief dangers of most political reporting is that too many
sources want to provide too much information that will serve their own
interests. In contrast, the investigative reporter tends to walk into a lot of
brick walls.

Are the brick walls new? Hardly. Even before the beginning of the
United States, one publisher created an adversary role for himself with
the government. In 1690, Benjamin Harris produced the first, and only,
issue of *Publick Occurrences, Both Forreign and Domestick*. Because some
of the "occurrences" were seen as criticism of colonial policy, and because
he was not printing "by authority"—that is, he was not licensed by the
General Court of Massachusetts—the newspaper was banned. The lesson
was not lost on future publishers, and it wasn't until 1721, with James
Franklin's establishment of the *New England Courant,* that a newspaper
dared oppose government policy. Franklin, Benjamin's older brother, was
the first to indulge in "crusade" journalism, and refused to print "by
authority." His crusade was against smallpox inoculation—in retrospect
the wrong side of the issue—but the cause became a rallying point for
those fighting local Puritan leaders. James Franklin ultimately spent
some time in jail (not unlike some modern journalists), but in the mean-
time he had made the singular contribution to American journalism of
establishing the principle of printing "without authority."

Clashes with authority have continued throughout journalism history, but an organized focus on wrongdoing didn't truly begin until the opening of the twentieth century; the first decade of the 1900s was the golden age of muckraking.

Muckrakers were a salient force in American journalism from about 1902 to 1912—though there were strong examples of such reporting both before and after that period. The era began with the *McClure's* magazine trio of Lincoln Steffens, Ida Tarbell, and Ray Stannard Baker, who started the pattern of what historian Judson Grenier calls the "systematic uncovery of sociopolitical corruption." Steffens's *Shame of the Cities* and Tarbell's *History of the Standard Oil Company* set the tone for a new literature of exposure. "Early in the century muckrakers had recognized that a sense of uneasiness about the malfunctioning political, economic, and social institutions which had begun to become evident several decades earlier was troubling increasing numbers of Americans," according to journalism researchers John Harrison and Harry Stein. "They found the medium for the message—more precisely, perhaps, the medium found them—in the popular magazines that represented one current manifestation of the communications revolution that had begun at least half a century earlier. An audience was there, and the means of reaching it was at hand. The muckrakers availed themselves of that fortuitous combination."

The label "muckrakers" wasn't pinned on that small group of writers until 1906, when President Theodore Roosevelt, angered at David Graham Phillips's series *The Treason of the Senate,* borrowed the term from *Pilgrim's Progress* and castigated "the writers who raked the muck of society and never looked up. . . ." At first upset by the obviously pejorative term, the writers soon took it as a badge of approbation, something to wear proudly. Their conversion of the term has been so complete that Webster now defines the verb *muckrake* as "to seek for, expose, or charge corruption, real or alleged, on the part of public men and corporations."

Carey McWilliams, retired editor of the *Nation,* claims there is a cyclical pattern to reform journalism that began in the late nineteenth century and continues through today. "Ongoing, it seems to disappear at certain times only to surface later," he wrote in 1970, adding that new communications technology and a mood of social concern usually herald an upsurge.

Remember the three golden words of investigative reporting: plan, plan, and plan.

> Research is an organized method of keeping
> you reasonably dissatisfied with what you
> have.
> —CHARLES F. KETTERING

One of the best of investigative reporters is Robert Greene of *Newsday,* who was once a regular lecturer in the seminars offered to newspapermen by the American Press Institute (API). Greene believes the ideal investigation is not based on a breaking news event, but on thorough planning. Reporters, Greene said:

> should be able to detect or at least smell unusual happenings, patterns of events, on their routine beats. And they should be able to learn what things are bothering people and what people suspect is going on, even though they cannot always prove it. It is largely from this net of information that investigative stories are born. And once a paper commits itself to this type of story, not only will one story lead to another, but also an encouraged general public will begin to generate tips leading to more.

In his lectures at the API seminars, Greene emphasizes the value of gathering complete background information on figures under investigation, especially the principal target:

> Who is he? What are his businesses? How did he purchase his home? What is his wife's maiden name? Who are his business partners? Who are his friends? What are his clubs? What are his sources of income? With whom or what other businesses or agencies do his businesses deal? A complete picture also requires a study of the milieu in which he operates, whether business or political. How does he fit? Who are the other powers in the field and how does he relate? Is his business or position controlled by a government or industry code of ethics? What is the code?
>
> *Sources.* In the course of backgrounding a subject, reporters will come across the names of many persons who may become excellent sources. Court files on litigation are particularly productive.
>
> *Records.* An excellent procedure is to require that the reporter or team members prepare complete memos on interviews or material they have obtained at the end of each working day. These memos should be reviewed by the team leader/or reporter and marked for duplication or cross-filing at the end of each working day.
>
> *Preparation for interview.* All major interviews should be timed (when possible) to come at the end of the investigation. Prior to the interviews, chronologies should be prepared on each deal file. If several deals are involved, chronologies should be compared.
>
> Once chronologies are compared, each deal file should be reviewed

for holes. All minor participants should have been interviewed by this time. Memos of all pertinent interviews should be in the file. Following the file review, a terse memo should be written summarizing the key points of each deal.

Interview. It is advisable to use two reporters at all interviews with investigation subjects. Open tapes of the interviews should be made, if agreeable to subjects. The presence of the extra reporter and tapes is to avoid any later claim of misquote.

If an investigation has been thoroughly prepared, the reporter already knows most of the answers to the questions he asks. The choice of material used in the questioning process alerts most investigative subjects to the fact that the reporter is already familiar with the answers. As a result, the subject is less likely to lie. If he does lie, however, repeat the question in several different ways, so that there is no possibility of misunderstanding.

This outline obviously prescribes an expensive and time-consuming investigative process. Relatively few investigators plan and carry out their work so thoroughly, and only the largest newspapers and magazines can support investigations on this scale. But investigative reporting is not limited to major productions. Marcia Knopf of the *Riverside Press-Enterprise* researched and wrote this story in a few days:

> What happens if you take a car with one bad spark plug and a poorly adjusted carburetor to 10 garages, tell each you don't know what's wrong, then ask what each would charge to fix it?
>
> Some disturbing—and expensive—things can happen in Riverside, a test by The Press shows.
>
> Only three of the 10 correctly diagnosed the trouble and charged accordingly ($3 to $4). Seven wanted to make unnecessary repairs and quoted prices as high as $45. Actual repair costs, at the seven where the work was authorized, ranged from $3 to $31.
>
> Most said the car needed either a minor or major tuneup—at $20 to $45—even though the car had been given a carburetor check two weeks before the test began and a minor tuneup (new plugs, points, condenser, timing check) a month before the test began. The competency of both of these repairs had been double-checked by two mechanics retained by The Press for the tests.
>
> Prior to the tests, the car idled and accelerated well, did not stall or miss—signs it did not need a tuneup.
>
> The Valiant, with 25,000 miles on it, was first put in top condition by two competent mechanics retained by the paper. Through use of an electronic motor tester, by manual and visual checks, all major working parts of the engine were checked and adjusted.
>
> Then a bit of pencil lead was broken off in the gap of one spark plug—making that plug dead—and the carburetor idling screw loosened, so that the gasoline mixture reaching the cylinder was too rich. These caused the motor to miss and stall, idle roughly and accelerate poorly.
>
> These simulate minor problems that often happen to engines. Bits of carbon often lodge in the spark plug gap, causing the plug to short out. Also, carburetor screws often get out of adjustment.

But the faults could be pinpointed easily by any mechanic going through the routine procedures. At most, one spark plug ($1.10) was the only new part needed to restore the car to good working order.

A woman motorist then took the car to four service stations, three garages and three new-car dealer shops selected at random from the telephone book. She told each that the car "shakes, makes noises, stalls and doesn't have much pickup."

After each shop worked on the car, it was returned to the two mechanics retained for the test, checked over again and "rebugged."

Here's what happened, shop by shop:

First test: Small downtown garage. The mechanic listened briefly to the motor and said, "It probably needs a major tuneup." An hour later, after checking it, he confirmed this, quoting a price of $37 for rebuilding the carburetor and for new condensor, points and plugs.

Though the plugs were almost new, he said, "When two or three plugs go, you might as well replace 'em all, 'cause they're about to go, too."

The major tuneup would take two hours, he said. (Repair manuals say this is a three and a half hour job.)

Second test: University area service station. The mechanic after checking, pinpointed the cause as "a pencil lead in the spark plug. It was done on purpose—someone's been playing with it." He added that the carburetor was "fooled with; it was way too rich."

He fixed the plug and adjusted the screw for $4.

Third test: Franchised new-car dealer. A service salesman—who makes the preliminary estimate and list of needed repairs when you bring your car in—said after listening to the motor: "It needs a good tuneup." Cost would be $40 to $45, he said. Asked if actual checking of the motor might show that less repair was needed, he said, "I'm certain I'm right."

Fourth test: Another franchised new-car dealer. The service salesman listened to the car, said a major tuneup, costing $43 to $44, was needed. "That's what we'd have to do to find out why it's missing."

On the work authorization order, however, he wrote: "Tune as need." A minor tuneup was done for about $21. "We didn't have to put in as much as we thought," the service salesman explained.

The two mechanics retained by the paper said new points, condensor and plugs were put in but the carburetor screw and the point gap had not been adjusted properly by the dealer's mechanic—as it is supposed to be done in tuneup. . . .

*Save your first investigative pieces to review
later. They'll show you how you improve.*

All experience is an arch to build upon.
—HENRY ADAMS

The student reporter who wrote the following investigative story had
alerted the university election commission to the candidate's violation of
election rules.

The Election Commission has declared junior Tom Todd "willingly
violated three campaign rules" in defeating Bill Wheel for the presidency
last week.

The by-laws provide no penalty for campaign violations discovered
after an election. So the senate held two days of open hearings on the
matter last weekend and decided that a new election will be held Thursday, open to all primary election candidates who wish to refile.

Theoretical loopholes abound in the by-laws, now 20 years old. But
two decades of complication-free elections have allowed the by-laws to
stand, unrevised.

This year the election commission caught a candidate clearly out of
line but was powerless to act because election by-laws provide no
penalty for violations after an election.

If Todd's campaign violations had been discovered 24 hours earlier,
before the election, Todd would have been disqualified from the election,
according to the rules.

"That would have been the greatest injustice imaginable," said
Steven Green, Todd's campaign manager. "The rules that the commission decided Tom had broken are completely outdated or irrational.

"Why should a candidate have to sign all his campaign material?
Tom's signature was left off his pamphlet through an oversight. Four
thousand pamphlets are not cheap, and Tom didn't have time to sign
them all, so we used them anyway.

"And a $75 limit on campaign spending is just ridiculous. The limit
may have bought a lot when it was set 20 years ago, but not today.

"The rules will be revamped when Tom takes office, to the benefit of
everyone."

Green declined to comment on Todd's third violation, that of promising two primary election candidates cabinet positions for withdrawing
their names from the ballot.

The new election Thursday was a compromise reached by the Senate after two days of heated arguments between Todd's supporters who
argued that the election should stand, and opponents who demanded
that Todd be disqualified.

After the hearings Green said that Todd will file for the new election
and that he expects to win.

Said Green, "The students know who's the best man for the job.
They won't let the senate keep Tom out over a few technicalities."

Apparently, Todd felt that it was worth breaking campaign rules he considered to be unfair to gain a position from which he could improve the rules.

"The similarities to Nixon and Watergate are really scary," said Dan Durham, Bill Wheel's campaign manager. "The Senate had the authority to can him and they didn't. Now he'll probably win again. This guy can talk his way out of anything."

Todd has displayed a flair for public speaking. He turned a 323-vote primary deficit into a 415-vote general election victory in just one week, largely through a flurry of visits to almost every dorm club and cafeteria on campus.

"He's always been a very bright, industrious boy. And he has a way of dealing with people," said Mrs. Harry Todd, Tom's mother.

Senator Bob Sadler said Todd "almost seems to have powers of mass hypnotism. But on an individual basis, well, he gives me the chills.

"One on one, he seems kind of nervous, like he's hiding something. It's definitely to his advantage to be at a school that's too large . . . to permit a lot of people to really meet him."

But Todd has been successful in the smaller setting of high school where he developed a reputation of wielding maximum power in governing situations.

Henry Bishop, a sophmore, was vice-president of his high school student council in 1974 when Todd was president.

"All this doesn't surprise me," said Bishop of the elections incident. "He's been a hard-core politico since I met him in the freshman year of high school.

"We ran together senior year and won. But working that close to him, I started seeing a lot of things I didn't like.

"The power grabs he tried to make were just incredible. He tried to install himself as head of the student judiciary committee. He tried to cut off funds to the school paper and almost did. He even tried to get rid of the cheerleading because, he said, the money could be better used elsewhere, but I think it was because his girlfriend got cut from tryouts."

Betty Anderson, Todd's high school girlfriend, is in her first year at the university. Concerning Todd's efforts to disband the cheerleaders, she said, "I don't think he would have tried it if I had made the squad, but he certainly didn't try because I was cut.

"He's really a sensitive person. He just had his own idea about how things should run.

"He often told me that student government is the only worthwhile organization in school. And he wanted to make it as strong as possible.

"He talked a lot about going to the university and becoming president of the student government there."

Manager Green feels Todd's goal of becoming president is in hand. Said Green, "The students know who they want and they won't change their minds by Thursday."

Wheel, loser in last week's election, announced he will not file in the new election. He said he hoped Todd would follow his example so that this week's elections would bear no "taint of scandal" from last week.

"It sounds like he's going to win again," said Wheel. "And I hate to say it, but if he does, the students deserve him and the friction he's going to create."

To cover local government well you must learn the territory very well.

I had six honest serving men who taught me
all they knew; their names where Where
and What and When, and Why and How
and Who.

—RUDYARD KIPLING

Reporters are often blind to opportunities for investigative reporting
because they must spend years on a beat before learning how and what to
investigate. Two great investigators, John Siegenthaler, editor of the
Nashville Tennessean, and Clark Mollenhoff, a Pulitzer Prize winner and
former head of the Washington bureau of the Cowles newspapers, have
provided a shortcut in this checklist, which is designed primarily to help
those who cover local government:

THE COUNTY OR CITY BOARD
OF SUPERVISORS, COMMISSIONERS, OR COUNCILMEN

1. *What is the budget making process?* Usually there is a provision
calling for the heads of the various departments and offices to submit
budget requests to the governing body, and there is a requirement for
public notice and a hearing. The supervisors or commissioners compare
the budget request with tax income and determine whether to grant the
request, or cut it. Sometimes budget requests come in lump sums or in
several sets of round figures that give no indication of how the money is
to be spent. Department heads like to be able to count on a surplus or an
average for an "emergency": This may mean money to hire some political pal or a commissioner—or it could mean actual fraud. Look for cor-
ners under which a department head can tuck money away. Make him
account for it.

What are the checks available on budget requests? Are there public
hearings? And do citizens bother to question or protest expenditures? Is
there a taxpayers association at the local level to make an objective
study of budget approvals and tax income? Who heads this group? Is he
so close to politics that he is no more than a rubber stamp for the politicians or special interest groups? Laws usually provide for a number of
checks to be made on the supervisors and departments. Are these laws
being observed?

2. *Conflicts of interest.* What are the side business interests of the
commissioners or supervisors? What businesses are their friends and
relatives in? Are commissioners or department heads using their positions in government to give contracts, insurance business, equipment
purchases, etc., to businesses in which they or their close friends or
relatives have a financial interest?

(A) What is the system in the various departments for purchasing equipment and property and awarding contracts and other business? Are sealed bids required in every department? Is the low bidder too frequently ignored and the contracts made with certain favored business interests? If a few firms have cornered all the business, what are the ties with the commissioners or department heads who are in charge of awarding the business? Are the laws governing the system being observed? If all bids are identical, this is an indication that competitors are conspiring to get a high price and are dividing the pie. If commissioners and department heads accept identical bids, it is an indication that somebody in government may be getting a piece of the pie. Also, check specification requirements. Specifications, if they are rigged, can throw business in the lap of a favored company and rule out competing companies.

(B) How about the system for approving bills for purchases made by the various departments? Is there any loophole in the system to allow false billing? Are dozens or hundreds of bills approved by the commissioners or councilmen by voice vote, without a close, or even occasional, spot check on what is being paid for? Is the responsibility for approving bills clearly established? If the commissioners have split up the responsibility among themselves by appointing each other to "committees"—is this practice a legal one? Is the system for approving bills so tight that a criminal case could be brought against a commissioner or department found guilty of false billing? Short of that, can you show negligence in the bill-approving procedure?

3. *Liquor and beer licenses.* What is the system for issuing and approving them? Is "spot zoning" prohibited by a provision that the planning commission must approve zone changes from agricultural to residential or to commercial or industrial? Such a provision provides just another check on the system. Is a particular councilman or supervisor or commissioner given the right to issue licenses for all bars and taverns and package stores in his district or ward? Are the commissioners ignoring the provisions which prohibit persons with criminal records from operating these establishments? Is there always a public hearing before these licenses are issued so the other businesses and property interests can be heard on whatever objections they may have?

(A) Who sells insurance to these establishments? Does the approving commissioner have any connection with firms which get this insurance business?

(B) Who is furnishing juke boxes and pin-ball machines to these establishments? The coin machine industry is a big one. There are all sorts of possibilities here for shakedown and kickbacks. If the industry in your community is controlled by one or two distributors it probably means there is a pipeline to the courthouse. Remember this: the tavern or bar cannot operate without the approval of the licensing authority.

SOME COMMON EVILS
FOUND IN LOCAL GOVERNMENT

1. *Zoning and planning.* Here are two areas of local government usually controlled by a board or commission and directed by a professional staff. Because of urban renewal, the interstate highway program, model cities and, in another direction, the development of special utility districts, a substantial amount of federal money and private capital is involved in various decisions affecting those who control zoning and planning. Questions which naturally arise are: Are the professional planners given final word in the laying out of subdivisions, the routing of roads and highways and in the changing of zoning restrictions? Or are these projects subject to arbitrary change by a politically appointed board or commission? If the commission or board usually supports the professional staff, does the executive or the legislative branch of the local government have the power to arbitrarily overrule professional planners for political reasons?

Sometimes the city council or its counterpart will grant, through councilmanic courtesy to its various members, the right of a member to decide on planning and zoning within a given ward or district. The full council supports the councilman in his district and in such cases the result is that the professional planners who make determinations on the basis of research, analysis and study can be overruled by the political caprice of a councilman who may be looking for a payoff from some special interest. The occasion for corruption here is quite obvious. Beyond that, long-range chaos will be inevitable unless planning and zoning follow professional guidelines. With increasing amounts of federal funds available to local governments and almost completely within the control of local governments, the temptation to flirt with bad planning and zoning will be strong among greedy politicians.

2. *Payroll padding.* Are the officials charged with setting your departmental budgets using the budgeting process to get political jobs for relatives, friends, or for political hacks? Check these various departments which submit budget requests. Look closely at their payrolls. Who are they employing? Anybody closely connected with the commissioners or councilmen who will approve the departmental budget? When there is a substantial budget increase for a department, and it is not explainable, check to see who this particular office recently hired. Does each employee in each office have a function? Are many killing time at taxpayer's expense? Do some have outside jobs which they work on government time?

3. *Personnel: hiring and qualifications.* Is there civil service status? If there isn't, these employees are nothing more than campaign workers at election time—and this includes sheriff's deputies and police officers. What is the method of promotion? What is the pay and background of those holding key jobs? Is there adequate protection of the local government retirement fund? Is there a provision to block the hiring of persons advanced in age who will be eligible to retire without making a substantial contribution to the retirement fund? Is there a provision to block

phony medical retirements from employees who plan to draw their retirement and go into other work?

4. *Vacation, sick leave, and work time.* Is this centrally supervised and controlled or does each office take care of its own workers without answering to anyone? Is there any possibility that your county or city is paying "dummy" or non-existent employees hired by a department pocketing the money? The auditor's office is the logical place for central control.

5. *Property management and inventory control.* What special services (such as automobiles) are furnished by the various offices and what services are bought and paid for? Who gets the business and why? Responsibility for property management should be lodged in the office of the County or City recorder. Any system for pinning down responsibility for property delivered to various offices can be perverted until it is meaningless, or until it is completely disregarded. This is a weakness which may encourage false billing.

6. *False billing.* This is a common practice for hiding the misuse of funds in government. Auditing systems won't usually catch it. A false bill accounts for each disbursement so that no shortage shows up in the records. The only way to pin this down is for a reporter to make a direct check of all questionable items.

7. *Expenses: travel per diem, etc.* Here is where padding can and frequently does occur. It is a simple matter to examine bills of officials when they turn them in after junkets or, in the case of police officers, after returning prisoners or serving warrants. Often there is a stipulated agreement for county and city employees traveling on government business to pick up a stipulated amount for mileage, and this in no way relates to the actual miles traveled.

8. *Private garbage collection contracts.* Privately owned companies sometimes have contracts with cities or with county governments to pick up garbage in suburbs (sometimes for the entire city) and the contract provides no control over service. Five thousand customers at $5 a week is a $100,000 monthly business. This is big money. Who approves the contracts; who regulates the firm's operation after the contract is signed; who has the power to suspend the operation if the firm provides poor service? These are the questions that need to be clearly spelled out if such private operations exist in your area. (In some areas snow removal contracts hold the same potential for the investigative reporter.)

The City or County Auditor

1. Under most systems records helpful in uncovering some of the "common evils" mentioned above will be found in this office. For instance, records applying to property management, false billing, travel expense padding and, especially if there is no civil service board, certain

personnel records. In checking billings, look at bills for long distance *toll calls*. This may tell a story about whom the office is talking to out of town and out of state.

2. What is the accounting setup on cash fees paid for dog licenses, automobile inspections, etc.? Is this a mere journal entry which can be doctored—or ignored? Or is there a cash receipt book and cash register with number licenses or stickers handed out to each person who pays money? Will the system permit an employee to pocket fees occasionally—or frequently at license renewal time—without having to show up in some book-balancing procedure?

3. This office may be helpful in furnishing data pertaining to conflicts of interest on the part of local government officials. Beer board and cigarette bond records will be recorded here, for example, and may reflect that a company in which a local government official has an interest on the side is getting this business because of his position with the city or county.

4. Since the employees in this department play a vital role in checking on the finances of other departments, it might be well to take a close look at the outside business interests of the key personnel in this office. Check *them* for possible conflicts of interest.

5. The county assessment function is often lodged in the office of auditor.

6. Examine fraud possibilities in the county election machinery in this office. In some cases, the League of Women Voters may offer a means of assistance in exposing voting irregularities.

The Sheriff's Office
and Police Department

1. *Is the sheriff on salary,* or does he receive a salary and *fees?* What are the possibilities for rackets to increase these fees?

2. *Illegal liquor seizures.* Does the system make it possible for seized and condemned liquor to get back into circulation? This takes a check of records from the time of seizure by law enforcement officials through the court condemnation, and to the actual destruction with witnesses. A basic question is this: is seized property identified by serial number or otherwise at the original time of seizure?

3. *Illegal gambling equipment.* Apply the same standards of checks on the system of seizure and final condemnation. Are the serial numbers on slot machines or other gambling equipment recorded at the seizure, and on the condemnation order?

EXERCISES

1. Consider the checklist for reporters prepared by John Siegenthaler and Clark Mollenhoff. What does it suggest about the adversary stance that the reporter takes? Is there a danger that observing such guidelines will turn the reporter into an adversary so suspicious of officials that his or her attitude closes off some avenues to information even as it opens others? Be prepared to discuss these questions in class.

2. Read the largest newspaper in your state, looking for investigative stories. Bring at least one story to the next class. Be prepared to describe how you decided that it is an investigative story rather than an interpretive one.

Communicating

II

Information:

SPECIALTY BEATS

7 Reporting Political Affairs

How little do they see what really is,
who frame their judgment upon that
which seems.

–ROBERT SOUTHEY

DURING THE LONG PERIOD when nearly every journalist was a generalist, reporters moved from specialty to specialty with some assurance that they could pick up in a few days or weeks whatever they needed to know. One of the highest compliments for any journalist was to have it said that he or she could cover almost anything. As a result, reporters often found themselves handling comically disparate topics: early in his career in the 1930s, James Reston was sent to London by the Associated Press to write sports news–and to cover the British Foreign Office when the sports scene was quiet.

Even reporters who took over a specialty as complex and demanding as politics without knowing much about it were likely to think that they could perform as competently as anyone had a right to expect. The assignment, after all, was not to address politicians but to relate provocative information to readers, most of whom shared the reporter's political innocence.

Although many small newspapers still rely on journalists who are generalists, larger news organizations employ fewer and fewer generalists, primarily for those stories that do not fit into specialties. Increasingly, news organizations expect reporters to write knowledgeably about one subject rather than sketchily about everything. Once assigned to veterans, political reporting now is often the work of reporters who have relatively little professional experience but who are capable of analyzing the political process.

This change has come about largely because many readers know much more about political trends; fewer journalists can afford to skim the surface of political news. Generalists risk misinforming the public and even inviting ridicule when they try to report politics in depth, exploring trends and interpreting political events.

Take into account the layers of interpretation that lie between the political story and the event.

Skim milk masquerades as cream.
— W. S. GILBERT

Consider what can occur between the time a political event breaks and the news reporter writes the story. These are the six steps to distorted information:

1. Something happens in government.
2. Government officials decide how to announce this occurrence; this may differ from what actually happened in (1).
3. A press secretary presents the news reporters with the government's announcement; this may differ not only from (1) but from (2) as well.
4. A reporter writes a story; this may differ from (1), (2), and (3).
5. A media organization processes the reporter's story for presentation to the public; this may differ from (1), (2), (3), and (4).
6. The public reads or hears the report.

Before it ever appears in print, a news story must hurdle four obstacles. First, the government official responsible for the news-making event constructs an announcement from the work of many subordinates, usually framing the facts to preserve a particular public image. The press secretary who gives this announcement to the journalists must also answer their questions — the second hurdle. If the journalists ask perceptive questions, the press secretary has an unusual opportunity to suggest that the journalist check with a higher official — or even to guide the journalist to an unhappy subordinate. The third hurdle is the journalist, who either reports what is given exactly as it was given or assumes an adversarial position, questioning closely and investigating beyond the announcement. Should the journalist find evidence of misinformation or corruption, the story faces a fourth hurdle, the editor. The editor has the say on whether the story reveals either a breach of ethics or excessive journalistic ardor.

Expect criticism from the politicians you cover.

Practical politics consists in ignoring facts.
—HENRY ADAMS

Dennis Kucinich, the former mayor of Cleveland, once categorized political reporters in the following way:

1. The creative instigators: These activists become directly involved in the political arena by generating conflict via certain reportorial tactics, including exaggeration, speculation, and doomsday prophecies.
2. The referee analysts: Didactic and conciliatory, these journalists emphasize political cooperation, instructive observations, and an analysis of political conflict in terms of governmental functions rather than personal confrontations; they will report on political fights but do not savor them.
3. The narrator-observers: Without taking sides or attempting to promote either political warfare or political peace, these reporters avoid exaggeration and report interrelating issues and political positions as dispassionately as possible; they work with identifiable facts and tend to be issue-oriented.

Thomas Vail, publisher and editor of the *Plain Dealer* in Cleveland, provides a journalist's perspective: "Politics and journalism do not mix."

Because they often depend on journalists to communicate their positions to the public, politicians are sensitive to even subtle shadings of meaning in the news story; hence Kucinich's characterization of journalists as instigators or referees. Most political reporters, who would put themselves in the third category, have little patience with these acute sensibilities.

For example, the following story is an apparently straightforward account of a council meeting on rental housing. Members of the city council, however, would disagree; their hypothetical objections appear as comments:

COMMENTS	STORY
MEMBER NO. 1: *I didn't entirely agree. I made a speech against this, favoring another plan, but I was outvoted.*	The city council agreed Tuesday with its planning commission that something must be done soon to increase the amount of affordable rental housing in the city.

MEMBER NO. 2: *As I said before every-one there, I don't trust the planning commission director—he's always travel-ing to another city to find out what they do.*

MAYOR KNOX: *He should have quoted me directly. After many hours of prac-ticing what I would say, I made those points tellingly.*

DIRECTOR TODD: *I knew what was coming, but I didn't attend the meeting where the council adopted the plan. I was out of town at the time.*

The council also asked the planning commission to study the effects of changes in zoning regulations on the city's comprehensive plan and on the character of individual neighborhoods.

The comprehensive plan, a guide to the city until 1992, states the city's policies and philosophies for future development. Though support for the preservation of rental housing and of neighborhood character was stated in this plan, it is only now, with the in-creasing demolition of rental housing and its replacement by larger and more expensive condominiums, that unforeseen problems with the plan have come to light.

The main problem with the com-prehensive plan is its ambiguity, said the council. In Tuesday's joint study session between the council and the planning commission, Mayor William Knox said he was concerned that homeowners and developers did not know exactly what rules and philo-sophies the comprehensive plan repre-sents.

Councilman Tom Landry and others agreed. "Whatever rules we decide upon should provide developers with certainty" as to what they can and cannot do, Landry said.

Planning Commission Director Ro-bert Todd suggested combining the existing zoning ordinances with added regulations to preserve rental hous-ing. In the commission's report to the council, Todd said that neighborhoods can be zoned either to prohibit high-priced condominiums altogether or just to limit them. . . .

No matter where reporters work, they should resign themselves to the inevitability of complaints, many from the offices of image-sensitive politicians.

Report on city politics by using the resources of the city clerk's office.

He that climbs a ladder must begin at the
first round.
— WALTER SCOTT

In San Jose, California,* the city clerk's office is the starting point for
city reporters. The city clerk, appointed by the city council, manages the
council agenda and keeps council records. Journalists who obtain copies
of reports and studies by contacting the relevant city departments should
be aware that the city clerk will also have a copy if the report or study has
appeared on the council agenda. The city clerk retains documents for two
years, after which they are moved to the archives in a nearby building.

The most important report is the annual budget of the city. The city
clerk keeps one copy that journalists can read, and the city manager
supplies other copies for journalists to take with them. The final budget is
adopted after public hearings and council approval.

The city clerk keeps files of city ordinances. Journalists with questions about the meaning of an ordinance, however, should consult the
appropriate department, not the city clerk or the city attorney. All regulatory, penal, and some administrative ordinances are compiled in the *Municipal Code,* available in the city clerk's office and all public libraries.

Journalists seeking resolutions, in which the city council takes positions that do not require an ordinance, should go to the city clerk. You
must request resolutions by number or give the city clerk the subject,
date, and agenda item number.

*Much of the material on San Jose was suggested by *Reliable Sources,* a booklet written
by Terry Christensen and self-published in 1980.

Use agendas, council packets, and research into past minutes and voting records when covering council or commission meetings.

Keep pounding away and the breaks will
come.
— ARNOLD GLASOW

Like most city councils, the San Jose council meets weekly in a public
session. The council also may meet informally in another session to discuss certain subjects in detail; these meetings are called the Committee of

the Whole (COW), and any decision COW takes must be formally acted upon at the regular meetings. Dates and subjects for COW meetings are published in the agendas for the council's regular meetings.

The city clerk publishes agendas for the city council meetings a week in advance. Journalists can pick up the agenda or have it mailed to them by supplying the city clerk with stamped, self-addressed envelopes.

Although the agenda provides only the subject of items to come before the city council, council packets carry detailed information about each item. Reporters may pick up the packets from the city clerk's office a few days before the council meeting. Packets are prepared for the mayor, each council member, the city manager, the press, and the public.

Journalists may have an interest in how the various city council members have voted on particular issues over time. To examine the general voting record of a member of the city council, reporters must go back through the minutes of meetings. Unfortunately, the council acts on dozens of items at each meeting, usually with a unanimous vote, and the minutes are so short that it is almost impossible to discern the meaning of the votes. Journalists must begin their research by knowing what they are looking for in the minutes, then using them knowledgeably. Reporters can also talk to various members of the city council or to those who know about the council. Finally, if reporters work for a local newspaper, they can learn a great deal by reading the past issues of their own newspaper.

As in most other cities, San Jose has dozens of commissions, boards, and committees to advise the city council. The city clerk manages the agendas and minutes for most of the commission meetings. The city clerk also publishes a list of commissions that describes functions, designates meeting times, and lists phone numbers of secretaries. Journalists can also call the city's information desk to learn the meeting times and places.

In San Jose and other cities, the planning commission is the most important. This commission advises the city council on land use decisions, which are becoming more and more crucial. Reporters may obtain agendas from the planning department in advance of the meetings and may study the minutes of past planning commission meetings. Like the city council minutes, these minutes include only terse descriptions of the items under consideration, how the commission voted, and a list of pro and con speakers, but not what they said.

The city council and the planning commission meetings are tape-recorded, but reporters should know that listening to these tapes is a time-consuming chore.

Draw on the resources of the clerk of the board of supervisors and commission secretaries when reporting on county politics.

> They fail, and they alone, who have not striven.
> —Thomas Bailey Aldrich

In Santa Clara County, reporters do not start with the county clerk but with the clerk of the board of supervisors. The county budget, reports, studies, ordinances, and resolutions can be read in the office of the clerk of the board of supervisors.

The board meets on Mondays and Tuesdays. After discussing transit issues at the beginning of the Monday morning sessions, the board turns to more general subjects, including public hearings. Health care and social services are usually the subjects during the Tuesday sessions. On the first Monday of each month, the board meets in the evening to discuss controversial items.

The clerk of the board of supervisors publishes agendas several days before each meeting. Reporters may pick them up each Thursday or request mailings from the clerk, specifying needed agendas: board of supervisors only or commissions, too.

Agendas carry short descriptions of each item, and board packets have additional memoranda and reports. Although the packets are not readily accessible to the public, the supervisors, their assistants, various county administrators, and the press receive them.

The clerk also keeps two versions of the minutes of the board of supervisors meetings. The first is the agenda with the board's vote added. The second, available a month or so after the meeting, provides more substantial detail. These detailed minutes should supply all the information a reporter needs. The meetings are also tape-recorded. Reporters can save time by starting with the written minutes, then focusing on specific agenda item numbers when they listen to the tapes.

Like those of city council members, the supervisors' voting records are difficult to obtain. Again, if reporters know what they are looking for, the clerk's librarian, who keeps an index of agenda items by subject, can assist them.

Santa Clara County has fifty-two boards, commissions, and committees. The board of supervisors usually appoints members to serve on citizen advisory bodies in particular policy areas. The clerk keeps a list of the commissions and their functions, including the secretaries of the various commissions and where to find them. Reporters must go to them to obtain further information, such as membership, meeting time, agendas, and minutes.

The planning commission advises the board of supervisors on land use decisions. The minutes and agendas of the planning commission are kept by the commission's secretary in the planning department.

Make a determined effort to penetrate and report on the activities of the Washington bureaucracy.

Great works are performed, not by strength, but by perseverance.
—SAMUEL JOHNSON

The building boom in Washington, D.C., at the end of World War II pushed the federal bureaucracy out into the suburbs of Maryland and Virginia. The National Institutes of Health, for instance, were established at Bethesda, Maryland, and the headquarters of the Central Intelligence Agency in McLean, Virginia. Add these headquarters to the scores of imposing buildings that spread out from the center of Pennsylvania Avenue, and reporters are justifiably confused: where can they find information they need to report on national politics?

In a light article, veteran reporter Lawrence Stern of the *Washington Post* wrote in 1976:

My apologies to you, National Commission for the Protection of Human Subjects for Biomedical and Behavioral Research. I didn't know where to find you and—sad to say—began to doubt your existence.

I called the Presidential Press Secretary and other authoritative White House sources and they couldn't help. The secretary wondered aloud, after vainly scanning his copy of the U.S. Governmental Organization Manual, whether it could be that you were a...CIA front.

Stern looked for two days and finally found it. Stern, who had been a reporter for the *Post* for fifteen years, was so amused by his own fumbling that he wrote an eleven-inch story recounting his adventures; the headline read, "On Reaching the End of an Odyssey through Bureaucracy."

No doubt many of those who read the *Post* laughed. Almost certainly, Dr. James H. Boren, who declared himself the founder and president of the International Association of Bureaucrats (INATAPROBU), found

Stern's article funny. Boren has been working at the State Department since 1968 and has spoofed the bureaucracy many times, including his own campaign for President of the United States on the Bureaucratic Ticket. To the hundreds of thousands of bureaucrats in government, however, Stern's story was not funny; it was an occasion for nodding and sighing. Members of the bureaucracy have been all but in hiding for years, appearing mostly as unnamed sources in the *Washington Post,* the *New York Times,* and other newspapers.

It is both crucial and difficult to cover the bureaucracy well. Newspaper coverage is improving as more and more reporters realize the bureaucracy's importance. Rich Jaroslavsky, a reporter who joined the Washington bureau of the *Wall Street Journal,* comments:

> The first thing that impressed me when I arrived in Washington was the sheer physical size of the government. Not just the White House and the Capitol, but also the three House and two Senate buildings, the Library of Congress and the Supreme Court, the massive Commerce building, and the labyrinth of the Pentagon. In every conceivable nook and cranny, some sort of decisions are being made that affect my life.
>
> Washington has been derided, somewhat unfairly, as a town of "Southern efficiency and Northern charm." But the fact is that many of the government buildings, massive and impenetrable, reflect the goings-on within them.
>
> While the civics books say that Congress makes the laws, the fact is that the various agencies, departments, and administrations—the agglomeration generally known as "the bureaucracy"—make a great many vital decisions. Yet to a newcomer (as well, I suspect, to many old hands), it's near impossible to tell precisely what the bureaucracy is up to.
>
> One problem is its size. Say you have a question on the safety of jet planes. Whom do you talk to? The Federal Aviation Administration? Civil Aeronautics Board? National Transportation Safety Board? Some agency is deciding whether banks can offer interest on checking accounts. Is it the Federal Reserve Board? Comptroller of Currency? Treasury Department? Federal Deposit Insurance Corporation?
>
> Still another problem is that so much of what the bureaucracy does is hidden from day-to-day public view. When an agency proposes a new regulation of some sort, it is usually in close-to-final form. But that regulation is often the result of weeks or months of staff work and internal deliberation within the agency—the records of which aren't often released to the public.
>
> The simple fact is this: If you don't know how the bureaucracy operates, you don't know how Washington operates.

*When reporting on the presidency, rein in
excessive advocacy to establish a relationship
of mutual trust, but do not acquiesce to
stonewalling or staged drama.*

> America is the only country in the world
> where you can go on the air and kid
> politicians—and where politicians go on the
> air and kid the people.
> —GROUCHO MARX

Helmut Sonnenfeldt, a bureaucrat who is a former White House aide,
made these points:

> What disturbs me about the relationship of the press to the govern-
> ment...is the press has come to regard itself increasingly as the opposi-
> tion to the executive branch of the government. There has developed an
> adversary relationship between the media and the government that has
> produced actions on both sides that have hindered each side in the
> proper performance of its functions. It is true that under our system the
> press has special immunities that the government does not enjoy. The
> press has the immunity of the First Amendment. . . . The executive
> branch normally uses other devices rather than legal devices, such as
> telling reporters that they can't cover events or misplacing their baggage
> when they are on trips. . . .

Although Sonnenfeldt is partly right about the advantages reporters
have over the president and members of the executive staff, presidential
evasion often aggravates an already uneasy relationship.

For example, members of the media believe President Lyndon Baines
Johnson resorted to any trick or gimmick to manipulate the facts. In the
end it was as if hardly a reporter in Washington believed much that
Johnson said. Correspondents stopped using euphemisms such as "news
management" and said frankly that the president was lying. Toward the
end of the Johnson presidency, a joke made its way around the Washington press corps: "Do you know how to tell when Lyndon Johnson is not
telling the truth? Well, when he goes like this [finger beside nose] he's
telling the truth. When he goes like this [pulling ear] he's telling the truth.
When he goes like this [stroking chin] he's telling the truth. But when he
starts moving his lips, he's *not* telling the truth."

David Broder of the *Washington Post* has written:

> I do not believe that the press of this country ever made it clear to
> the readers and viewers what the essential issue was in the "credibility
> gap" controversy. It was not that President Johnson tried to manage the
> news: all politicians and all Presidents try to do that. It was that in a

systematic way he attempted to close down the channels of information from his office and his Administration, so that decisions could be made without public debate and controversy.

President Ronald Reagan seems to have continued in this tradition. The following edited story gives some insight into presidential behavior:

COMMENTS

This lead might be more effective if the writer took one thing at a time, dealing first with Boorstin's four ideas, then showing how the press conference conformed to Boorstin's definition. Also, more specific discussion would strengthen the case for conformance to the first two criteria.

STORY

In The Image, Daniel J. Boorstin cites four criteria for classifying a happening as a pseudo-event. President Reagan's recent press conference meets all four criteria:

(1) It was not spontaneous but rather planned, planted, or incited. Obviously, Reagan's press conference was planned.

(2) It was planned primarily for the immediate purpose of being reported. Again, obviously this was the case.

(3) Its relation to the underlying reality of the situation was ambiguous. What was Reagan's real motive in announcing his support of a Republican tax reform?

(4) It was intended to be a self-fulfilling prophecy. For example, the Republicans will be forced to come up with some acceptable tax reform, since Reagan has indicated that he will support their efforts.

Before the press conference, cameramen were scurrying around, taking light readings, setting up their equipment for the best possible angle. Newsmen were conferring with one another and their camera-men, checking over their questions for the best possible angle. There was a general air of artificiality pervaded about the proceedings. Most of the correspondents acted as if they were preparing for an exciting

A stage production is real even if it is an artifice; one reference to "stage production" is enough; hopefully *means "with hope": "He asked for a loan, then looked at her hopefully."*

The revisions make these sentences crisper and more readable.

stage production. But even with the cameras fixed upon the proscenium, the newsmen were obviously going to play an essential role~~, in the drama~~. Reagan was not creating this non-spontaneous event by himself--he was only an actor; the journalists were producers, directors, narrators and editors ~~of the production~~. Both Reagan and the newsmen were using the press conference, in a sense each leeching off the other: Reagan, to create a favorable image of the workings of his administration; and the press, to generate some ~~hopefully~~ newsworthy copy.

~~Note:~~ if the pr~~o~~ceeding sounds like a diabolical plot, ~~let me caution you that~~ it isn't. It's just the way things are. An institution--the press conference--has developed, and the participants have ~~a~~ legitimate need~~s~~ for it ~~to continuing to exist~~. Reagan needs it to keep himself in the public eye, to re-establish, on a regular basis, the favorable image which ~~the~~ *many* voters have of him. Newsmen need the press conference to ~~have~~ *win* access to someone who might not otherwise grant them interviews. Even the public is afforded some glimpse of the workings of government. Although ~~practically no~~ policy deci- sions are *seldom* made in a (thirty)-minute press conference, the public is informed as to the president's position on major issues. ~~In spite of the fact that~~ *And although* the public misses out on, or even is deluded about, the behind- the-scenes workings of government, it ~~is informed~~ *does learn* ~~as to~~ the result, even if not the process, of policy-making. *The show begins as* ~~Back to the show.~~ Reagan enters the room, surrounded by what seems to be a crowd of admirers

(~~they are~~ actually his staff members). Bulbs flash

blindingly as Reagan walks to the speaker's plat-

form. ~~Reagan,~~ an incredibly perfect example of

rosy-cheeked health, *The president* smiles winningly as the cameras

whirl. The first question is asked, and Reagan

considers it carefully, or anyway as carefully as

possible *in this age of instant answers* ~~given the nature of the split second response.~~

He wrinkles his forehead slightly, just enough to

look thoughtful, intellectually in control ~~of the~~

~~situation.~~ Reagan looks marvellous and looks way

above average in physical appearance. Reagan has

a distinct and unfair advantage over his less well

endowed opponents and detractors. Next to Reagan,

almost any other politician would look positively

disreputable.

As the conference continues, several points

become apparent. One is that the newsmen ~~very much~~

see themselves as *pivotal* ~~crucial factors in the proceedings.~~

They do not see themselves as catalysts, say, to

force Reagan to address issues which he may have

heretofore successfully avoided. In fact, such

considerations become almost peripheral as the

journalists, in a ~~very~~ real sense, become actors

in the drama. *A television reporter also* ~~The journalist, too~~, looks thoughtful

as he asks his carefully phrased question, *knowing* ~~cognizant~~

~~of the fact~~ *one of* that the cameraman from his news team

is filming his question as well as Reagan's response.

In fact, ~~it is obvious that~~ the cameraman are

obviously ~~quite~~ selective about the questions they do film:

covering not ~~they do not film~~ the ~~entire~~ thirty-minute press

conference, but ~~rather~~ "highlights" ~~from it.~~ And

besides the basic and controversial, they film the

When you begin with a name, then use a comma, consider including the name into the sentence. This relieves the monotony of opening each sentence with the subject and removes one pause from the sentence flow. At the end of this paragraph "Reagan" is used too often.

An example of how the journalists do not force issues would help.

The revisions help the readers move swiftly from point to point.

```
questions "their man" asks.  During the less news-
         periods,
worthy portions of the press conference, the camera-

men run around filming each other.  One cameraman

obligingly posed, squinting into the eyepiece of
                                  it was not operating
his camera, even though he was not filming anything

at the time and his equipment was off....
```

    From the time of George Washington to today, the
president has professed to want a free and independent press
as a check on government; in practice, they have wanted no
such thing.

From the time of George Washington to today, presidents have professed to want a free and independent press as a check on government; in
practice, they have wanted no such thing.

Look to congressional staffers for news in the House and Senate.

> The first essence of journalism is to know
> what you want to know; the second, is to
> find out who will tell you.
> —JOHN GUNTHER

Most of the real news in the legislative branch is made in committee.
Yet even committee meetings, no matter what bargains are struck there,
generally serve only as public outlets for the work of congressional staff-
ers. These staff assistants are to Congress more or less what bureaucrats
are to the cabinet. More than 11,000 staff assistants serve in the House
and another 7,000 in the Senate, but as hard as they work, and as crucial
as they are to congressional action and policy, these staff members are
virtually invisible to the public.

Although almost never identified in news reports, congressional staff-
ers are frequently paraphrased, sometimes quoted ("a highly authoritative
source"), and nearly always the main source of any news that issues from
a congressional office. Major legislative ideas have originated with staf-
fers and been executed by them—in the name of the senator and representative who employs them. For example, some years ago Senator William Proxmire received a letter from a constituent complaining about

bank credit practices. The senator "investigated" the problem by saying five words to Kenneth McLean, the staff director of the Senate Banking Committee, of which Proxmire is chairman: "Let's do something about this." As a result, McLean drafted the pioneering and much lauded truth-in-lending legislation that carries Senator Proxmire's name.

Staff assistants also provide valuable and anonymous services in the more venal field of day-to-day political maneuvering. Consider the teamwork of Texas Representative Jake Pickle and his administrative assistant Michael Keeling back in the politically explosive Watergate period. Congressman Pickle had steadfastly opposed most of the early investigative moves against President Nixon. But as the scandal expanded and evidence became more damning to the Nixon administration, a growing liberal constituency in Pickle's district began working hard to unseat him. Congressman Pickle needed badly to put distance between himself and the Republican administration.

Several months earlier, International Telephone and Telegraph (ITT) had merged with the Hartford Insurance Company through a foreign intermediary, Mediobanca of Italy; because of that, the Internal Revenue Service had awarded the merger a tax-free status, saving ITT several hundred million dollars. Pickle, involved in the congressional investigation of that merger as a senior member of the House Commerce Investigating Subcommittee, had publicly voiced the opinion that ITT had been awarded the tax-free status as a political plum from the Nixon administration, but the committee had taken no action.

Michael Keeling developed the idea of publicizing Pickle's criticism of the ITT merger to put a lot of ground beween Pickle and Nixon. Keeling began simply by writing a series of letters (recounted in press releases) to the IRS protesting the tax-free status of the ITT-Hartford Insurance merger and demanding that it be revoked. Pickle and Keeling made sure to send every letter and release to the liberal opposition in Pickle's district.

Ned Kenworthy, a Washington correspondent for the *New York Times,* became interested in the Pickle releases and helped to publicize them nationally, although neither Pickle, Keeling, nor Kenworthy thought the protests would have any practical impact on the ITT case. They were all astounded, as was the boardroom of ITT, when an IRS spokesman announced that the ITT decision had been reversed and that ITT would be liable for the full amount of back taxes.

Historians probably will never know for sure whether it was the Keeling-Pickle campaign or some political calculations by the Nixon White House that motivated the IRS to move on Pickle's protests. At any rate, Pickle ended up with a good deal of favorable news space in the national press, ITT had to pay off its tax bill, and the Nixon administration's embarassments were compounded – all because Congressman Pickle needed some anti-Nixon press in his district. Keeling, of course, was never mentioned in any of the press reports.

EXERCISES

1. Read the various bylined stories in the local newspaper (or a newspaper in a nearby city) and try to determine how many of the reporters are specialists and how many are generalists. Report your findings in the next class.

2. Having decided which are the specialists in exercise 1, invite at least two to the next class. Include these questions:
a. How well would you have done if you had written specialist stories as a beginning reporter?
b. Which classes in college have helped you in becoming a specialist?
c. What must you read in addition to your reporting to keep up with your specialty?
d. Are you interested enough in your specialty to go to lectures and workshops that your competitors do not deem necessary?

3. Describe for a government reporter the six steps to distortion and ask him or her whether this is accurate.

4. Again test the six-steps illustration by asking a high-level politician whether this is true. If the politician says it is not, ask him or her what is wrong with it.

5. Find out whether your college or university city (or a nearby city) government is like that described for San Jose. Make a list of the differences between San Jose and your city and turn them in at the next class meeting.

6. Prepare to cover the next city council meeting by reading stories about the council in the local newspaper. Also check with the city clerk to determine whether the council meets in informal sessions to discuss major subjects. If so, and if the clerk publishes agendas for the council meetings, ask the clerk for a copy.
Having prepared to report on the city council, attend the next meeting, arriving early to acquaint yourself with the session room and the council members. Type a story about the meeting in more than 1,000 words.

7. Prepare to cover the next meeting of the county supervisors (or other governing body) by reading stories in the local newspaper or in the newspaper published in the county seat. Also check whether the clerk of the board of supervisors publishes the agendas in advance. If so, ask the clerk for a copy.
Having prepared to report on the county board of supervisors, attend the next meeting, again arriving early. Type a story about the meeting in more than 1,000 words.

8. Write a story on either the city planning commission or the county planning commission. Prepare yourself by reading stories in the local newspaper or in a newspaper published in a nearby city and obtaining information from the planning department. Go early to the next meeting to acquaint yourself with the session room and the planners, and afterwards type a story about the meeting in more than 700 words.

Reporting on the Law: Police to Prison

The four branches of government are the executive, the legislative, the judicial, and the investigative.

—ANONYMOUS

THOSE WHO ASSUME a person in prison was delivered there via a policeman and a court are usually right, but they have overlooked many of the steps of law enforcement. Much of criminal law and the many people who are involved with it are captivating, which is why so many television programs are devoted to law enforcement. For example, chances are that anyone in any of the following positions could tell some highly intriguing stories: police chief, police watch commander (officer in charge of a shift), head of detectives, head of crime prevention, district attorney, deputy district attorney, city attorney, deputy city attorney, district judge, and director of the rape crisis center.

Combine the workings of the system with your own good sense: how can I get the most and best information from the police over the long haul?

If at first you don't succeed, try someone else.
—ANONYMOUS

Here is a story about a police reporter:

Diane Miller is a police reporter who has less than a year of reporting, but she conducts her beat as though she is a professional reporter. Miller covers the criminal justice beat for the *Gazette,* and works as if she were born to it.

Although Miller is aware of the problems of being a police reporter, she also knows that everyone wants only good publicity. "I've got to make it clear to my sources that this is a business relationship. I'm not their public relations agent," she emphasized.

Her primary difficulty is maintaining a continuous flow of stories. She stressed that it is important to have a good relationship with her news sources.

"Covering the police, you do a lot of joking," Miller said. This part of her job is the name of the game. "I have to get people to talk, and then I can ask my questions." One tactic she takes is to "show some interest" in anyone she talks to, far beyond just trying to pump sources for information.

Some of the police, she said, are much more accessible than others. In the police department, Miller finds that the police are open and approachable. "Down in the next town, you have to request the detective you want to talk to through a locked door," she said. "I don't just walk in there and talk to people the way I do here."

Miller's life as a police reporter includes inconvenient hours. She has received calls at midnight about breaking stories. More often than not, a police officer is calling. Nonetheless, Miller has found that her reputation as a fair reporter has helped her to establish valuable working relationships. As a result, she often receives tips on breaking stories from her sources.

About half of her work involves traveling to the police stations and courthouses to find news. This tedious work sometimes yields important stories. "Just being visible is all-important," she asserts. "My sources most of the time won't call me up." Miller makes herself visible in the stations and courthouses by sitting at a desk and writing notes.

On some occasions, Miller finds herself dealing with key administrators who have told their personnel to tell the reporters to check with the administrators. She has found a way, however, to get around dealing only with the top people. When she needs to talk to a detective or a uniformed officer, Miller makes certain to mention it first to the supervisor. Using this ploy, she is certain that the administrators feel in control.

Miller inherited her beat from a previous reporter who said he covered stories from a different point of view. "I have to be careful that I don't take over the other reporter's biases," she said.

This story introduces only some of the tactics of a police reporter, but these actions are important.

Although most police organizations in medium-sized and large cities have many divisions—communications division, identification bureau, records department, bureau of missing persons, juvenile bureau, and several others—the most important parts of the organizations are traffic and detective bureaus. Reporters might find themselves using all the divisions for information for their stories, but traffic and detective bureaus rank first.

The traffic bureau has many policemen assigned to controlling traffic, to enforcing traffic laws, and to investigating accidents. Almost all accidents are investigated, and the police try to reach an accident within a few minutes after it occurs. They investigate the cause and also gather information for citations or arrests. When the police make reports, the reports usually include statements of those who are involved in accidents.

The most interesting news for the reporters grows out of the detective bureau. In medium-sized cities, the bureau is divided into at least these details or divisions: burglary, robbery, homicide, auto theft, bank and check, vice squad, and general work. In larger cities, the police organizations are divided into more than a dozen details or divisions.

Occasionally an innocuous-appearing record will contain a much bigger story. The officer writing the report will either not have disguised it sufficiently or will not be aware of a story.

Research is to see what everybody else has seen, and to think what nobody else has thought.
—ALBERT SZENT-GYÖRGYI

Records are made of all *complaints* and of all *arrests*. These records carry few details, but the officers indicated can supply information about the cases. Although these are central headquarters records, district stations usually have similar records. In some cities, the district stations transfer records to central headquarters when the prisoner is taken there. Reporters find that these records are usually open to inspection, but some records, such as a report of a homicide detail detective to his or her superior, are not.

Police records are privileged. An interview with a police sergeant, however, is not privileged in many states. The fact of an arrest is privileged in all states, but the law varies in all states as to whether or not complaints are privileged.

Many, or most, police reporters ordinarily begin their days by checking complaints received during the night, and they determine who has been arrested and booked. Reporters look especially for names, because they know that "names make news." If they find any generally recognized celebrity, or almost any name that their readers know, the reporters will fix their next efforts to finding out what happened. In nearly all cases, the reporters will ask for details from appropriate officers.

Next, reporters make telephone calls to the district police stations, the hospitals, the coroner's office, the state highway patrol, the fire department, and in coastal cities, the Coast Guard. In some cases, the reporters will call the same numbers again and again. Many reporters never leave central headquarters, but they call the city desk to have other reporters do on-the-spot reporting. The police reporters in small cities often accompany police officers to the places to which the police are called.

The reporters always try to verify names taken from police records or given to them in conversation with the police, hospital workers, or eyewitnesses. Often those who supply names to reporters are not accustomed to spelling names properly; they may make guesses that they think are accurate. All reporters are (or should be) cautioned by their editors to make certain that the names are correct.

Notice the errors in the following story, written by a beginning reporter:

COMMENTS	STORY
It is better to have "found dead" together.	A U.S. serviceman was found *dead* early yesterday morning at the bottom of a local motel swimming pool ~~dead~~. Police said it was an accidental drowning.
No need to repeat "morning" in the next paragraph. The phrase "discovered at 3:30 a.m." is false. The body was discovered four hours later. *"Mac" is misspelled. The name is "Mack."* *The police did not learn this "after." It was "while" they were questioning occupants.*	The body of Tom Boyd, 25, was discovered at 3:30 a.m. yesterday ~~morning~~ in the pool of the Flamingo Motel, 339 Elm Rd. The body was first seen by John Mac*k* a swimmer staying at the motel. *While* ~~After~~ questioning motel occupants, police learned that the victim was a guest in the room of Mr. and Mrs. William Chandler. They had met at the Jacksonville Airport and had gone out for drinks. The victim was en route to a base in Fort Bragg, North Carolina.
How much is "much"? Make it "some." *State the victim's name again.* *"Awhile" is one word.*	After consuming ~~much~~ *some* alcohol the trio had returned to the motel. ~~Victim~~ *Boyd* stated that he wanted to wade in the swimming pool for a while, the police report said. The next time he was seen was at the bottom of the pool. He had previously
Do not use contractions.	told the Chandlers he could*n't not* swim.

The writer is guessing, not using facts in writing that lung purges are "common in drowning cases."

```
A coroner's examination found the cause of
death to be lung purge. common in drowning cases.
His body will be taken to Rabenhorst's Mortuary
which handles all Military personnel.
```

Contrast this with an accurate story about the same events:

A 25-year-old soldier returning from Korea drowned early yesterday when swimming alone in a motel pool, police said.

The body of Tom Boyd, a soldier en route to Fort Bragg, N.C., was found at the bottom of the swimming pool of the Flamingo Motel, 339 Elm Rd. Boyd, who was not a registered guest at the motel, reportedly was wading at approximately 3:30 a.m. John Mack, a professional swimmer staying at the motel, discovered the body four hours later.

Boyd was a guest of an Augusta couple he had met at the Jacksonville Airport earlier that evening. Mr. and Mrs. William Chandler told police that they went drinking with Boyd at the airport before inviting him back to the motel. They had learned the next flight to Boyd's destination was not until the following day.

Boyd, who had told the Chandlers he could not swim, went to the pool after the Chandlers retired. Motel guest Roger Snapp of Gainesville, Georgia, told police that he heard loud splashing at about 3:30 a.m., but thought it was an underwater swimmer. No other guests reported hearing anything.

Criminal police work is 10 per cent inspiration, 90 per cent perspiration. Little glamour is involved.

What the police department doesn't know would fill a jail.
— ANONYMOUS

Detectives solve a high percentage of criminal cases in these ways:

1. They give many hours or days to long, drawn-out investigations.
2. They derive information, usually from petty criminals, who attempt to stand high with the police in return for important information.

Detectives often have to question many persons and visit many places, such as hotels, pawnshops, bars, and taxi stations and headquarters.

In using clues that point to a motive for a crime, detectives imagine beyond the mere physical clues. They must connect the clues with at least one person. When they find someone that seems to have the motive, the detectives try to unearth other clues about the suspect. So it is that the detectives must combine hard facts with imagination—provided they will not let their imaginations go too far.

Be prepared for increasing pressure limiting media exposure of police work.

> Everybody belongs to one of two classes: those who always know more than they tell, and those who always tell more than they know.
>
> —ANONYMOUS

An accused swindler named Billie Sol Estes, who already had been convicted in a federal court and sentenced to fifteen years in prison, was tried in a state court in Texas on additional charges. Estes's attorneys argued before the pretrial hearing that television, radio, and news photography should be banned from the courtroom. But the case had attracted national attention, and the judge denied the motion. Estes was found guilty.

The U.S. Supreme Court reviewed the case and reversed Estes's conviction. In a decision written by Tom Clark, the Court held:

> These initial hearings were carried live by both radio and television and news photography was permitted throughout. The videotapes of these hearings clearly illustrate that the picture presented was not one of judicial serenity and calm to which petitioner was entitled. Indeed, at least 12 cameramen were engaged in the courtroom throughout the hearing taking motion and still pictures and televising the proceedings. Cables and wires were snaked across the courtroom floor, three microphones were on the judge's bench and others were beamed at the jury box and the counsel table. It is conceded that the activities of the television crews and news photographers led to considerable disruption of the hearings. . . .
>
> Pretrial publicity can create a major problem for the defendant in a criminal case. Indeed, it may be more harmful than publicity during the trial for it may well set the community opinion as to guilt or innocence. . . . The trial witnesses present at the hearing, as well as the original jury panel, were undoubtedly made aware of the peculiar public importance of the case by the press and television.

In a five to four decision, the Supreme Court ruled that Estes deserved a trial without such extravagant coverage.

All signs point to stronger restrictions on law-enforcement coverage by all the media. The real dangers have been spelled out plainly by Nicholas Horrock, a reporter who formerly was a journalist in New Jersey. He claims that "prosecutors, police, and other mechanics of the law enforcement business spend much of their time and effort now in endeavoring to conduct their business with as little public scrutiny as possible." Recalling his days as a cub reporter in New Jersey, Horrock told of the arrest of a Newark black for the rape of a suburban housewife. Horrock and a veteran reporter were at the police station when the man was brought in at 2 A.M. Said the veteran: "Look around–do you see any lawyers–anybody from the American Civil Liberties Union? Sure you don't. You and I are it."

When all break-ins, rapes, and hit-and-runs look about the same to you, ask yourself how you can make an otherwise common crime stand out.

Whatever our theme in writing, it is old and tried. Whatever our place, it has been visited by the stranger, it will never be new again. It is only the vision that can be new; but that is enough.
    —EUDORA WELTY

Although most crimes are not intriguing, the unusual crimes need the reporter's literary skill. Often, though, these interesting crime stories are written by reporters who are too accustomed to grinding out their stories, one after the other.

Here is a story written by a student reporter who is beginning to understand that he must use all his skills:

> On almost any afternoon, neighbors can be seen jogging, washing their cars, or chatting over the fence.
> "I have a wonderful feeling about this neighborhood," a longtime resident, Mary Timmons, said. "My neighbors on either side are looking out for me, just as I'm looking out for them."
> Ann Maddorf, who lives with her daughter, said emphatically, "I feel protected all the time. If anyone approached me, I could run to any house because the houses are so close together. It's especially nice here because a policeman lives across the street."
> Although people seem generally safe, University Park has changed. Most of the residents now own dogs and the people are more aware of crime. . . .

The writer of this story knew that he had to observe University Park carefully and some of the actions of the residents.

The following story deserves special attention because the student writer knows that some of the vividness of an event can be achieved only through painstaking research. This form of the story is known as "suspended interest" because the central action occurs near the end of the story:

> That morning, burly Bill Doran hurried through breakfast and left his home at 9:00—to get a good seat for the double-header between the Giants and the Dodgers. Doran, 47, a ship's carpenter, was a faithful fan; whenever he could, he went to watch his favorites. He took along a friend's son, Dennis Kye, 15.
>
> From their seats in the upper grandstand, they faced home plate and, above it, rising over the top of the grandstand, a row of apartment houses. In one of these houses, a young black with a .45 pistol he had found that day, was preparing for a celebration all by himself; he had saved his only bullet for July 4.
>
> In the ballpark, Doran, Kye, and more than 55,000 others sat watching as the Dodgers, at 15 minutes after noon, walked onto the bright green grass of the field.
>
> Meanwhile, 15-year-old Robert Coogan had climbed onto the roof of his apartment house, raised his .45 pistol and fired it, for the fun of it, into the air.
>
> His bullet looped swiftly over the playing field, sped toward Seat 5, Row D, Section 21. Just as Bill Doran, his score card in hand, turned to speak to young Dennis Kye, the bullet smashed into Doran's left temple, sank into his brain, and stayed there. Doran, suddenly bleeding, slumped forward.
>
> "What's the matter?" asked Dennis, and got no answer. Doran was already dead. After the police carried off the body and helped Dennis away, two fans scrambled to the two vacant seats, and the game began.

Jump through the regular hoops to get information from hospitals. Then use your resources and wits.

> Bureaucrats are all alike: they think it's their business to delay other people's business.
> —ANONYMOUS

Police reporters often obtain news from hospitals. Upon checking police records and finding that the victims of accidents or crimes have been taken to hospitals, reporters usually make telephone calls. Usually they talk to hospital attendants, but in some cases they talk to the hospital directors. Physicians and other hospital personnel observe rules that protect the privacy of patients, but hospitals ordinarily give the names and addresses of the patients, the names of the physicians, and the illnesses or injuries of the patients. In some cases reporters can get additional information from the attending physicians. In important cases reporters usually find that they must get more information from sources other than the hospital.

From time to time reporters almost anywhere learn that airlines, railroads, and industries try to protect themselves in accidents. One must be resourceful in reporting such cases. Excellent reporting can be accomplished by getting information from other sources, then confronting the executives. Because the information already obtained will be published, the executives ordinarily think that it would be best for them to make statements for publication.

Stories about fires merit the same attention as criminal stories: be fair, be accurate, and use your good sense.

> He is never lucky in the coincidence of his facts with the truth.
> —WINSTON CHURCHILL

At many newspapers, police reporters also cover news about fires. Fire alarms are transmitted to police stations, and patrolmen race to fires to protect lives and property. The patrolmen also must find the name of the owner of the property, the name of the tenant, the amount of damage, and the cause of the fire. Reporters must, however, obtain some or all of this information from the chief of the fire department, his assistants, or from representatives of the underwriters.

Here is a badly flawed story about a fire:

COMMENTS	STORY
The children are not infants. *Loss of life should be mentioned first:* *"Two children died last night in a fire that destroyed a $2.5 million apartment building in Pinedale."*	A fire ~~totally~~ destroyed an apartment building worth $2.5 million and killed two infant brothers last night in the Pinedale section of the city. Firefighters from the city and two neighboring suburbs fought the blaze.

The writer should place higher the phrase "All other residents escaped unharmed . . ." and who the dead are.

This sentence is written as though the firefighters are residents of the building.

The six-story building is ~~located~~ at Oak and 11th Street.

All other residents escaped unharmed in in the blaze, except for three firefighters who suffered smoke inhalation. The brothers, identified as Joe and Bobby Rogers, aged 6 and 4, burned to death before their mother, Nancy, could reach them.

A state fire inspection official said that his office had recently cited the building's owner, Jay Cooper, for three violations of the state fire code: ~~The~~

It is better to revise this sentence in a way that would have the readers make the connection instantly.

~~violations are:~~ bad electrical wiring on the first floor, flammable material on the siding, and faulty fire escapes. Cooper would not comment *about the violations.* ~~on the official's~~

~~statements.~~

This revision is important. When an investigation is being conducted, it is to determine whether someone should be charged, not to determine if the person is guilty.

If the fire resulted from failure ~~District Attorney William Fox said he~~ *to bring the building up to required* ~~would investigate the fire to see if~~ *standards, the owner could be charged* ~~Cooper is guilty of negligent manslaughter~~ *with negligent manslaughter.* ~~for failing to make all of the required~~

~~changes.~~

First, remember these changes indicated in the comments section, especially in the last statement. Second, read again the four comments on the first three paragraphs. These tell beginning reporters how to order many of their fire stories.

When reporting crimes, learn the language your first day and keep yourself and those you work for out of serious trouble.

> Accuracy is to a newspaper what virtue is to a lady, but a newspaper can always print a retraction.
>
> — ADLAI STEVENSON

Arrests. An arrest is a serious matter, especially for reporters. The exact charge against the arrested person must be documented by a police record or must be attributed to a police official.

Arson. Reporters should memorize this definition because arson is spreading daily: usually to collect insurance, someone must willfully burn a building or property for an improper purpose. Also, someone must maliciously burn a building or property that belongs to another.

Booking. The formal police act of charging a suspect is called booking.

Breathalyzer Test. Police must make an at-the-scenes test of a suspect's blood for intoxication.

Bunco. This is a term for swindles and cheating.

Burglary. This is the act of breaking into a building or property to commit a theft.

Confessions. With few exceptions, police must tell defendants of their right to remain silent and to obtain counsel. The Miranda Rule is the first thing reporters must think of here. The rule came into effect in 1966 when the U.S. Supreme Court reversed the conviction of Ernesto Miranda, a young, mentally retarded truck driver. Police had failed to warn him, prior to his confession to raping an 18-year-old girl, of his right to counsel or that his statements might be used against him. Reporters must remember that individuals are presumed to be innocent until they are found guilty. Many editors will tell new reporters not to use confessions until they are admitted in open court.

Felony. Reporters should know that this general term includes major crimes, such as arson, armed robbery, and murder.

Homicide. This term includes murder and manslaughter. *Murder* is defined as the unlawful killing of one person by another. *Manslaughter* is defined as the taking of a human life without premeditation.

Investigations. During the course of police investigations, reporters are almost always confined to lists of witnesses who have entered the police stations. Reporters have the right to interview the witnesses if they will talk. Some stages of police investigations require secrecy and almost all reporters respect this.

Identifications. Many reporters use this phrase for identifications in important cases: "This person gave his name as. . . ." Nonetheless, if an identification is inaccurate, the reporter may be in trouble. Often, reporters can be reasonably certain of identifications by using papers in the suspect's possession or by questioning relatives or friends.

Larceny. Grand larceny is theft of property of value greater than that specified by state law. Petit larceny is theft of property valued at less than that amount.

Misdemeanors. This term applies to crimes less serious than felonies, such as speeding an automobile.

Robbery. This differs from burglary in that robberies take other people's property from them personally through force or threat of force.

These are some of the abbreviations police officers use in their reports: **Actor:** suspect; **AKA:** also known as; **b.f.:** black female; **b.m.:** black male; **complainant:** victim; **d.o.a.:** dead on arrival; **d.o.b.:** date of birth; **LSW:** last seen wearing; **n/a:** not available; **NFD:** no further description; **r.p.:** reporting party; **s.:** suspect; **t/p/o:** time and place of occurrence; **v.:** victim; **w.:** witness; **w.f.:** white female; **w.m.:** white male.

Some experience helps in covering criminal courts. Prepare for it.

> When I was young I observed that nine out of every ten things I did were failures, so I did ten times more work.
> —George Bernard Shaw

The federal court system is much less complicated than the many diverse state systems. It consists of district courts, courts of appeals, and the U.S. Supreme Court. District courts are trial courts that try all cases involving violations of federal laws. Courts of appeals hear only appeals from a district court or from state supreme court decisions if the cases involve constitutional questions. Usually, the Supreme Court hears only cases appealed from the courts of appeals. In a few cases, decisions of district courts may be appealed directly to the Supreme Court.

State courts are divided into inferior courts, courts of original general jurisdiction, and state supreme courts. Inferior courts are ordinarily made up by the justices-of-the-peace or magistrate courts who hear all claims between citizens to a maximum fixed by the state, usually up to $500. Courts of original general jurisdiction hear all cases that involve disputes between two or more parties and criminal offenses against the state. These courts are sometimes called "trial courts" and "courts of record," but in most states the official name is "circuit court." In most states, the highest tribunal is the state supreme court; it hears appeals from trial courts.

Both federal and state systems have special courts. In each system, special courts are strictly limited to certain kinds of actions. In the federal system, the special courts are created by Congress, such as the customs court, which hears only cases about the rates of duty on many classes of imported goods. In the state systems, there are probate courts to probate wills, juvenile courts to try cases when children are charged with a crime, and many other special courts.

The chief officer of an inferior court is called the trial justice, the justice of the peace, or a similar name. The executive officer of an inferior court is the constable. In a state court of record—those usually known as the circuit court—the chief officer is the judge, the executive officer is the sheriff, and the recorder is the clerk of the court. Like the state courts, the federal courts have the same names, except that the executive officer is a marshal.

Lawyers or attorneys are officers of the court and can be punished for breaches of duty. Many states permit the parties, although they are not lawyers, to conduct their own trials. In nearly all cases, however, lawyers represent the parties in civil or criminal trials.

Like police work, the covering of criminal trials has its own official sources. Use them to start.

A live wire is never dead, especially if he has connections.

– Anonymous

Over the years reporters develop many sources in addition to those actively involved in the trial itself. Beginning reporters, too, should introduce themselves to as many sources as possible. Here are most of them:

Clerk of the court. The clerks are basic foundations for all reporters. In nearly all cases the clerks prepare trial calendars, handle dockets, have records of all proceedings, and receive applications, motions, and fines. Ordinarily the clerks make arrangements with the reporters for trial coverage.

United States attorney. In the federal system, the United States attorney and his or her assistants are major sources for news.

Judges. Those who are judges at the federal and state levels vary widely when they are confronted by reporters. Although most judges will decline to be interviewed on pending legal cases, veteran reporters will introduce themselves nonetheless.

Prosecutors. Reporters know that the offices of prosecutors are among the foundations of news. Reporters also cultivate many of the minor officials: bailiffs, special police, court stenographers, and the like.

Defense counsels. Reporters know that some judges will seal off access to prosecutors and defense counsels at the beginning of trials. In many criminal cases, however, reporters can maintain contacts with the opposing lawyers during recesses in the courtroom and before and after court sessions.

Plea bargaining — a necessary if sometimes unpopular practice.

> Children are innocent and love justice, while
> most adults are wicked and prefer mercy.
> —G. K. CHESTERTON

Court reporters have learned over the years that plea bargaining, in which the defendant agrees to plead guilty to a lesser charge than the original one, has increased dramatically. "I don't think that there is anything sinister or improper in negotiating in a criminal case any more than in a civil case," Robin Wakshull, a lawyer in Santa Clara County, has said. He has estimated that 90–95 percent of cases filed are handled by negotiating a settlement.

Nonetheless, in many states citizens have been outraged by plea bargaining, and in some states, like California, provisions have been placed in propositions that would virtually eliminate plea bargaining. Frequently city leaders are arrested for drunken driving and escape being convicted on this charge by pleading to fail to stop for a traffic sign.

Increasingly, reporters state in their stories whether plea bargaining was involved and cite both the original and reduced charges. The increasing crime rate, however, seems to ensure that plea bargaining will continue.

Generally there are eleven steps in the civil trial process—less sensational than in criminal litigation but equally important.

A lawsuit is a machine which you go into as a pig and come out of as a sausage.
—AMBROSE BIERCE

One who starts a civil suit by filing a complaint or a petition is the *plaintiff,* and the one against whom the action is brought is the *defendant.* Less than half of all civil suits go to court. In most cases, reporters ignore the suits that do not. Here is what happens during a civil suit in court:

1. The plaintiff files a complaint with the clerk of the court. The nature of the claim and the remedy sought is stated in the complaint.

2. The clerk issues a *summons,* which tells the defendant to appear in court and files his or her answer.

3. The jury is empaneled, and the trial begins.

4. The plaintiff's lawyer makes a first statement to the jury, indicating the nature of the action.

5. Ordinarily, the defense lawyer also makes a first statement.

6. The plaintiff's lawyer gives the evidence: witnesses and documents.

7. The defendant's lawyer gives the evidence: witnesses and documents.

8. Lawyers for each side summarize the evidence and argue in an attempt to win the jury to their version of the case.

9. The judge tells the jury the points of law governing the case. The jury decides how much weight is to be given to the points of evidence.

10. The jury goes to the jury room and secretly arrives at its *verdict.* After this is announced, the judge either sets it aside (uncommon) or renders judgment.

11. If neither side requests a jury, the judge alone would act as both judge and jury.

Learn these terms:
Accessory. One who assists in committing a crime.
Affiant. One who makes an affidavit.
Affidavit. A written statement of facts.
Allegation. An assertion, which a person says will be supported by evidence.
Alias. A fictitious name assumed by a person.

Arraignment. An appearance of a defendant before a judge to hear the charges and to enter a plea of guilty or not guilty.

Bail bond. Security to guarantee the appearance of an accused person in court.

Bailiff. An attendant who preserves order in a courtroom and has custody of prisoners during a trial.

Change of venue. This changes the place of a trial.

Contempt of court. Any willful disobedience to a court order or any misconduct in the presence of the court.

Deposition. A written statement from a witness before trial.

Eminent domain. The right of a government to take private property for public use.

Grand jury. A panel of twelve to twenty-three citizens that investigates in secrecy the accusations against a person.

Habeas corpus. A writ signed by a judge requiring production of a detained person to inquire into legality.

Injunction. A court order requiring those named either to act or not to act in certain actions.

Lien. A charge imposed upon a specific property, which is security for a debt or for a duty to perform an act.

Malfeasance. The wrongful doing of an act.

Parole. A release of prisoners before their term expires, on condition that they behave properly.

Perjury. Willfully making false statements while under oath.

Power of attorney. A written statement that authorizes another to act as one's agent.

EXERCISES

1. Invite two detectives to your class for interviews. Ask them questions such as whether most of their work requires long investigations and/or whether they use petty criminals as informers. Also, ask them to illustrate how they conduct investigations by telling the class how many different places they must visit and their relationships with their informers.

2. Visit the library and determine the law of your state with respect to the publication of the names of juvenile offenders. Record your findings and bring them to the next class.

3. While at the library, determine whether newspapers in your state can publish the names of raped women. Record your findings and bring them to the next class.

4. Imagine that you are a reporter making some routine calls. While calling an outlying district police station, you are told that a truckload of dynamite has blown up just off Highway 11. List all of the questions you ask of the police department.

5. Invite the local fire chief to your class to answer these questions and others of your own. Afterwards write up the interview in a story of at least 700 words.
a. Which is the most frustrating, dealing with reporters, the public, or the police?
b. If everyone in this class were to become reporters, how would you advise us about covering fires?
c. In your fire department, do you ordinarily attend the scene of large fires? Or do you delegate the work of answering questions from reporters at the scene to an assistant?

6. Write a news story based on the following facts:
Louis Chama, aged 40, entered the home of T. D. Ford, 1703 Elm Street, on January 21 (according to his own testimony) at about 4:55 P.M., stealing a radio and some jewelry. He aided the police in recovering his loot. His attorney was John Lyons. Chama was born in Puerto Rico, attended school up to the sixth grade, came to New York in 1957. He had served two terms in the penitentiary. Burglary after sunset constitutes first-degree burglary. Second-degree burglary is burglary during daylight. Chama was tried yesterday in district court, presided over by Judge Tom Jackson. If he had been convicted of first-degree burglary, he would automatically have been a third offender and his sentence would have been 12 years to life. Second-degree burglary carries a sentence of one to five years. It was held by Judge Jackson that he had committed the burglary in daylight although the prosecutor conjectured that Chama would certainly have been seen carrying away property in daylight. Sunset, it was stipulated in the evidence, was 5:22 P.M. The defendant was convicted of second-degree burglary and sentenced to the penitentiary for one to five years.

7. Rewrite the following news story:

> With a bill of exceptions to proceedings of the third district court being filed by Oscar Klugger, 39, rancher, convicted of involuntary manslaughter, the matter will now be taken over by the state supreme court, William Hertl, district court clerk, said today.
> Klugger was convicted of the manslaughter charge in connection with the fatal shooting of Ernest Gilmore, a railroad section hand. He was sentenced to one year in the county jail with nine months being suspended. He was charged originally with second-degree murder, but this was reduced to the manslaughter charge through plea bargaining.

8. When a judge who wants to be reelected deliberately performs unusual actions in the courtroom, such as eating sandwiches on the bench, in order to obtain publicity, should the newspapers assist in those plans? Formulate a definition of news that would require that the judge's behavior be reported.

9. Clip from newspapers three stories reporting civil trials and three stories reporting criminal trials. Bring these reports to class, and be prepared to read any of these.

10. Write a news story from these facts. This is a police accident report.

a. **Place:** Elm and Oak Streets.

b. **Time:** 11/11/83, 9:50 A.M.

c. **Vehicle 1:** Driver, Elmer Powell, 32, 1703 Ross Road, Gainesville, Georgia. 1976 Ford. **Direction of travel:** N-S on Elm. **Damage:** Moderate, driver's side, door, front fender.

Vehicle 2: Driver, Robert B. Rogerson, 38, 591 N. Cowper St., Gainesville, Georgia. 1975 Dodge. **Direction of travel:** W-E on Oak. **Damage:** Major, front end.

Injured: Robert B. Rogerson, injured forehead, complaint of dizziness. Taken to Elwood Hospital.

Collision narrative: D-1 (Powell) said he was traveling southbound on Elm in the number two lane of traffic and heard nothing about the crash until V-2 hit his car. D-2 said he was traveling eastward on Oak and could see very little because it was raining. D-2 (Rogerson) said his foot slipped from the brake pedal and compressed the gas pedal. His car hit the V-1 car.

d. **Cause:** V-2 was at fault.

Recommendation: None.

9 Reporting on the Environment and Energy

Man is a complex being; he makes
deserts bloom and lakes die.

—GIL STERN

FEW SPECIALTY AREAS OF REPORTING can mark their birthdays as clearly as can the environmental, which for all practical purposes was born April 22, 1970, when magazines, television, radio, and newspapers all focused on the many carefully planned protests and teach-ins that were part of Earth Day. Four years later the Arab oil embargo ensured the rise of the environmental writer's most important beat-within-a-beat, that of covering energy production and use. Few stories so dominated the 1970s as the effects of industry upon the natural environment and of its parallel discovery of the apparent coming of an age of scarcity in those raw materials so needed to support modern society. The importance of the environment has been clear not only in stories directly about it, but also in those that lie on other beats—the foreign correspondent's report from the Middle East, for example, which is now laced with considerations of oil, or the economic articles from Brazil that also carry scientific warnings about the global impact of "developing" the Amazon industrially.

Although some of the media's initial enthusiasm for the beat has waned, the fact remains that in the coming decades few specialty areas are likely to be of more importance or have as wide-ranging implications; while other beats cover the mechanisms and relationships that exist within human civilization, the environmental beat claims as its territory the very question of whether technological culture can survive. In the environment lie the limits and the resources that set the agenda for discussion on other beats.

Few specialty areas demand as much familiarity with technical documents or as much patience and fortitude in pushing through the clouds of confusion raised by well-meaning scientists and partisans. Few have as many sub-beats, any of which could be a specialty in itself—and often is—and any of which can have not only local, but national or even global, implications. It is not unusual on the environmental beat for a reporter to look well beyond the geographical area covered by one's own newspaper or broadcast station to find information about, say, the effects of certain toxic chemicals or air pollutants. In fact, an environmental reporter who does *not* look beyond the immediate geographic area for information can usually be assumed to be doing an inadequate job. After all, the tall power plant stacks emitting the sulfur dioxide that turns to acid rain over New Jersey may well be four or five states away.

Some critics suggest that the environmental beat, for all its importance, has been one of the worst-covered and worst-written, trumpeted in doomsday language and cast as humorous battles between dams and fish. Unfortunately, much of the criticism is accurate. Often reporters who have simply been tossed into writing about an environmental topic have approached the subject as they would a car wreck – as a one-shot event. To some extent the event-oriented Earth Day heritage lingers, ironically working against substantive environmental coverage. The complexity of the beat does not lend itself well to event-oriented reporting; what is required is patient, ongoing, well-crafted *process* coverage, for what happens and has happened to the environment is much more a process than a sudden event.

More on that later. For now, consider some of the many aspects of the environment with which a reporter pursuing this specialty may have to be familiar:

Population growth and change. Locally, this may mean the growth or shifting about of people within a city or a region. Specific increases or decreases may be left to the urban affairs reporter, but it is up to the environmental reporter to bring a perspective to the impact shifts have upon land, water, air, forests, and food supply. (The urban affairs reporter will be busy enough documenting the increased demand for sewers, roads, schools, utility services, etc.) Globally, the population is expected to *triple* to about 12 billion within the lifetimes of many of those reading this book. Where will the people go? Few communities, even in industrialized nations with low birthrates, can expect to escape the direct and indirect effects.

Food supply. If the problem of putting the people somewhere seems immense, consider feeding them. Because the United States has had a history of having ample food supplies, journalists here never were much concerned about the ways in which the food was produced. That has been changing in recent years as more citizen groups and reporters have begun analyzing the effects of agricultural techniques, water reclamation, pest control, agribusiness, agricultural research, and so forth. Agriculture requires land, and land is in fixed supply. Many say the land is deteriorating, too.

The question of who controls the land is also of interest to the environmental reporter. Is the land being taken over by agribusiness corporations or is it still owned by people who live in your county? Different ownership may mean different effects upon the land and the water: heavier pesticide use, for example, or less concern for the land itself.

Air and water quality. Pollution and *environment* became almost synonymous in the 1970s, to the extent that on some media the environment beat was more properly called the air pollution or water pollution beat. Either filled the journalist's work week quite adequately. Indeed, journalistic consciousness about the environment was first aroused by concerns about the "tail end" of the industrial cycle — pollution, waste disposal, and health questions. With smog omnipresent in most cities, reporters have had to learn the language of oxidents and photochemical reactions and particulate control. But the "front end" of the cycle is important, too. Where the water will come from to cool the new power plant is as significant as what will happen to the water once the plant cools its turbines. Similarly, the effects of mining coal and uranium upon air and water quality are as important as the effects of their use.

Waste disposal. Ever since the discovery of the Love Canal tragedy (in which a school and New York suburb were built over a dump site filled with toxic chemicals), reporters have grown more sensitive to the fact that industries generate not only air and water pollution but poisonous wastes, which have to be disposed of somewhere. Even normal waste disposal of both the liquid and solid kind poses substantial environmental problems for a community.

Environmental health. This topic has become so familiar that probably little needs to be said. The phrases themselves are evocative: brown lung; black lung; gray lung (from uranium); cancer-causing chemicals in the workplace or in food; the effect of pesticides on pregnant mothers; the effects of lead on children. The environmental reporter also has the task of questioning the safety of man-made changes in the environment. The health of readers is at stake.

Natural resource conservation. Much of an environmental reporter's time can be spent covering controversies about how certain resources, such as forests, rivers, shorelines, and wilderness land, should or should not be used. The shoreline habitat of unique and even endangered species makes a dandy dumpsite for the superheated water from nuclear power plants, for example. Few battles are more emotional than those in which individuals claim ownership and use of that which is common heritage — the world's limited resources.

Energy. No environmental reporter these days can afford *not* to be familiar with the close link between energy and environment. The two are intertwined as certainly as the physical laws of the universe say they are. If the environment is composed of "matter," then energy is a vital part of that relationship between different types of matter. Some argue that humans can extend scarce material resources by the application of ever more energy; the reporter has to ask where that energy will come from. Is it to come from fossil fuels such as coal and oil? Nuclear power? Geothermal or wind power? Solar energy? Some of the biggest construction projects ever attempted are associated with the present human endeavor to ensure a source of energy for itself in the coming decades. As a result, decisions being made in a utility company boardroom can now have as much, if not more, impact than decisions being made in the statehouse. In the early 1980s one of the biggest stories was that of the collapse of the Washington Public Power Supply System. This consortium of utilities in three states attempted to build a string of nuclear power plants but, because of cost overruns and mismanagement, ended up abandoning some of the plants half-completed. The effects rumbled through bond markets and banking houses all the way back to New York City.

Because of its complexity, the environmental beat demands that the journalist formulate a framework to keep efforts directed and goals clearly in mind.

America once had the clarity of a pioneer axe.
–ROBERT OSBORN

What exactly will be the goal of environmental coverage? Is it to present as much of the scientific information about ecological effects as possible? Is it to cover each meeting held to develop a new wilderness plan or each hearing scheduled on an environmental impact statement? Is it to always look at any environmental issue from a "human-centered" standpoint, focusing primarily on, for example, public health effects? Is it to concentrate on a "non–human centered" approach, conveying the importance of meeting animal or plant needs even at the sacrifice of immediate human needs? Is it to cover the end of the industrial cycle – pollution or waste disposal – or starting points of the biological cycle – food production, groundwater protection, species conservation?

Some journalists simply surrender, without telling their editors, of course. For example, a reporter in one of the biggest oil boomtowns in the United States commented that he saw no reason to do any environmental writing because the *business* reporter did an adequate job of covering the petroleum industry. Other reporters throw up their pencils or pound their VDTs in dismay and fall back on the beginning reporter's caveat of attribution: they say it, I just quote it. As critic Dennis Chase has written: "By and large, journalists have been content to report the crisis by attributing it—to a study, a report, or the judgment of a prominent scientist or government spokesman—with no serious attempt to verify the conclusions or locate flaws in the findings. . . . Eco-journalism is the journalistic practice of reporting ecological crises by ignoring, treating as unimportant, or mishandling the evidence on which the crises are based."

Part of the difficulty of the beat is that the journalist covering the environment is much like the human ecologist studying it. The subject matter is that of the relationship between organisms and their environment. The academic disciplines involved in the study include anthropology, biology, physics, chemistry, sociology, psychology, engineering, political science, economics, law—and even, as we will see in a bit, religion and philosophical history. One must be as conversant with the legalese of the National Environmental Policy Act as with the physics of the second law of thermodynamics. Some familiarity with marketplace economics and bond rating systems helps, too.

Without a clear purpose in mind, an environmental journalist can easily be sidetracked into writing dull tomes filled with technical information or, alternatively, vapid poems to the beauty of some marsh. Worse, they can become listers of the "Fifty Best Hikes" or sensationalists ever out to "get the bad guy." What follows are some items to keep in mind in formulating a purpose and framework for environmental reporting.

Keep in mind the history of how the environmental "crisis" developed when defining what aspects of the "crisis" warrant attention.

The problems of preserving the carrying capacity of the earth and sustaining the possibility of a decent life for the human beings that inhabit it are enormous and close upon us.
—GLOBAL 2000 REPORT TO THE PRESIDENT

No good reporter begins work on a beat without first learning the history and context of that beat. A political reporter who has not read the U.S. Constitution, some Federalist Papers, and at least a little political philosophy and history is a poor political reporter. This familiarization with the context is not going to translate into paragraphs in every story, of course; "contexts" are particularly hard to work into straight news stories that are focused more on the current event than on the processes shaping that event. But the historical context can be invaluable for intelligently questioning the current event and for deciding which of many stories is the most important to pursue. Usually the context is a vital part of any interpretive or in-depth research story, too.

Though the environmental beat is a complicated one, certain information can be kept in mind, and even repeated to the public when appropriate.

Modern society faces a severe environmental and social crisis. On the one hand, critical resources are becoming scarcer. These include minerals for our furnaces, water for our developments, air for our lungs. The list also includes adequate topsoil for food production and millions of plant and animal species vital to a diverse and ecologically stable world. On the other hand, the increasing human population is intruding upon balanced ecological relationships. This ever-increasing human population also wants a level of material sustenance that the earth may not be able to sustain. Within these two facts lie serious questions about economic and social justice—who gets what and how much—and the likelihood of present and future inhabitants living in peace with each other. To quote the *Global 2000 Report to the President* (produced in 1980 by the federal Council on Environmental Quality and the State Department):

> If present trends continue, the world in 2000 will be more crowded, more polluted, less stable ecologically and more vulnerable to disruption than the world we live in now. Serious stresses involving population, resources and environment are clearly visible ahead. Despite greater material output, the world's people will be poorer in many ways than they are today.

Another report, this one prepared in 1980 for the United Nations Environment Programme, warns that "living resources essential for human survival and sustainable development are increasingly being destroyed or depleted. . . . The planet's capacity to support people is being irreversibly reduced in both developed and developing countries."

The crisis, in other words, is real, and environmental journalists must keep that fact before the public—even if some critics complain about "doomsday reporting." But, odd as it might sound, there is certainly a difference between "responsible" doomsday reporting and "irresponsible" doomsday reporting. Critics who want to wish the crisis away by charging reporters with sensationalizing it can be ignored. More thoughtful critics are right in saying that it is not enough to point at the sky and cry that it will fall—according to so-and-so. That is especially true when the journalist then quotes XX saying it won't and YY who says it may fall, but not for twenty-five years. The public is only confused, and ultimately jaded, by such reporting. Comes the rejoinder: but scientists disagree! What is a journalist to do?

Consider: logic alone makes it clear that infinite growth on a finite planet is not possible. Eventually, as political scientist William Ophuls points out in *Ecology and the Politics of Scarcity* (recommended reading for all environmental journalists), we may have to live in societies more frugal than the ones we are in now. The resources of this planet are limited and we are pressing the limits. Among thoughtful, well-educated scientists and leaders, on that much there seems to be a fair consensus.

The consensus collapses over the time scale involved: optimists believe that the current situation is not that bad and that technology can overcome some of the limits; pessimists, Ophuls says, believe the situation is already worse than we realize and that whatever extensions of time technology can grant us will be too little, too costly, and too much an "answer" that has actually created the problem.

The responsible environmental journalist does well to keep the ultimate problem firmly before his public: *Biological, physical, and resource limits do exist. Past policies and habits are causing us to exceed those limits. The dispute is over what to do about those limits and how quickly action must be taken.* A public inured to disputes between Scientist A and Scientist B tends to wish the entire environmental crisis away with statements like these: The oil shortage is not real; it's just because of the Arabs. There is plenty of natural gas; the big companies are hoarding it. Without becoming strident about "doomsday," the environmental reporter must help readers make choices—and the first step in doing so is to make certain they know that choices *have* to be made.

The journalist will probably want to remind the reading audience that the present age of abundance is relatively new. Historically, as Ophuls points out, human societies have lived very much on the edge of scarcity; goods have never been available in an abundance that can match human wants. The very foundation of the state—and thus of politics—lies in ecology: the first function of the state is to maintain order by seeing that limited goods are allocated nonviolently and by restraining the human passion for collecting and hoarding. If the state cannot do that, then disorder reigns and collapse is assured. (How the state allocates goods is, of course, part of the question of justice.)

In centuries past, occurrences such as the discovery of America and the Industrial Revolution removed the pressing issue of scarcity from Western consciousness for a time.

The philosophy of the Enlightenment, to which we are heirs, is based upon that initial tremendous expansion of abundance and that confident eighteenth-century faith in the ability of Newtonian physics to manipulate and control the natural world. Religion colors our thinking, too, particularly Protestantism with its emphasis on work and on the domination of nature. Our world view is one based upon an assumption of abundance. Recall John Locke's argument for private property; it could be had by all because there was such an abundance of land. Recall economist Adam Smith's praise for the marketplace and its "invisible hand," which would right the abuses of any single greedy merchant; the marketplace did not have to worry about environmental costs that would be absorbed by the common air and water, without charge to the producer. Recall David Hume, wistfully fantasizing that all could share the earth as "man and wife" if goods were as abundant as air and water—both of which are now threatened. Recall, too, the utopian Karl Marx, who believed that with a bit of tinkering, the state—that arbiter of scarce goods—could completely disappear, the abundance would be so great. All three dominant world views—capitalist, socialist, and communist—seem to assume that abundance is guaranteed; the question is just how to distribute it.

Now, with the dawning of a New Age of Scarcity, the conflict lies between the Enlightenment viewpoint, with its "technological fix" to scarceness, and the still-developing philosophies of the "small-is-better" and "steady-state economy" schools of thought.

Thus, the environmental journalist is concerned not just with scientific information, but with that conflict between world views that can be represented in even the most microcosmic of environmental decisions. If only technical information is emphasized, the reading public is likely to be discouraged from participating in environmental decisions, preferring to surrender them to technical elites. (The environmental journalist is likely to encounter technical elites who believe that is what *should* happen anyway, as well as those who want to maintain their own power by refusing to release information to the public.)

The role of the environmental journalist is to insist upon access to all relevant technical information, but not to swamp the audience with it; one must strive to provide sufficient context about the environmental limits, about the conflicting world views *and* about the relevant technical information to enable readers to participate in public policy decisions. These have to be made, not by technical elites (because turning the decision over to them means, in essence, opting for one world view) but by prudent men and women trying to guide a community toward some kind of common good. As Ophuls notes, the questions being raised by the environmental crisis—and thus the questions that the public must understand—are those that political philosophy began with in the days of Plato and Aristotle:

What is in the common interest, now and in the future? What actions will we take to ensure survival and some measure of the good life, not only for us but for our descendants and our companions in the global state? What actions and policies of the past now seem unwise for the future?

The journalist covering conflicting answers to such questions might remind readers of the historical context from which each answer derives. Some argue (and are dutifully reported) for colonizing space or, at least, for bringing raw materials back from space. Such stories are occasions for reminding readers of the limits faced here on earth, for recalling similarities to the "extension of the known world" that occurred when the Americas were discovered. That New World bought Western society four centuries of time, because the Industrial Revolution had not yet occurred and the population was small by today's standards. Today a similarly rich new world might buy us only twenty-five or fifty years. How long will be needed to find it? How much will it cost? How many more will we need to keep finding? Is this really the long-range solution? Such questions can help place what seems like a logical solution into its proper context. In this case, of course, the answer that many readers might have jumped for initially begins to look like a very costly, temporary solution at best, and a further fueling of the problem at worst.

To summarize, an environmental reporter should avoid frustrating self and audience with seemingly endless disputes by reporting them as if they are about the problem itself. The disputes are about the answer to the problem. The environmental reporter needs, first of all, to constantly educate readers about the problem itself. A second need is to put the answers into their historical contexts. One should not be awed by those who, because of their command of technical information, try to turn a public policy decision about the common good into an elitist decision. The story writer needs to examine not only controversies over scientific information, but conflicts between values. Finally, the writer should point out what the end result of maintaining a certain set of values will be.

Characterizing environmental disputes as shoot-outs between the "good guys" and the "bad guys" will almost certainly trivialize what is really at issue.

So many men, so many minds.
— TERENCE

"Bad guys" can be environmentalists who are bow-legged bird watchers, or they can be off-road motorcyclists, the twentieth-century answer to Attila the Hun. "Good guys" can be developers who promise jobs and electricity, or they can be environmentalists who stand as chivalrous knights, resisting the onslaught of rapers of the land. Caricaturing one side or the other seldom conveys useful information or insight; it simply allows the reporter to vent personal opinions while pretending to be objective.

Consider the Tellico Dam case, in which the entire issue – not just the opposing sides – was subjected to caricature. Much of the media portrayal of the controversy over whether the Tennessee Valley Authority should build a new dam focused on the seemingly comical confrontation between a three-inch fish called a snail darter and a $100-million hydroelectric Goliath. The media focused on the dramatic cartoon and failed to look beneath the surface, as David Sleeper, an associate of the Conservation Foundation, pointed out in a 1980 article. Predictions by the TVA about the dam's potential and the need for its electricity went largely unquestioned. So did the fact that 16,000 acres of prime farmland and several important archeological sites would be flooded, and that one of the area's last remaining free-flowing rivers would be plugged. Excellent questions could have been raised: How accurate were the predictions about how much electricity the dam would produce? Would the electricity truly be needed? Would it be needed as much as that farmland? How much food did that land produce? What contributions to knowledge or historical appreciation were the archeological sites likely to make? How much energy would it take to build the dam? Of how much social and psychological value to humans is a free-flowing river – especially if it is a region's last?

Instead, the focus centered on the halting of a major project – one that was simply presumed to be needed and of benefit to humans – by a tiny fish championed by selfish environmentalists.

At the same time the Tellico Dam story was unfolding, Sleeper points out that a similar dispute was occurring on the Platte River in Wyoming and Nebraska, at the Grayrocks Dam and reservoir. When a federal judge ordered construction stopped because of a faulty environmental impact statement (it failed to take into account the project's effect on groundwater, farming, and wildlife habitats), some newspapers headlined only one item: the dam had been stopped because it might disturb whooping crane habitats. A *Washington Star* head read: "Whooping Cranes Stall a Dam." The *New York Times,* reporting a recommendation that Tellico not be completed and that Grayrocks be modified, said in its head: "Snail Darter and Whooping Crane Win the First Test of Species Act."

In effect, as Sleeper points out, the media manufactured an environmental drama, trivialized the values at stake by casting it as an "us versus them" or "David versus Goliath" human interest story, and skipped the important value considerations: the careful weighing of answers to those questions about what is in the common interest.

Note the difference between the *Washington Star* lead on the Grayrocks Dam decision and a more thoughtful attempt to establish the issues about a proposed hydroelectric dam in New England:

> It's seven power agencies versus 70 whooping cranes for control of the Platte River in Nebraska—in a fight with stakes of more than $1.2 billion.
> — *Washington Star*

> Last winter's energy scare made an almost magic word of Dickey-Lincoln [the name of the New England hydroelectric project].
> The project, which would flood the wild Saint John River to generate electricity, is being touted as the answer to Maine and New England's long quest for a cheap and plentiful source of power.
> The truth is somewhat less dramatic. Dickey-Lincoln would produce useful volumes of power. But construction of the dams won't solve either the energy crisis in general or New England's need in particular.
> — *Maine Sunday Telegram*

The *Star* allows its readers to escape reality, even if only for a moment. The energy crisis could be solved if it were not for those darned environmentalists and their birds! The second writer offers a more balanced picture: the hydroelectric project will produce "useful volumes of power," but it is no complete answer to national or even regional needs. The second reporter has begun to establish a needed context, which can be explored in more detail throughout the rest of the story. The first lead focuses on the *conflict* that is so strong a news value for reporters. In this case, the conflict is hyped for mass consumption. The second lead offers a serious look at some hard decisions that will have to be made.

The goal of a responsible environmental journalist must not be just to play Henny Penny, to trivialize real drama, or to hype confrontations.

Instead, one must promote a public understanding of ecology and provide careful analyses that help the public actively and intelligently participate in shaping public policy.

Addressing the psychology of environmental use and misuse can help journalists and their readers to understand the real difficulties in correcting problems.

> The mastery of nature is vainly believed to be an adequate substitute for self-mastery.
> —REINHOLD NEIBUHR

In 1968, in an article in *Science* magazine, microbiologist Garrett Hardin revived a useful concept that had been first published in the 1800s by a mathematician. The concept is a valuable one for environmental journalists and their audiences.

Imagine a pasture open to many cattle ranchers. Each rancher can be expected to keep as many cattle as possible on the open range even when the addition of an extra cow means a slight deterioration of the pasture, and, thus, of all the cattle. The rancher rightly figures that while he will get all the benefit of adding that extra cow, the losses that occur to the range will be equally shared by all the other ranches. Thus, he loses far less than he gains.

Following such logic, each rancher keeps adding extra animals, regardless of the ability of the pasture to feed them. If one attempts responsibility by reducing herd size, he risks suffering more than the others, as well as losing his "share" of the market. The system compels each to increase herd size without limit, even though the pasture is clearly limited.

This is the "tragedy of the commons" and, in a nutshell, the story of the current ecological crisis. The psychology that is at work in a commons has long been known; Aristotle pointed out that "what is common to the greatest number gets the least amount of care." The logic of the system dictates that the limits be ignored and that expansion go on until restraint is either mutually agreed upon or externally imposed—or until the commons is destroyed. Commenting on the tragedy of the commons, political scientist Ophuls points out that the individual contribution to the damage seems tiny, so there is little incentive for any individual to act responsibly. In fact, acting responsibly only provokes frustration: for an individual to decide to not use a car in Los Angeles, where the common air has been seriously damaged already, is to cause substantial personal hardship with no palpable gain. "The essence of the tragedy of the commons," Ophuls writes, "is that one's own contribution to the problem (assuming that one is aware of it) seems infinitesimally small, while the disadvantages of self-denial loom very large. Self-restraint therefore appears to be both unprofitable and ultimately futile. . . . Thus we are being destroyed ecologically not so much by the evil acts of selfish men as by the everyday acts of ordinary men whose behavior is dominated, usually unconsciously, by the remorseless, self-destructive logic of the commons."

This last point the environmental journalist would do well to emblazon upon the wall above the typewriter. It is easily forgotten, particularly in the heat of investigations.

Consider again the cattle and the pasture. Suppose that one rancher, by virtue of great capital resources (maybe he owns a bank), has been able to increase herd size more rapidly than the other forty-nine ranchers sharing the range. His herd accounts for 5 percent of the total cattle rather than the proper 2 percent.

Enter the environmental journalist. The range is clearly overgrazed and the commons is almost destroyed. Should you, the journalist, write the story about the one whose herd is bigger, and thus is causing more damage than any other single herd? Shall you investigate the manner in which the rancher has been able to expand herd size more rapidly than the others (maybe some stories about bribes, kickbacks, or illegal loans can be had)? Or shall you write the story about all the ranchers? About the fact that even if everyone's herd accounted for only 2 percent, the commons would still be destroyed?

Ideally, both stories will be written. Often, though, the temptation is to focus solely on the "bad guy." Although a certain amount of public good may be done if the "bad guy" acts more temperately, or is removed entirely, the logic of the commons will ultimately render that good quite useless. The public will have been lured into thinking the problem solved — and another "bad guy" will emerge to take the place of the other.

More important than the "bad guy" story is the effort to bring the public face to face with the logic of the commons itself and then to provide information about possible solutions. The environmental reporter who spends time on "white knight" investigations, tracking down single polluters, may not do as much good as the reporter who patiently and Pulitzerlessly explores why a certain bay has become polluted by a lot of little users and what will have to be done to correct the system that encourages pollution.

Investigations of single polluters are useful, especially in those cases when one company or one person *is* responsible for a significant amount of the damage. But even then the danger is that readers will be allowed to simply shift the blame for environmental degradation to "the other guy" and to continue acting as puppets of the logic of the commons.

In reporting about the commons, a reporter will encounter – and must then put into context – various rhetorical claims. One of the most common is that any limit upon the use of the commons is an unacceptable limit upon "freedom." For example, when the U.S. Forest Service started demanding land use plans from miners who were filing claims in the national forests, the miners cried that their freedom was being eroded. Armed attacks were even launched on Forest Service personnel by people who saw themselves as twentieth-century descendants of the Sons of Liberty. Similarly, when the federal Bureau of Land Management started trying to determine which land in the California desert would be made available or designated off-limits to off-road-vehicle use, ORVers – who had been able to operate without limits previously – raised the cry of "freedom." Some took to their motorcycles and ran cross-country races in defiance of the BLM.

It is not just the "developers" or the "conservatives" who protest, either. Some back-country hikers have not been especially happy about the wilderness permit systems that have been used to limit the number of backpackers who can go into overused areas of national forests or parks. Even liberal thinkers cringe at the idea of restricting the "right to develop" claimed by Third World countries and some American Indian reservations. (After all, the reasoning goes, by what right does an affluent, environmentally minded person tell a less affluent tribe or country not to strip mine a valuable mineral that will provide much-needed jobs and money?)

Freedom! Reporters, who have a heritage of considering themselves defenders of the concept, are often easily persuaded to lend a megaphone to the cries. Because the same word is used for both, no distinction is made between the political and social freedom essential for justice and the personal "right to do as I please" that may lead to castastrophe in the commons. The example of the pasture is all too real: public grazing lands in the United States have been severely overgrazed as ranchers have added larger herds with little regard for maintaining an ecological balance. The tragedy of the commons is being repeated day after day: in developing countries where people scour forests for wood to burn, in industrial countries where factories gulp that which is common – clean air or water – and return it soiled and sometimes unusable.

Cries of "freedom" are worth reporting and abuses of the public's right to participate in decision-making are worth investigating, but the reporter who enters the ravaged pasture and simply broadcasts ranchers' cries of "freedom" – or who portrays such ranchers as heroic individualists standing against a monolithic government – will be doing neither the pasture, the reading audience, nor even the ranchers, any good. The reporter will, instead, be contributing to the "tragedy of the commons."

Background information about basic scientific laws can also help a journalist's audience to understand why the environment has been degraded and to evaluate proposed solutions.

> We cannot command Nature except by obeying her.
> —FRANCIS BACON

Along with the inscription about the psychology of the commons, environmental reporters might also attach to their walls a few reminders about basic natural laws, to be worked into news and interpretive stories when possible.

The first reminder would be about the first law of thermodynamics: the Law of Conservation of Energy. Simply stated, it means that energy can be neither created nor destroyed.

Yet how many stories in newspapers refer to power plants that "produce" energy? How many refer to energy "consumers"? Journalists write—and their audiences think—as though energy is being *created* and then is *disappearing.* Not so. As Paul Ehrlich points out in the book *Ecoscience,* "If energy in one form or one place disappears, the same amount must show up in another form or another place. . . . Although transformations can alter the *distribution* of amounts of energy among its different forms, the *total* amount of energy, when all forms are taken into account, remains the same." Light from the sun turns into thermal energy in the soil and plants, into the heat of vaporization as water evaporates, and into chemical energy through photosynthesis. Then it is transformed into electromagnetic energy heading skyward.

The ledger sheet must always balance; no exception has ever been observed. When gasoline is burned, the chemical energy potential is transformed into mechanical energy, thermal energy, and electromagnetic radiation; combined, the forms are exactly equal to the amount of chemical energy potential that disappears.

Energy is not consumed, then, but its *availability to do work* is transformed; high-grade energy (those sources in which a large amount of the stored work can be transformed into applied work) are converted into low-grade forms of energy (those sources in which only a small part of the stored work can be converted to applied work). Electricity is a high-grade form of energy; the heat from a light bulb is a low-grade form.

At this point, the second law of thermodynamics takes over: all physical processes, natural and man-made, proceed in such a way that the availability of energy decreases. An increase in the availability of energy is *not* possible. Ehrlich notes these consequences:

• In any transformation, some energy is degraded.

• No process converts a given quantity of heat (thermal energy) into an equal amount of useful work.

• The availability of a given quantity of energy can be used only once; it cannot be converted time after time into useful work.

These two laws make it possible for scientists to calculate the efficiency of various transformations of energy. For example, as Ehrlich notes, scientists can specify how much energy is needed to separate salt from seawater (to produce fresh water for domestic or agricultural consumption) *regardless* of the exact details of future inventions. In other words, the fixed laws of nature put fixed limits on technological innovations. Yet many in the journalist's audience do not understand that. Indeed, sometimes even a journalist can be misled into writing a story about a "new invention" that will cure the water availability problem by desalting; in all the hoopla, the journalist fails to ask how much *energy* will be required to make the transformation and where that energy will come from.

Journalists daily fail to point out to readers that most fossil-fuel plants convert only about 40 percent of the energy available in the fuel into electricity. That leaves 60 percent to go elsewhere—as gases up the stack, or as particulates into the air, or as heat into a nearby lake or ocean. Nuclear power plants are even less efficient. Audiences, though, are left with the impression that energy is somehow being "manufactured."

Journalists may also fail to point out that as electricity travels along transmission wires, more available energy is lost. The longer the transmission line, the greater the loss. Such a simple fact may help a reporter effectively question what, initially, may seem like a good idea: locating a power plant and its pollution far from the urban area that will use the electricity. Finally, once electricity reaches the light bulb in a person's reading lamp, another 90 percent or so of the electric energy is released not as light, but as heat.

Taken together, the two laws of thermodynamics mean that all that technology can ever hope to do is exchange one form of energy for another, and one form of pollution for another. Thus, it should have been no surprise—though the media reacted as if it were—when Californians discovered that the catalytic converters on their automobiles controlled one kind of emission, but released another, also harmful.

The two laws can also help a journalist evaluate plans for overcoming natural limits. Proposals for capturing low-grade energy will almost certainly be expensive. Similarly, proposals for using ever more technology will assuredly put ever greater financial burdens on a community: it is terribly difficult to control or reuse low-grade energy. Power plants in this country, for example, can achieve about 90–95 percent control of stack emissions (low-grade energy), but to go another four or five percentage points would cost as much if not more than control of the first ninety. Of course, even a single percentage point means the release of several tons of pollutants a day, and so the tolerance of the commons can be reached quickly, even when there is 90–95 percent control.

Natural laws impose limits; the environmental journalist must educate readers about those limits.

The environmental beat often demands more "process coverage" than "event coverage." Sometimes catastrophes occur; more often the damage is gradual and the repair seemingly requires forever.

> If some great catastrophe is not announced every morning, we feel a certain void. "Nothing in the paper today," we sigh.
> —PAUL VALERY

What does "process coverage" entail? First, it most assuredly includes event coverage, at least significant event coverage. An environmental journalist is still in the news business. If an oil pipeline is planned, then the reporter will be expected to cover the stages by which government permission is given. The most important stories, however, will be those in which attempts are made to explore the need for and the effects of such a pipeline.

Sometimes the need for "process coverage" gives an enterprising local reporter an edge over national reporters, who often can spare only a parsimonious amount of time to a particular controversy. Thus, though the environment beat demands almost a global familiarity with ecological issues, the best performance on the beat often occurs at the most local level.

For example, in September 1974 one such local issue surfaced on the ABC network news, an item about 175 children in the small Idaho town of Kellogg having dangerous concentrations of lead in their blood. The report quoted Idaho's director of health and welfare saying that a lead and zinc smelter run by the Bunker Hill Company was the probable cause of the lead concentrations. NBC carried a report, too, but in total the national reports ran about seven minutes. The *Lewiston Morning Tribune,* a small daily (25,000-plus circulation) in a town 150 miles south of Kellogg was intrigued, and even though Kellogg was outside the *Tribune's* circulation area, the newspaper assigned reporter Cassandra Tate to the story. As free-lance writer Dwight Jensen points out in a 1977 *Columbia Journalism Review* article about Tate's investigation, over the course of the next two years, this small-town, local reporter executed a style of journalism and public service that outshone anything the larger media did. Her coverage included

• An article explaining that the hazard of airborne lead pollution was not limited to Kellogg alone. A similar hazard had arisen near El Paso, Texas, two years earlier, in which 101 of 138 children had lead levels exceeding the public health standard. (This is a good example of the way in which an environmental reporter must look beyond the local neighborhood to present vital background information.)

• A story in which nationally known health officials called for blood tests to be run on children living near the nation's six major lead smelters. The story noted another effect: lead absorption is related to a high rate of stillbirths and spontaneous abortions.

• An article revealing that as of that time, 1974, the Environmental Protection Agency had neither set nor even proposed regulations governing the amount of lead that smelters could discharge. The story also pointed out that sometimes the air around Kellogg contained almost twenty times more lead than was considered normal by state health officials.

As Jensen notes, Tate expanded the story far beyond what the national press had done, "beyond children to childbearing women, and of course to thousands of workers; beyond Kellogg to the other communities located near primary and secondary lead-smelting plants; beyond Boise, the state capital, to Washington, D.C." She even brought the story home to her own newspaper with a report on the health effects of the lead used in the newspaper's production process.

A good example of Tate's skill came when she was confronted with the usual contradictory statements of scientists. Presented with such possible contradictions, many environmental reporters simply retreat into the "he-said-it, he-denies-it" style of reporting. Shortly after the lead-poisoning story broke, the industry-supported International Lead-Zinc Research Organization announced it would conduct a study of the effects of lead absorption on children in Kellogg. Other papers simply reported the announcement; Tate, drawing on information she had obtained while studying the El Paso case, reported that a "medical brouhaha" had developed in Texas when a similar study by the organization had concluded that the children had not been harmed. The findings contradicted those of a study by the U.S. Center for Communicable Disease Control, run by the U.S. Public Health Service. Tate's account presented both sides of the brouhaha, but concluded with a simple obituary for the tiny town that had been affected: "The 120 or so families living in the area were eventually moved out and the town [was] purchased by the smelting company and later levelled." The proposal by the industry-supported scientists was shown to be the public relations gesture it was.

In all, Tate wrote about 175 articles on the lead poisoning, making full use of the journalist's repertoire of reporting and writing skills. (She even included a feature profile on James Halley, president of the Bunker Hill Company.)

Process, not event alone. Readers gain more understanding if the reporter presents more depth.

Here is another example: in the mid-1970s, the federal Bureau of Land Management embarked upon a massive program to inventory the natural and social resources of the California desert, as a prelude to deciding how the desert should be administered. The area affected, about the size of Ohio, had begun to receive intensive use from recreationists, conservationists, the military, and energy companies—and their uses were colliding. The planning, predictably, sparked intensely emotional contests of competing interests. Motorcyclists who feared losing their ability to ride wherever they chose defied the BLM and its small force of desert rangers. Ranchers complained about new grazing proposals. Energy companies demanded transmission corridors. Health resorts wanted "their" clean air protected. Scientists complained about sightseers trampling rare fringe-toed lizards. Cities wanted some guarantee they could continue to expand their populations, drawing further on the desert's meager water resources.

Staged events (such as picket marches and motorcycle protest rides) and scintillating rhetoric were abundant enough to tempt any event-oriented reporter, but the real service to be performed lay in covering the process: an exercise in land use decision-making and a confrontation in values on a major scale.

The *Riverside Press-Enterprise,* located in the urbanized zone of Southern California, about sixty miles from the desert, examined the process in a series of articles over a period of several years. Again the stories made use of the full range of writing styles available. Here is the beginning of one of the interpretive, overview stories:

It is a quarter to four and it is raining, raining for God's sake in the desert, and when it isn't raining the mosquitos swirl from the pools left by last month's rain and come into the truck and dance across the windows. At long last, Jim surrenders and comes from the outside to join those who hours ago left their beds to the elements. It is not a night for sleep.

So this is how the fate of the California desert is being decided. This, and in other ways too.

In El Centro, at mealtime, the publisher of *Sunset* magazine, who has a presence befitting his white mane, incongruously stood eating yet another box lunch on yet another 16-hour day, part of his job on a citizens' committee Congress chartered to help determine the desert's future. The long days were almost ended. The suitcases had been packed. But for Bill Lane, the publisher, the day would end differently, because his chest would hurt and he would leave and when he would be found, he would be on the floor of a nearby office.

In other ways, the future of one-quarter of California is being decided: in Pasadena, where satellite signals are being translated into computer "photographs"; in Riverside, where the headquarters of a special federal planning staff resembles a war room with transect sketches and U-2 photographs; in the desert itself, where archeologists are flown onto isolated mountain ridges. . . .

The California desert. It doesn't really exist at all, certainly not as a geological or biological area distinct from others. Many deserts are here squeezed into one, within an expanse the size of Ohio, 39,000 square miles intruded from the north by the Great Basin, from the east by the Mojave and from the south by the Salton trough and the Yuha and Colorado deserts. Taken as a whole, it is not one of the world's harsher deserts; indeed, as time and human building go on, it seems to grow tamer and for many it has become only a fleeting obstacle to be crossed on the way to Las Vegas or to the ski resorts at Mammoth.

What sets it apart is its variety. More than 200 different kinds of animals exist here, for instance—and more than 1,000 types of plants. Some are rarely seen, having retreated into a tenuous existence as anachronisms left from a day millions of years ago when the desert was an ocean. Life for the fairy shrimp, for example, may come only once every decade, as their eggs, the size of sand grains, lay waiting for the right amount of rain, at the right time of year, so they can hatch and in the few days before the rain pool evaporates, grow, reproduce, and insure the uncertain continuity of the species for yet a few more years. To scientists, the adaptations here, to all variety of arid climes, say much about evolution and life.

What sets the California desert apart, too, is pressure. Human pressure. There are 1,200 miles of pipelines, 100 microwave repeater sites, and 3,500 miles of power lines. Almost a half-million people live in more than 100 settlements. Areas such as the Coachella and Imperial Valleys have become rich farming lands or resorts, and urbanization, which once only crept, now at the very least saunters, and in some cases, races. Hundreds of mining claims are staked; geothermal developments are considered next to mineral springs held sacred by Indians; power plants are suggested in the midst of scenic vistas; jeeps smash the eggs of the fairy shrimp and motorcyclists occasionally crash into sand-sailing recreationists using the same playas.

For each pressure, there is an interest group and an emotion. Probably no other property so often considered wasteland has caused so many lawsuits and so many speeches.

Finally, what sets the California desert apart is that here the federal government has begun what is generally acknowledged to be the biggest environmental planning effort yet attempted. The effects go beyond California. The methods used, the millions of dollars spent, the scientific techniques developed and the new scientific knowledge produced are already being used to determine the way natural resources will be allocated elsewhere in the country. . . .

That story went on to explore the planners and their efforts, the strains that were being created between the "old guard" BLM officials who were "use-oriented" and the "new guard" who were "conservation-oriented." Others explored the lives of those who were on the front-line of the effort, out in the jeeps. Still others explored the conflicts between the "oldtimers" of the desert and the new, urban users.

The *Press-Enterprise* series centered on the process that was unfolding, more so than on a single event or series of events: the process of determining what the human relationship to the desert and its ecosystems was going to be, and the significance of that process to urban and desert dwellers alike.

Again, the local press was able to provide far better coverage than the regional or national press, which afforded scanty, event-oriented reports at best.

Exponential growth in demand for a particular resource can rapidly turn what seems to be a "non-issue" into a hot controversy.

> In nature, there are neither rewards nor punishments – there are consequences.
> —ROBERT G. INGERSOLL

Suppose, as an environmental reporter, you are asked to write a story about the prospects of a brizzig shortage ("brizzig" being an imaginary material for this example). Your circulation or broadcast area happens to include several factories that use brizzig.

You discover that there are 50,000 tons of brizzig remaining in the world reserve. Since the current demand is only 100 tons per year, you are told that there really is no likelihood of a brizzig shortage any time soon. In fact, at 100 tons per year, 500 years will be needed to exhaust the current reserve. You tell your editor, "No story."

A few months later, Consolidated Brizzig Products releases its annual report, noting that the demand for brizzig is growing at a rate of 3.5 percent a year. You know that will shorten the time brizzig is available, but you still figure that any shortage is four or five generations away—by which time brizzig will probably have been replaced by some other mineral anyway. No story.

Did you ever play the child's prank of asking a friend to put a penny on the first square of a checkerboard, two pennies on the second square, four pennies on the next, and so on, doubling each time? Perhaps your friend, thinking she would not owe you much money at the end, fell for the prank. By the last square, the amount would have been nothing short of astronomical.

That is exponential growth, and that is what is happening with brizzig.

With a 3.5 percent annual growth rate, demand will double every twenty years. Doubling, and redoubling, the absolute demand for brizzig rises from a mere 100 tons per year to sixteen times that amount by the fourth doubling. At the end of that fourth doubling (eighty years), the supply of brizzig will be exhausted. Eighty years may still be a generation away, but obviously, any planning and conserving had best start *now*. Sound like a story?

As William Ophuls points out, once exponential growth begins and once the demand for a certain material is high, even increasing the reserve of that material by a substantial amount makes little difference. Suppose, with new technology (deep mining for brizzig?), the accessible reserve can be raised from 50,000 tons to 500,000 tons, a tenfold increase. With the same 3.5 percent growth rate, brizzig still will be exhausted by the time of the seventh doubling (140 years). With even a hundredfold increase in the reserve, brizzig will last only until the tenth doubling.

Change the scenario a bit. Suppose instead of being at the starting point, you are actually living in an age toward the end of the doublings—say, at the fourth or fifth doubling. Even though your reserve may seem large, it may be exhausted by even a single additional doubling of the demand.

The *static reserve,* as it is called (the amount of the reserve of brizzig divided by the current annual demand), is an extremely poor indicator of how long a certain material will last, especially if demand for that material (or mineral) is already high and increasing. A more important figure — and the one the environmental reporter should look for — is the *exponential reserve.* In the example above, the exponential reserve turns out to be less than 20 percent of the static reserve.

Environmental reporters can draw two lessons from the exponential reserve. First, even promises of enormous increases in reserves cannot offset a steadily growing, high demand and cannot extend the useful life of the reserve by many lives. Reporters who focus only on the latest big oil discovery, without noting the small effect that discovery has on the exponential reserve, may mislead readers into a false sense of security. So will reporters who communicate statements like this: "At present levels of demand, the reserve of XX is expected to last 400 years." That is the static reserve figure.

The second lesson exponential growth teaches is that even if a no-growth policy is adopted in the years just before the final doubling, there will be very little effect. For example, if the original reserve of brizzig is five million tons and will be exhausted by the tenth doubling, the adoption of a no-growth policy at the time of the ninth doubling will extend the life of the reserve by only thirty or so years. This is so, Ophuls notes, even though at the time of the ninth doubling, *nearly 70 percent of the original reserve still remains* (about 3.5 million tons). That is the problem with exponential growth: it is much like a farmer who watches a lily pad double in size each day (an example that became popular after the publication of *The Limits to Growth,* a 1972 Club of Rome study that was one of the first to focus on the problem of the scarcity of many resources). At first, the pad is so small that it seems of no concern. Even when it covers a quarter of the pond, the remaining free area of water seems so great in comparison that the farmer does not realize only two days remain before the entire pond is covered.

As is the case with the tragedy of the commons, a failure to keep the exponential growth problem before the public plays into the hands of those who want to simply blame "bad guys" for one shortage or another. Even reporters fall into that trap; news accounts for the past decades have been laced with innuendos about the Arab nations. "Bad guys" there certainly are, and a good reporter will reveal them. Still, revealing those who manipulate current shortages to their own advantage is no solution to the shortages themselves.

RECOMMENDED RESOURCES

Some of these sources are mentioned in the chapter. Others are recommended by authors in the field of human ecology.

Highly recommended is William Ophuls's *Ecology and the Politics of Scarcity* (W. H. Freeman and Company, San Francisco, 1977), a well-written treatise on the political and economic viewpoints that have shaped the environmental issue and the political changes that are likely to be necessary to cope with scarcity. Herman Daly's *Economics, Ecology, Ethics: Essays Toward a Steady-State Economy* (W. H. Freeman and Company, San Francisco, 1980) is a useful anthology of essays by economists concerned with the problem of growth. The book includes Garrett Hardin's article, "The Tragedy of the Commons," originally published in *Science* magazine in 1968, as well as a concise explanation of the laws of thermodynamics, originally published in *Ecoscience* (W. H. Freeman and Company, San Francisco, 1977) by Paul and Anne Ehrlich and John Holdren.

Works by Rene Dubos are always recommended for a biologist's viewpoint, particularly *So Human an Animal* and *A God Within. The Limits to Growth*, a Club of Rome study published in 1972, was one of the first to explore the global nature of the environmental crisis.

Several excellent articles analyzing the media's performance on the environmental beat have appeared in recent years. Among them are Dwight Jensen, "The Loneliness of the Environmental Reporter," *Columbia Journalism Review*, January/February 1977; Roger Morris, "Buffaloed by the Energy Boom," *Columbia Journalism Review*, November/December 1981, and "Whatever Happened to the Natural Gas Crisis?" *Columbia Journalism Review*, March/April 1976; John S. Rosenberg, "Land Use Coverage: A Connecticut Sampler," *Columbia Journalism Review*, May/June 1978; David Sleeper, "Media Coverage of the Environment: The News May Not Be the Truth," *USA Today*, January 1980; and Jon Swan, "Uncovering Love Canal," *Columbia Journalism Review*, January/February 1979.

Magazines that focus on environmental issues include *Science*, the official organ of the American Association for the Advancement of Science; *Technology Review*, from the Massachusetts Institute of Technology; *Environment*, which examines the technical side of issues but is written for the layman; the *Bulletin of Atomic Scientists*, with news of the nuclear industry; *Not Man Apart*, the Friends of the Earth publication, which contains news items about legislation as well as in-depth features; *Environmental Action*, focusing on legislative and administrative actions; *Oil & Gas Journal*, a respected industry journal; *Public Utilities Fortnightly*, examining regulatory agencies and financing problems; the *Sierra Club Bulletin* and *Audubon*, both published by their respective conservation societies.

Private organizations that can be invaluable sources of data and background include the American Petroleum Institute, Washington, D.C., the primary lobbying arm of the oil industry; Center for Science in the Public Interest, Washington, D.C., which includes scientists interested in energy and pollution issues; the Edison Electric Institute, New York City, the utilities' equivalent of the American Petroleum Institute; the Conservation Foundation, Washington, D.C., which runs information and research programs; the Environmental Defense Fund, with offices across the country, including Washington, D.C., and New York City; Friends of the Earth, San Francisco; Sierra Club, San Francisco; National Audubon Society, New York City; National Coal Association, Washington, D.C., the coal industry's trade association; Natural Resources Defense Council, New York City, a public interest law firm; and the American Institute of Mining, Metallurgical and Petroleum Engineers, New York City, a large professional group of engineers involved with energy matters.

Among the government agencies heavily involved in environmental matters are the Environmental Protection Agency, with jurisdiction over air and water pollution; the U.S. Department of the Interior's quartet of the Bureau of Land Management, the National Park Service, the Bureau of Reclamation, and the Bureau of Indian Affairs; the Department of Agriculture's Forest Service; the Department of Commerce's National Oceanic and Atmospheric Administration; the Department of Defense's Army Corps of Engineers; the Department of Energy; the Department of Health and Human Services' National Institute of Environmental Health Sciences; and the Department of Transportation's Federal Highway Administration.

State governments often have parallel agencies.

Reporters considering the environmental beat would be wise to enroll in university courses in ecology. A number of schools have begun interdisciplinary programs in environmental education.

EXERCISES

1. Build a foundation for environmental reporting by preparing a source chart (as described in the exercises for Chap. 1) listing local, state, and federal agencies that have responsibility for protecting the environment in your area. This usually can be done by working with a telephone book and by making several phone calls to the agencies themselves to confirm their roles. You might also talk to a local environmental reporter. Once the chart is complete, test yourself: Which agency would investigate accidental chemical spills in a nearby river or lake? Which could tell you where to find the most polluted and least polluted air in your region? Which would be responsible for deciding whether a planned housing development would harm already endangered plant species?

2. Complement the source list created in exercise 1 with other lists of citizen environmental groups and private research agencies. Are there nongovernmental authorities on water pollution at your university? Does the local Audubon Society chapter engage primarily in bird-watching, or has it also begun lobbying efforts and research on sensitive environmental issues in your own community?

3. Having familiarized yourself with the background of the environmental beat in your community, begin to examine specific issues. These could be pursued individually or in teams; each should produce usable and interesting stories about the environment that even the local media may have overlooked:
a. *Food resources.* What is the status of food-growing land in your area? Is it being encroached upon by suburban development? How much farmland was lost last year? Is the land owned by individuals who live in your community or is it controlled by absentee landlords or corporations? Does the ownership pattern seem to have affected the environment in any beneficial or adverse ways? How does food get to your city? Are there environmental side effects of that manner of transportation?
b. *Water resources.* Where does your drinking water come from? Is it being mined from groundwater reservoirs? Are they being replenished as fast as they are

being drained? What is the industrial and residential demand for water in your area likely to be in the next ten years? What is the quality of the rainwater upon which nearby farmers and possibly even urban communities are dependent? Have lakes and rivers gotten cleaner in the last decade or dirtier? Who are the chief polluters? What have they been doing to reduce their pollution?

c. *Waste disposal.* How is liquid and solid waste disposed of in your community? What about hazardous wastes? Radioactive wastes from hospitals and universities? Are the sewage plants up to date in technology or are major improvements needed or planned? How much waste does your community produce each day?

d. *Population growth and distribution.* Compare the 1980 and 1970 censuses for your area. Have there been shifts in population distribution? Have those had any environmental effects?

4. Analyze the media coverage given to a recent environmental issue in your own or another community, asking yourself the following questions:

a. Did the reporter make use of a variety of journalistic styles to cover the controversy (straight news? interpretive stories? features? investigations?)? Were there process-oriented stories as well as event-oriented stories? Or did the bulk of the coverage consist of "quote-slinging," which simply quoted one side or the other?

b. Was the information presented in a sufficiently thorough and interesting fashion as to enable a lay audience to follow the issue and even participate in the policy decisions that had to be made? Was it too technical? Not technical enough?

c. Did the coverage focus primarily on the "tail end" of a pollution-creating process, or did it also take account of the "front end" of the pollution cycle?

d. Was the controversy trivialized into a "bad guy" versus "good guy" confrontation?

e. Were the values of the opposing sides examined? Did the reporter probe those values and raise the fundamental question of the common good?

f. Did the journalist explore the logic of the system involved, making use of the notion of the "tragedy of the commons" if it was appropriate?

g. How did the reporter handle rhetorical claims about freedom? Were the claims of "the right to do as I please" handled analytically or did the reporter primarily act as a megaphone for such claims? Did the reporter create "heroic individualists" on either side?

5. The formula for calculating the doubling time for exponential growth is seventy divided by the growth rate, usually expressed as percent per year. Thus, a 3.5 percent rate of growth in the demand for a certain material means that the demand will double every twenty years (seventy divided by 3.5). If the demand for brizzig is 100 tons per year and the demand is growing at a rate of 3.5 percent per year, then in twenty years, the demand will be up to 200 tons. In forty years, the demand will be up to 400 tons; in sixty years, up to 800 tons, and so forth.

From some quick and rough calculations, you can then figure that if there are only 100,000 tons of brizzig in the world, the static reserve is 1,000 years (100,000 divided by 100), but the exponential reserve is somewhat less than 115 years.

Figure the doubling rates and static reserves and make an approximation of the exponential reserve given the following information:

a. Demand for Mineral A is 200 tons per year and 75,000 tons are believed recoverable. Demand is growing at a rate of 2 percent per year.
b. Demand for Mineral B is 500 tons per year, and 600,000 tons are known to be recoverable. The demand for the mineral is growing at an astonishing rate of 10 percent a year.
c. Demand for Mineral C is 1,000 tons per year; the recoverable reserve is 1,000,000 tons. Demand is growing at a rate of 5 percent a year.
d. Demand for Mineral D is also 1,000 tons per year, but the recoverable resource is only 500,000 tons. Demand has been growing at 5 percent a year. You are assigned to cover a major new discovery of Mineral D, which adds 25,000 tons to the recoverable reserve. The public relations officer is trumpeting it as a major extension of the mineral's availability and as the solution to the impending shortage of D. How many years does the discovery add to the exponential reserve?

10 Reporting about Business and Economics

> Big business is basic to the very life of this country, and yet many – perhaps most – Americans have a deep-seated fear and an emotional repugnance to it. Here is a monumental contradiction.
>
> – DAVID LILIENTHAL

JOURNALISTS HAVE TRADITIONALLY FOCUSED most of their efforts upon the coverage of political affairs and, much like political scientists in universities, they have sometimes defined *politics* rather narrowly. The work of government – especially the elected and judicial branches of government – along with the antics and strategies of politicians have been the bread and butter of the news columns.

In the mid-1970s, however, a significant change began. Partly it entailed the discovery of the need for new beats, such as environment and energy, and partly it reflected the emergence of old beats from their former ghettos at the back of the news pages or the bottom of the newscasts. The latter was true of religion reporting, which is discussed in a separate chapter. Both elements of discovery and emergence were valid in the case of the subject of this chapter: business and economics reporting.

Until the mid-1970s, business news tended to be a dull affair, assigned to worn-out city hall reporters and hidden, as *Washington Post* columnist Nicholas von Hoffman once wrote, "down the corridor behind the partition next to the water cooler." Economics reporting faired even worse; except for the stock market reports, few publications or broadcast outlets cared about issues of money supply, interest rates, gross national products, or international trade. Any talk about M-1 or M-2 would have sent most reporters to the local armory in search of a new weapon. And if someone mentioned talking to "Fanny Mae," most journalists surely would have thought the name referred to a lady of the night.

Chris Welles, a former reporter and editor for *Life* magazine, once noted in a *Columbia Journalism Review* article, appropriately titled "The Bleak Wasteland of Financial Journalism":

> The average consumer today knows much more about the operation of the Los Angeles Rams than Gulf Oil Corp., much more about the strategy and tactics of basketball teams than cereal manufacturers . . . much more about the track record and competitive performance of Secretariat [a prize-winning horse] than the 1973 Buick. . . .
>
> Platoons of reporters are regularly dispatched to cover the most miniscule election [but] many residents of a state intimately acquainted with the background, character, views and ethics of the main contenders in a congressional race will not even know the name of the chief executive of the state's largest corporation.

Von Hoffman suggests that one reason public affairs reporters have traditionally ignored business and economics news is that Americans have been taught, repeatedly, that business and government are separate entities. Mention the words *feudalism* or *communism* and chances are good that a typical American will envision *both* a government system and a particular kind of economic structure. *Feudalism,* for example, calls to mind not only a government of lords and disenfranchised peasants, but an economy of barons and serfs. Mention the word *democracy,* however, and chances are good that the resulting vision will encompass *only* a system of elections, political checks and balances, widespread voting rights, and so forth. Mention *capitalism,* and the vision includes free enterprise, competition, profits, and Wall Street, but no assumptions about government, other than that "politics" is something separate.

Yet, as the chapter on environmental reporting indicates, the very foundation of the concept of government lies in the management of limited goods and in the maintenance of order in the distribution of those goods. Journalist von Hoffman makes the same point as political scientist William Ophuls, quoted in the environmental chapter: "Politics, be it under a Western democracy or communism, is primarily a matter of government supervision of the society's economic activities."

The era of abundance—as well as the long period of American isolation from the world because of its immense natural resources and its geographic independence—allowed Americans and American journalists to pretend for decades that there was a separation between government and economics. Just as the passing of that era has given new significance to the environmental beat, it has pushed business and economics reporting from the ghetto onto the front pages of every daily newspaper and into the opening minutes of every broadcast.

Several events shocked the American press from its complacency about business and economics: the 1971 decision to end the link between the dollar and gold, marking the collapse of a three-decade-old system of international finance; the stiff price hikes in Arab oil in 1973 and 1974, revealing the interdependence of the American and world economies and the way in which natural resources could be manipulated; soaring federal deficits and record unfavorable balances of trade; levels of inflation unheard of in the post–World War II period; and the ever-lengthening unemployment lines during the mid-1970s and early 1980s recessions. The virtual collapse of the American auto and steel industries in the face of cheaper foreign imports only helped to emphasize the importance of trying to understand what was happening to the American *material* dream, as well as the American political dream.

Thus, business and economics became important for much the same reason as did environment and energy news: Americans were forcefully and suddenly reminded of the essentials of survival. In prosperous times such essentials can be taken for granted; in a less prosperous age they become the focus. It is not simply coincidental, then, that news of the economy and of the environment became important during the same years; one deals with the survival of the resources of the earth, while the other deals with the way in which people use those resources to build economies and ensure the survival of complex societies. They are two sides of the same coin.

Some journalists now go so far as to suggest that business and economics reporting is and will continue to be the real bread and butter of late twentieth-century journalism. Whether that claim is true or not, certainly one of the key challenges faced by journalists in the coming decades is the mastery of the intricacies of the new global economic interdependence. That is as likely to shape and reshape local communities as single powerful mayors or governors supposedly did in the past.

Meeting that challenge will not be easy. Corporation officials and bankers are not always inclined to talk to reporters, and many do not believe they should. There is no corporate freedom of information act and there are no sunshine laws to let light into the meetings of boards of directors. Most of all, economics has not been called the "dismal science" just in jest.

The beat is sometimes pursued with an emphasis on either "business," "finance," or "economics." Increasingly, the good news media cover all.

Writing is at the same time perceiving well, thinking well, and saying well.
—GEORGES BUFFON

Business news typically refers to that concerned with the activities of various corporations, partnerships, and proprietorships. In the ghetto days it meant reporting the latest stock dividend or producing a "business office special," a puff piece that might please an advertiser. Stock dividend stories are still with us—and they should be—but today they are often placed in the context of a business's overall profitability, its competitive strategy, its corporate personality, and its marketing ability. Business news never needed to be dull or obtuse, of interest only to those with a predilection for reading agate charts of statistics, for business is an arena of "high drama, basic emotion, and elemental conflict," as *Esquire* editor Clay Felker once noted. For all of the pin-striped stereotype of blandness, business people and their strategies, be they the competitive tactics of ice cream parlors or cereal manufacturers, can be every bit as interesting as the competing strategies of professional football teams—and probably more significant. The audience for such stories is automatic; not only will the employees of the company be interested, but so will that company's consumers and the employees and consumers of its competitors.

Here is an excerpt from one such story about a new competitor in that boom business of the early 1980s, the video game industry. The story ran in November 1982, in the *New York Times:*

> Attack and defend: In the fantasy world of video games that is the theme played out daily on millions of American television screens. And much like the characters in those electronic conflicts, Coleco Industries is bent on conquest—the $5 billion home video game market—at the expense of two well-entrenched rivals, Atari Inc. and Mattel Inc.
> To that end, the Hartford-based company recently introduced its Colecovision home video game system, a cartridge-playing console, to face Atari, the industry leader, and Mattel, the marketer of Intellivision, in the marketing arena.
> Industry analysts and toy store owners say Colecovision's graphics—especially color quality—are generally superior to those of its competitors, and that in many stores it also enjoys a price advantage. But marketing battles, especially at Christmas, are never easy.

The rest of the story goes on to include dollar comparisons of the sales prices of the Atari, Mattel, and Coleco equipment; the obstacles faced by Coleco in trying to establish its market share; and a detailed chart giving the financial background on Coleco and its assets and liabilities.

Although the story about Coleco ran in a national newspaper, it would have made interesting reading in practically any newspaper in the United States – certainly in any city with a toy store. In the hands of a less experienced or less aggressive reporter, the subject could easily become just a puff piece: an article about a new product being carried by a local merchant. In the hands of a reporter who is interested in the marketing strategy and in the statistics indicating Coleco's likelihood of establishing a foothold in the video war against Atari, the story becomes an informative paradigm of what business news is about.

The terms *financial* and *economic news* are sometimes used interchangeably by journalists, but in a narrow sense "financial" news refers to the various movements of money and credit, as well as to the ways in which business and government try to provide for the accumulation of capital to fuel the American economy. Transactions on the stock market, banking policies, and Federal Reserve decisions on controlling the money supply are all part of the province of the financial reporter. Increasingly, journalists are also developing "personal finance" stories, aimed at helping consumers decide how to plan their own investments, retirements, and savings. Such stories used to be left to the personal finance columnists, such as Sylvia Porter, but now reportorial pieces on money market funds, home budget planning, and real estate buying can be found in the news columns, too.

In its broader sense, "financial" news becomes synonymous with "economic" news, which focuses on reports about economic processes that affect all businesses and all citizens. Included are such items as unemployment, inflation, taxes and tax breaks, international trade, shrinking natural resources, and government management of the economy. In the ghetto days, business reporters tended to leave such stories to the national wire services; too often, that is still the tendency. With the increased economic interdependence of the world, such geographic parochialism – such a failure to look beyond the bounds of one's own community to understand and report about the processes that will affect that community's economic health – is untenable and unconscionable. Decisions being made by international diplomats in Tokyo and Washington, D.C., to determine whether Japan will increase its imports of American farm products to offset its exports of Datsuns will determine what price the orange growers in Corona, California, and the apple growers in Wenatchee, Washington, get for their crop. That is something both the *Corona Daily Independent* and the *Wenatchee World* have to be concerned about. Similarly, it is not only Third World governments that have to decide economic strategies; local governments are increasingly in the position of having to decide whether to give significant tax breaks to businesses, whether to use taxpayer money to redevelop business districts, and whether to subsidize businesses through low utility rates. The formulation of such policies—or the lack of them—is of paramount concern to the local economics reporter.

The most important rule for a business reporter is to continue to apply the techniques of good reporting and writing.

> The difference between the right word and the almost right word is the difference between lightning and the lightning bug.
> —MARK TWAIN

That sounds commonsensical, but sometimes lazy reporters forget, resigning themselves to writing little more than "business-office specials" that are neither interesting nor probing. Suppose the *New York Times* story about Coleco's fight with Mattel and Atari had begun in either of these two ways:

> Coleco Industries' stock price fell four points yesterday, to a price of $44.75, even though the company posted third-quarter earnings of $17.6 million, more than eight times the profit reported a year ago. The company is engaged in a major marketing battle with Atari Inc. and Mattel Inc. to establish a share of the $5 billion home video game market.

> "It's got great color graphics," Joe Blydon, of Blydon Toy Store, 5435 Main St., said yesterday. He was talking about the new Colecovision Video Game that he has added to his stock of video equipment.
> Blydon also carries equipment from Atari Inc. and Mattel Inc., Coleco Industries' two principal competitors. Coleco is a relative newcomer to the field of video game toys.
> "We expect to sell a lot of them," Blydon said, adding that he thought Coleco was doing very well financially because of its new entry into the video market.

In the first case, the reporter let the numbers become the focus of the story rather than letting them serve as *evidence* for the theme of the story, Coleco's competition with Mattel and Atari. Such numbers will be interesting to Coleco's stockholders, but not to a general audience.

In the second example, the reporter has focused too much on the local angle, promoting one local merchant at the expense of the broader, and more significant, story about Coleco's strategy and its financial strength. The local focus is not bad in itself (if it can be handled in a manner less promoting of Blydon's Toy Store), but it needs to be fleshed out with figures the reporter can easily obtain, either from a quick phone call to the Coleco public relations department or from a standard reference source such as Standard and Poor's Register of Corporations, Directors, and Executives.

The first reporting rule, then, is *keep the audience in mind.* On this beat, as in other specialty areas, a reporter actually has at least two possible audiences: an elite audience familiar with the journalist's specialty and with the terminology, history, and functioning of various institutions of concern to that area; and a general audience that knows none of those items. Which should be the target? An elite audience does not need to be told what "M-1" or "Fanny Mae" is. An audience familiar with Coleco may not need to be told that it is engaged in a major marketing war over video games. But the general audience does.

The degree to which the reporter can eliminate background depends upon the audience served by the particular publication or broadcast outlet, but the safest rule is that a reporter—especially in this very complex area of business and economics—should explain, explain, and explain. When the explanations are well crafted, those in the elite audience will not be bothered by reminders of what they already know. Indeed, they will probably be happy to have their knowledge reinforced. The *Wall Street Journal* seems to recognize this, even though it caters strictly to an elite audience that knows business. The *Journal* typically includes more explanation of basic economic terms than do many stories in periodicals aimed at a more general audience. For example, in a 1982 story about the Reagan administration's economic forecasts, the *Journal* very carefully reminded its readers of the difference between economists of the "monetarist" school and those of the "supply-side" school:

> The monetarists stress the importance of slow, steady growth in the nation's money supply to curb inflation. This group...believes the Fed's [Federal Reserve Board's] tight monetary policy leaves little room for real economic growth until inflation slows further. They forecast slower growth and larger deficits than the administration has projected. . . .
>
> The supply-siders...still think the tax cuts [passed earlier in the year] will produce rapid growth and high enough tax receipts to hold down the deficit.

Even popular economic terms, such as *recession,* need to be specifically defined. Short paragraphs such as this one should be standard in news stories: "Economists define a 'recession' as six or more months of declining economic activity, marked by a reduction in the amount of goods and services consumed."

A second step in applying good reporting techniques to the business and economics beat entails *personalizing* the news when appropriate. Corporations are not just faceless entities, despite popular myths about the pin-striped corporate identity. Businesses are run by people, and it is in their competition, their conflicts, their successes, their failures, their emotions that the nitty-gritty essence of business reporting lies.

The third reporting technique to apply is that of *simplification*. The more complicated the subject, the simpler the lead. A reader or viewer first should be able to grasp a very simple and very concrete example or image before plunging into abstractions. The *Wall Street Journal,* for example, once began a story about a federal government regulation affecting potato chips made of dehydrated potatoes with this simple, catchy lead: "When is a potato chip a potato chip?"

The *Journal* started a story about a federal lawsuit against one of the nation's most influential accounting firms this way:

> In Lewis Carroll's "Through the Looking Glass," Humpty Dumpty says in scornful tones, "When I use a word, it means just what I choose it to mean . . . Impenetrability. . . . When I make a word do a lot of work like that, I always pay it extra."
>
> Humpty's broad face undoubtedly would display a look of blissful pleasure if he could riffle through the documents of a hotly contested tax case on file at a federal court here [in Atlanta].
>
> He would see a fire-alarm bell described as a "combustion enunciator," doors referred to as "movable partitions," a manhole dubbed an "equipment access" and windows called "decorative fixtures."
>
> These terms, and dozens more, were the heart of a civil lawsuit filed last March by the Justice Department on behalf of the Internal Revenue Service against Cleveland-based Ernst & Whinney, one of the nation's "Big Eight" accounting firms. The suit accused the firm of willfully using misleading terminology to improperly qualify property for investment tax credits on portions of new buildings.

Imagine if the *Journal* reporter had forgotten to simplify by beginning with the concrete image of Humpty Dumpty: "A particularly complex area of tax law, that involving what 'tangible personal property' can be applied as a credit against federal income taxes, is being debated in a federal lawsuit filed against one of the nation's most influential accounting firms."

Such a lead demands that readers grasp the abstractions first. Chances are good that they will simply read another story instead.

The fourth reporting rule of thumb to recall is that journalism emphasizes *change,* so a reporter always needs to place today's dividend report

or economic prediction into a historical context. Does the dividend declared by the Blam Corporation represent an increase or decrease from
last year? Does a new advertisement or commercial signify a change in
marketing strategies? Was that same strategy tried, successfully or un-
successfully, fifteen years ago?

Finally, as in other specialty areas, a reporter needs a firm grounding
in knowledge about the beat; that means both a general knowledge about
economics and business and specific knowledge about the particular industry or region being covered. The preparation—which is on-going,
since the subject matter changes—includes study in economic history,
micro- and macroeconomics, political economy, finance, pricing theory,
international trade, economic theory, marketing, accounting, and
management. Because of the obvious complexity of such topics, numerous reporters are going back to college, participating in fellowships specifically aimed at improving economic journalism, or in regular class of-
ferings in business and economics. Many skipped those subjects back in
the days when journalism focused so heavily on politics. Undergraduate
and graduate students in journalism now have the advantage of being
able to get an early start.

---

*Businesses—even those privately owned—
leave paper trails. As with other beats, the
first step on this specialty is often toward
the library.*

> The Bell System is like a damn big dragon.
> You kick it in the tail and two years later it
> feels it in its head.
> —FREDERICK KAPPEL

Often, the first question posed by a reporter new to the business and
economics beat is, where do I find information about a company? Say that
AMAX, Inc., a major multinational mining corporation, plans to construct a mine in your region. Besides the corporate public relations office,
which may or may not cooperate, where can you turn for background on
an unknown company? In this age of mergers, corporate diversifications
and business takeovers, how can you even find out who owns whom?

The paper trail for business and economics begins at the reference
section of the nearest city or university library with these books:

- *The Directory of Corporate Affiliations,* with its guide to 4,000 parent companies and more than 40,000 subsidiaries and affiliates. It will answer that question of who owns whom.

• *Moody's manuals on industries, public utilities, transportation companies, and banking and finance institutions.* These manuals contain reports on finances, history, profits, sales, dividends, assets, etc. of corporations that are traded on the major stock exchanges.

• *Standard and Poor's Register of Corporations, Directors, and Executives,* listing thousands of public and private companies along with the names and titles of hundreds of thousands of corporate officials. Like the Moody's manuals, this is a basic reference source, updated every few months with supplements. It will quickly give you great amounts of information that even a public relations officer would take hours to dig up—unless, of course, she referred to the *Register.*

• *Dunn and Bradstreet's Million Dollar Directory, and the same company's Middle Market Directory.* The first contains information similar to the *Standard and Poor's Register* for companies with sales of more than $1 million. The second covers the smaller companies, with sales between $500,000 and $1 million.

• *Thomas's Register of American Manufacturers,* an invaluable work that can be used as a sort of "reverse directory" for locating companies that produce certain products. If you are doing a story on ball bearings, for example—rather than concentrating specifically on the Acme Bearing Co.—this book can help you locate other manufacturers you might want to phone. It provides indices to manufacturers, trade names, and specific products.

• *The Encyclopedia of Banking and Finance and the McGraw-Hill Dictionary of Modern Economics: A Handbook of Terms and Organizations* can help you through the economic jargon as well as the world of private and government agencies concerned with the economy. The first provides a comprehensive examination of the financial system, with information about money and credit, banking history, trusts, securities, and a variety of other subjects. The latter combines a dictionary of jargon with a guide to public and private agencies.

• *The Who's Who reference books* provide information on prominent business leaders, letting you know about who it is that controls the company planning an expansion in your community. *Who's Who in Commerce and Industry* and *Who's Who in America* can quickly give information about the business leader's background, public service, and links with other companies.

Once you have gleaned what you can from the basic reference sources, you may be ready to move on to the immense amounts of paper generated at every spot where government and business intersect. Usually there is a goodly amount of public paper. Those corporations that trade stock on the exchanges (and therefore are considered publicly owned) must file quarterly and annual reports with the federal Securities and Exchange Commission (SEC).

In fact, perhaps the most comprehensive public document filed by any company is the SEC Form 10-K, an annual report to the federal government. (The company's own annual report to its stockholders is worth examining, too; usually it is a leaner and graphically more interesting publication that substitutes propaganda for facts, but on occasion a company will tell stockholders something not considered worth mentioning to the government.) A corporate public relations office normally has access to the 10-K's and should—emphasize *should*—be willing to provide copies to reporters. If not, the documents are available from the Washington, D.C., and regional offices of the SEC.

The 10-K includes the following information:

• The address of principal executive officers, along with background data and the kinds of remunerations given to each. (Salaries are just a part of the remuneration; usually it includes participation in stock plans, expense accounts, cars and perhaps airplanes, etc.)

• The kinds of stock issued and the largest stockholders.

• The principal products and services of the company and the principal markets it serves.

• Background on any major legal proceedings in which the company is involved.

• Financial data on sales, operating revenue, income, losses, assets, long-term obligations and so forth.

• Mergers, market conditions, etc., that either are affecting or might affect the company's performance.

In addition to the 10-K, the SEC requires several other documents, many of them updates of information contained in the 10-K or notifications of any changes that might affect the company's stock. These include:

• The 8-K, which must be filed within fifteen days after any significant change in the company's operation or finances, including such changes as bankruptcy, the closing of a manufacturing plant, a shift in who controls the company, the selection of new auditors, and so forth.

• The 10-Q, filed within forty-five days after the close of a fiscal quarter. This report keeps the 10-K up to date, although 10-Q's do not have to be approved by an independent auditor, meaning that their information may be somewhat more suspect. A company can get away with more accounting shenanigans in a 10-Q.

• The N-1R, an annual report equivalent to a 10-K for management and investment firms. The report will show portfolio turnovers, capital gains, and diversification of assets by the firm, giving a reporter some insight into whether the firm is being soundly managed.

• The N-1Q, the equivalent of a 10-Q for management and investment firms. To be filed within one month after a fiscal quarter has ended, it shows the number of shares bought and sold by the firm, the portfolio breakdown at the time, etc.

State and local government offices are also valuable mines for information about corporations. The corporate division of the secretary of state's office can provide official corporation records listing names and addresses of officers and directors. (These are available in the state in which the company is incorporated. It may well be that a company you consider "local" turns out to be incorporated elsewhere, though, so you may have to do some searching.)

Financing statements, written when a company borrows money and offers real property as collateral, are often filed in the county registry of deeds and mortgages. These can provide information about the borrower, the lender, the date of the loan, and the collateral offered, though they may not tell you how much was borrowed.

The courts provide another valuable resource for corporate information. In the court indices rest details about who has sued the company, whom the company has sued, whether the company has filed for bankruptcy, etc. The answers may require much time and many trips and telephone calls to various superior courts and federal district courts— especially to bankruptcy courts. However, if you suspect the company you are interested in has been involved in significant legal action, you are likely to come away with stories, or at least ideas for stories, that you did not have before.

The administrative agencies of government are another type of source. Companies that lay pipelines, build roads, dig mines, market new drugs or toys, plan factories, or contemplate just about anything that might affect the environment often have to file voluminous reports with such agencies as the Federal Environmental Protection Agency, the Federal Trade Commission, the Federal Communications Commission, the U.S. Forest Service, and all the local government counterparts. Even small businesses have to be concerned about zoning changes, land use variances, community master plans, etc. Although such reports usually focus on whatever project or product the company is proposing, sometimes the administrative agencies ask for financial and ownership information that not even the SEC requests. (If the company involved does not trade stock on an exchange, and thus is considered "privately held," such reports to administrative agencies may be the only avenue to the financial data, since privately held companies do not need to issue annual reports or file 10-K's.)

If the business you are concerned with is an insurance company—and these days, insurance companies control billions of dollars in capital, thanks largely to the pension funds they administer—you are in great luck. Every insurance company has to file very detailed annual reports with each state insurance commission, documenting every investment, all the salaries of its officers, its income from properties held in your state, the amount of money deposited in state banks, and so forth.

If it is a banking company you are following, the comptroller of the currency gathers information about national banks through filings similar to those corporations make to the SEC. You can also request annual reports on specific banks from the Federal Deposit Insurance Corporation, which insures the deposits in member banks. The semiannual reports to the FDIC show the financial health of different banks and give statistics on the number of employees, total salaries and benefits, etc. For savings and loan associations, the companion federal agency is the Federal Savings and Loan Insurance Commission, which collects semiannual reports on such details as advertising expenses (how much are the S & Ls in your community spending to attract customers, and is that more than in the past?), consultant and legal fees, income, assets, and so forth.

Each bank holding company participating in the federal reserve system files annual reports to the Federal Reserve Board. Like the other documents, it shows directorship information, balance sheets, affiliations, and so forth. State-chartered banks report to state banking commissions.

Whenever a bank wants to build, relocate, merge with or acquire another bank, application forms must go to the proper federal or state regulatory agency. Such applications include predictions about the bank's performance, the number of employees to be hired, who the potential customers may be, etc. Each bank by law must also have on file a Community Reinvestment file, showing how the bank is supposed to help the local community, provide loans to low-income residents, and fulfill its duty of public service.

If information about corporate pensions is what you are seeking, you can request the forms required by the Department of Labor and the Internal Revenue Service. These include the Form 5500, which provides information about the number of participants in a company plan, the contributions and benefits, the income and expenditures, rebates on group insurance premiums, and investments made by the plan administrators.

Finally, if you are confronted with a nonprofit organization, which may be heavily involved in business activities, you can turn to the Internal Revenue Service Form 990, which gives details on sales, assets, liabilities, and net worth. It also often includes a breakdown of consultant fees, administrators' salaries, and so forth. The 990s for foundations also list contributions. Some states have active charitable trust divisions in the secretary of state's office; they may have copies of the 990s or have similar reports required by the state.

Information sources abound. Documents will never replace a good human source, of course; you may or may not be able to construct a good story around a set of financial figures alone. But knowing where to turn for *some* information if you meet a brick wall at a public relations office can help you begin.

Here is an example of part of a background story written by an undergraduate journalism student who relied primarily on document sources to construct a picture of AMAX. The story appeared in the *Seattle University Spectator.*

> The molybdenum mine planned for Mount Tolman may be the biggest industrial project ever to come to the Colville Indian reservation, but it is only one of many such projects worldwide for AMAX Inc., the largest diversified mining company in the United States and the world's leading molybdenum producer.
>
> Pick a mineral—copper, molybdenum, zinc, lead, nickel—and you'll probably find AMAX involved in mining, refining and/or selling it. Pick a continent, any but the Antarctic, and AMAX has a project, a company or a business partner there.
>
> A list of AMAX wholly- or partly-owned subsidiaries reads like a geography textbook: AMAX Asia, AMAX Botswana Ltd., AMAX de Chile, AMAX Indonesia, AMAX Japan, AMAX Phillippines. Under other company names, such as Climax Molybdenum, AMAX Petroleum and AMAX Exploration, the corporation also owns subsidiaries in countries from New Zealand to Norway, in Ireland, Fiji, Brazil, Liberia, Luxembourg, Bermuda—the list goes on. And in the United States, AMAX's influence stretches from its headquarters in Connecticut to California, with businesses or projects in more than 25 states in between.
>
> AMAX has had international ties since its beginning. The company was formed in 1887 as American Metal Co. Ltd., a New York branch of the German metals trading firm Metallgesellschaft—literally, Metal Company. The U.S. corporation's name became American Metal Climax Inc. in 1957 when it merged with an affiliate, Climax Molybdenum, and was finally shortened to AMAX in 1974.
>
> Except for the new name, everything about AMAX is big. It produces about 40 percent of the world's molybdenum and 64 percent of the U.S. total in 1979, almost 100 million pounds out of the U.S. total of

143.9 million pounds. The company is the third largest producer of coal in the United States, although in 1979 coal represented only 15 percent of its sales revenue. It has petroleum and natural gas interests in 23 states and in Canada, Australia and the North Sea, off the coasts of Norway and the Netherlands. According to the Wall Street Journal, 1980 was a record year for AMAX in earnings: the company made $470.4 million on revenues of $2.95 billion. And AMAX employs more than 17,000 people – almost three times the number of Colville Indians.

But although it is a huge business and owns many subsidiaries, AMAX itself is partially owned by even larger corporations. Standard Oil of California (Socal), the nation's fourth largest oil company, controls about 20 percent of AMAX's stock – and wants more. In 1978, Socal tried to buy the remaining 80 percent but was turned down; this March, it tried again, offering AMAX $4 billion, but was again rejected. Another company, Selection Trust Ltd., owns about 9 percent of AMAX. The role of both firms is reflected in the AMAX board of directors: three AMAX directors are also vice presidents of Socal, while two more board members are also directors of Selection Trust.

Few corporate boards can boast of a former U.S. president as a member, but Gerald Ford, elected to AMAX's board in September 1980, is not untypical of an AMAX director. Along with most of his fellow members of the board, Ford is white, male, in his 60s, and an influential man.

Unlike Ford, most of AMAX's directors are lifelong businessmen, including several whose careers have been within AMAX and its subsidiaries, and several more who have worked their way through the ranks of Socal. Typically, an AMAX board member has one or more college degrees, with mining and law the most common fields; seven of the 19 men hold master's or doctoral degrees in law. Five directors are foreign-born, including the top present and past AMAX executives: Pierre Gousseland, a Frenchman who is AMAX chairman; Ian MacGregor, born and educated in Scotland, who was Gousseland's predecessor and the company's former chief executive officer; and John Towers, also a Scot, who joined American Metal in 1949 and rose to be its president, and who is now a director of several AMAX subsidiaries in Africa. . . .

*Statistics and economic indicators play a
key role on the business and economics beat.
Journalists have to be able to interpret
them.*

> There are three kinds of lies: lies, damned
> lies, and statistics.
> —ATTRIBUTED TO BENJAMIN DISRAELI

"For better or worse, statistics are the bread and butter of economic
reporting," says Robert Samuelson, a free-lance business reporter, in a
1975 article in the *Columbia Journalism Review.* "You may not like them,
but you've got to live with them." Samuelson was, and is, right. The hard
evidence of how well or poorly a business or an entire economy is faring
comes in the form of inflation rates, unemployment statistics, profit
margins, and productivity scores. This is a specialty grounded in quanti-
tative measures, and the sooner the journalist masters the language, sim-
plifies it for his audience, and uses it to explain business actions, the
quicker he begins to sense the important shifts that herald either the rise
or downfall of a company or an economic policy.

Statistics are not ends in themselves, however, and reporters err
when they become overly fascinated solely by the raw figures. Emphasis
should be on "using economic indicators" rather than "reporting economic
statistics" for a very good reason: to remind the beginning reporter especially that the numbers are a *means* to an end, a means to understanding
and reporting about economic activity. They are indicators, symptoms if
you will, and the best use of them is as an aid to understanding what has
happened in the past and what may happen in the future. "It's usually a
mistake," Samuelson warned in his article, "to focus exclusively on the
latest statistical spasm. Don't ignore it, but don't overplay it. Putting
numbers into perspective takes a longer view."

Often a single statistic makes no sense without comparison with
others. Statistics about low inflation may need to be balanced by reference to high unemployment. Reductions in company inventories may
mean a very rapidly increasing demand for the product or a reduction in
the rate at which the product is being manufactured. A steady unemployment rate may not mean a stable economy since the total employment
could be either rising or dropping.

The first statistical indicator with which a journalist must be concerned is the Gross National Product.

Everyone lives by selling something.
—ROBERT LOUIS STEVENSON

Gross National Product (GNP) is one of the most popular of the economic indicators and is, perhaps, the most useful measure of a nation's total economic activity. However, simply because it is so sweeping, the GNP statistic has to be used carefully; it will not pinpoint for a reporter how a local community or region is faring, nor will it highlight specific areas of trouble within the economy.

The GNP is defined as the total value of goods and services produced in a nation, measured by their retail—not wholesale—price. In computing GNP economists would, for example, add together the retail prices of all automobiles produced, but would not include the money the auto manufacturer paid for the steel or for the salaries of the workers. The economists assume that retail prices include such costs.

Four major components are added to get the GNP: total consumer spending on retail goods and services; business investments, primarily in new housing, new industrial development, and inventories; government spending for goods or services, such as parks, defense weapons, police, and schools; and net exports, defined as the difference in value between what a nation imports and what it exports.

Statistics on GNP always need to be adjusted for inflation. The fact that more money might have been spent on loaves of bread in 1979 than in 1975 does not necessarily indicate that the country was producing and consuming more loaves of bread; it might just mean that bread cost more. Journalists need to always check to make certain they are comparing what is called "real GNP" (adjusted for inflation) rather than "nominal GNP" (not adjusted for inflation) unless they are deliberately pointing out how much of the GNP is being eaten by inflation.

Sometimes increases or decreases in the GNP will be cited as proof of either an improvement or a decline in the well-being of individual citizens. Journalists who use or quote such statements are on extremely shaky ground; an individual statistic is an indicator, but not complete proof. For years, steady increases in the GNP were presumed to reflect steady increases in American well-being, but in the past decade many economists have been critical of such a simplistic viewpoint. The GNP, they point out, does not actually measure the *total* cost involved in producing an item or delivering a service, because the retail sales price does not include the cost of the damage that might have occurred to the "commons"—as was noted in the chapter on environmental reporting. The cost of the harm to air or water quality is borne by everyone. The GNP also does not distinguish the social value of the goods being produced: the sales of pesticides that may pollute the environment are valued equally with the sales of medical equipment that saves lives. Thus, the GNP is only one small indicator of a nation's social and economic well-being—and it may not be the best.

In reporting the GNP, journalists sometimes wonder how rapidly it should be increasing. Is a 2 percent raise over last year good or bad? For years, one economic rule of thumb was that the GNP should advance by about 4 percent each year, a figure that assumed an increase in the labor force of 1 percent a year and an improvement in worker productivity of about 3 percent each year. However, in recent decades little in the economy has stayed stable enough to provide for such orderly growth. Inflation has soared, raising the cost of both goods and labor. Worker productivity gains have slowed or even disappeared in some industries. The labor force has changed radically with the entry of more women. The best context to add to a story explaining whether a gain in the GNP is adequate or not may thus be statements about the economy's past performance, explanations of the economic theories about what the GNP should be doing, and samples of some of the less sweeping economic indicators—rather than any simple statement that the GNP did or did not attain the 4 percent standard.

In years of high inflation, the second indicator—the Consumer Price Index—commands wide attention.

> A study of economics usually reveals that
> the best time to buy anything is last year.
> —MARTY ALLEN

One of the economic indicators less sweeping than the GNP—and perhaps of more interest during the 1970s—was the Consumer Price Index (CPI), designed to measure changes in retail prices and so the best indicator of the inflation that racked the American economy during those years. The CPI is computed by comparing the price of thousands of goods and services in a "retail marketbasket" from a base year (currently 1967) to subsequent years. The base year is assigned a value of 100 and if the CPI is 157 in a later year, that means the price of goods and services has

risen 57 percent. The Bureau of Labor Statistics (BLS), which calculates
the CPI, also breaks the statistic into various categories, enabling a reporter to pinpoint areas in which prices are rising or falling.

The CPI categories include housing costs (composing about one-third
of the index); food costs (about one-fourth); health and leisure spending
(about one-fifth); transportation (slightly more than one-tenth); and
clothing (one-tenth). To the extent that an individual consumer's spending
matches that breakdown, the CPI is a fairly good measure of the increases or decreases in one's own budget. However, this breakdown is
meant to reflect the spending habits of typical urban workers and so is
not as good a mirror of the often very different habits of executives,
students, rural families, impoverished inner-city dwellers, and so forth. In
reporting the CPI, the journalist should take note of the price rises in
different categories because of that variation. If food prices are rising
rapidly, then the impoverished and the migrants, who usually spend more
than a fourth of their total income on groceries, are being hit much harder
than the upper-middle-class executives who typically spend less than a
fourth of their income on food items. When leisure costs are rising more
rapidly, then the reporter can look at the crunch on the upper middle
class, and the readjustment in family activities that may be occurring.

The Bureau of Labor Statistics also publishes regional CPIs for some
metropolitan areas, and journalists in those regions may be fortunate
enough to have a local CPI to compare with the national figure. However,
even if a regional CPI is not available, a local reporter can do more than
just leave the accounts of changes to the national wire services. Remember that you want to localize the story: every time the CPI changes, the
significance goes far beyond individual pocketbooks. Many government
and industry contracts, as well as social service and pension programs,
have cost-of-living clauses written into them; whenever the CPI goes up
or down even one percentage point, the result is a multi-million-dollar
transfer of income—automatically. If the CPI goes up 8 percent in one
year, how much more will your local government be forced to pay in
automatic salary increases in police or fire personnel? How much more
will Social Security pensioners receive? How much more will factory
workers in your city get? And where will the money come from? Even the
leads of your stories about the CPI can reflect this impact and make the
story much more meaningful than just another report about numbers:

> The federal government announced that the Consumer Price Index
> had risen 8 percent last year, meaning that the Terrytown City Council
> will have to find another $3 million to pay police and fire personnel this
> year. Terrytown senior citizens who receive Social Security payments
> are expected to begin receiving an extra $5.5 million in benefits next
> July because of the rise.

One cautionary note about the CPI is in order. As the Associated Press Stylebook makes clear, it should not be called a cost-of-living index, because it does not include the effect of income taxes or Social Security payments. Thus, even though the agreements in contracts are very properly called cost-of-living clauses, the CPI should not be referred to in that manner.

Unemployment, the third statistical indicator, is much more than a number. It may well be a record of happiness and discontent.

> Employment is nature's physician, and is essential to human happiness.
>
> —GALEN

Along with the CPI, the unemployment rate has the greatest impact on the public mind. Technically, it is defined as a form of economic instability caused when demand falls below supply, thus leaving part of a nation's labor force and some of its industrial plant idle. The rate is calculated by simple division: the number of people out of work who want to work is divided by the number of people working. But, as you might expect, the indicator has several definitional limits that a good reporter will keep in mind.

The first and perhaps most important is that the rate does not reflect all of those who do not hold jobs. For obvious reasons, it is not meant to include homemakers, students, prison inmates, and hospital wards who are either unable or unwilling to work. The BLS includes in the rate only those who have actively sought work in the weeks preceding the release of the figure. When substantial portions of the unemployed give up looking for work, as occurred during the 1981–1982 recession, their numbers will not be included in the rate.

The second important limit on the use of this indicator stems from its tie to another statistic, that on the total number of people working. This latter number lets you know whether the work force (and thus the number of jobs) is actually expanding or contracting. At times the unemployment rate may remain high even though the economy is expanding; perhaps the opening of a large number of new jobs will induce people who had dropped out of the work force or who had given up looking to return and compete for the new positions. The rapid entry of new elements of the population into the work force can also drive the rate up abnormally fast, even in years when the economy is healthy. The sudden reduction of government financial aid to students, for example, or the entry of large numbers of women or of personnel from the armed services, can drive hundreds of thousands into the job market.

Another important qualification on using the unemployment rate as an indicator of economic health is its tendency to reflect the state of the economy several months ago, rather than right now. The rate lags behind developments in the business world. Employers, for example, may not lay off workers until after a recession has firmly taken hold; instead, they may reduce overtime payments. Similarly, they may not rehire employees until a recovery is fully under way, preferring to offer overtime payment to their current workers instead. To the extent that employers do so, statistics on overtime payments may be a better leading indicator—one that points the direction in which the economy seems to be moving—than the unemployment rate.

As with the growth of the GNP, journalists sometimes question what the unemployment rate should be. In the 1946 Employment Act the United States made a commitment to full employment, although the commitment was a vague one. Full employment, though, did not necessarily mean a zero unemployment rate: in 1964, Congress passed the Humphrey-Hawkins Act which set a "full employment" goal of 4 percent unemployment. How practical that goal is has been disputed; numerous economic thinkers believe that striving for the 4 percent target, given the substantial changes that have occurred in the American work force in the past twenty years, creates too much inflationary pressure by fueling a demand that supply cannot possibly meet.

The fourth indicator, profits, can be the source of confusion and sensationalism.

> Few of us can stand prosperity. Another man's, I mean.
>
> —MARK TWAIN

Even though it should be the easiest to understand, the fourth major indicator, profits, may be not only the most maligned but, some business executives would argue, the least understood by journalists. Reporters write continually about soaring or plummeting profits, often failing to establish any context for the raw figures they include in their stories. A $10 million profit sounds enviable, especially if compared with a $5 million profit the previous year, but sometimes even a $10 million profit can ensure that a company is on the way to bankruptcy.

Simply defined, profit is the difference between what a company takes in and the total of what it spends. Sometimes it is called net income, net profit, or net earnings. Profit is an essential part of a capitalistic business system in that it is one of the most important sources of money a business has available for re-investment, expansion, updating old equipment, and so forth. Even so, Americans—and American journalists in particular—sometimes reflect a very suspicious attitude that links all profits with a stereotype of robber barons. Surveys have shown, for example, that Americans tend to think that profits are considerably larger than they are, that they believe that upwards of thirty cents of every dollar spent for a service or a product goes to profit. The real figure is closer to five cents. Large numbers on financial statements and headlines about "soaring" profits and "record" profits tend to reinforce the misconception. Consider what could be a typical, misleading lead: "The National Nabbit Oil Company yesterday reported that its annual profit this year is expected to set a record, doubling the $5 million in profits earned last year. Critics of Nabbit charged that the sizable profits were a 'ripoff' of consumers."

The mistake is to report only raw figures, the $10 million versus the $5 million. Profit reports, it should be remembered, are *indicators;* they are not an end in themselves but a means—a means to examining a company's *profitability.* It is upon the profitability, rather than the profits alone, that the story should focus. To understand profitability, a journalist must compare raw profit figures with other statistics. Usually that means looking at the profits as a ratio, or a percentage, of return, either on sales, on the amount of money that stockholders have invested, or on the assets held by the company.

Did Nabbit Oil really better its financial picture by doubling its profits? Suppose in the previous year Nabbit had total sales of $100 million. Its net profit ratio (net profit of $5 million divided by the total sales of $100 million) would be 5 percent. In other words, it netted about a nickel on every dollar of sales. Suppose that this year Nabbit sold $250 million of oil. Its net profit ratio ($10 million divided by $250 million) would have actually dropped to 4 percent. The company would have netted only four cents on every dollar of sales.

Suppose, too, that using figures provided by the Federal Trade Commission, which calculates industrywide averages, you find that most petroleum companies have a net profit ratio of 7 percent.

Finally, suppose you discover on the annual report that Nabbit has tried to increase the amount of capital available to the company by selling extra shares of stock. The number of Nabbit shares has increased from 6 million last year to 20 million outstanding common stock shares this year. A little simple division tells you that the earnings-per-share ratio was eighty-three cents last year ($5 million in profits divided by 6 million shares) while this year the ratio is fifty cents per share ($10 million in profits divided by 20 million shares).

Contrary to the impression left by the first lead, then, you may have a story about a very sick company.

Productivity, the fifth indicator, can say as much about white-collar management as about blue-collar labor.

> Going to work for a large company is like getting on a train. Are you going sixty miles an hour or is the train going sixty miles an hour and you're just sitting still?
> —J. PAUL GETTY

The American worker once was regarded as the most efficient and most productive in the world, but as the United States began to be barraged by more cheaply produced imports—chiefly from Japan—the American worker took on a new and considerably less prestigious image. Workers, the media reported, seemed to no longer be as interested as before. They smoked marijuana, drank heavily, were more interested in ripping the company off than in company loyalty. Productivity, in a word, was miserable.

That is an exaggerated picture and an unfair one, but it is the image that helped put productivity statistics into the public mind. Productivity is a measure of how much people can produce in a certain amount of working time. To calculate it, the Bureau of Labor Statistics divides the nation's total output by the total number of hours worked. If the output rises faster than the hours worked, productivity is said to have increased; if the output stays the same while the number of hours rises, or if output does not increase as rapidly as work hours, then productivity declines. When the statistic is tied to numbers on wage increases, it produces a valuable indicator of whether prices will have to rise in order to cover salary costs.

Suppose, for example, that the Nabbit Oil Company also owns a barrel factory in which it employs twenty workers. If those twenty workers are given a 5 percent wage increase, productivity must increase by 5 percent for the per-barrel cost of labor to remain the same. If the workers get a 5 percent pay boost and increase productivity only 2 percent, then it costs the company more to produce each barrel. Consequently, prices are likely to rise.

If productivity in a company or an entire economy is declining or is not advancing as rapidly as that of its competitors, then profitability will decline and investors will probably take their money elsewhere.

In the United States, productivity grew about 2 percent each year for decades, but by the 1970s that average was showing signs of declining. Workers in other countries could outproduce their American counterparts (more barrels per hour, for example) *and* were being paid less per hour. The result was inevitable: major American industries (such as the auto and steel industries) began facing serious financial difficulties or collapsing altogether—*or* moving their operations out of the United States.

In its initial discovery of the problem, the media did paint a poor picture of the American worker. Questions were raised about whether Americans were becoming self-indulgent and lazy, giving up the dedication to hard work that was said to have always marked the American laborer and instead turning to drugs, alcohol, or simply pleasurable hobbies. However, the problem of productivity goes beyond the individual laborer, as the media began to discover in the latter part of the 1970s and early 1980s. More important factors affecting worker productivity are the quality of the machinery available to aid in production and the quality of the management. Increasingly journalists began to explore not just the eager attitudes of Japanese workers (versus the somewhat bored attitudes of Americans) but also the Japanese theory of business management and the availability of modern technology to aid workers in production. The media also began to examine the link between low defense spending (Japan is limited by its American-designed constitution to spending no more than 1 percent of its GNP on defense, while other nations typically spend a far greater percentage) and the availability of money for funding capital improvements. Through numerous articles about the need to "retool" aging American machinery and to experiment with less hierarchical and rigid models of corporate management, the emphasis began to shift from sensationalistic articles about pot-smoking auto line workers—who were only a symptom of the declining productivity—to stories that addressed actual economic causes.

The lesson, even for the local business and economics reporter, was written clearly: faced by a business with declining productivity, do not look only at superficial signs of that decline and accept corporate explanations that emphasize worker boredom; look, too, at the manner in which the corporation encourages workers to participate in management and at the tools the corporation gives to workers.

*By manipulating the money supply, the
government can stimulate a lagging
economy or repress an overbounding one.
Keep an eye on this sixth indicator of
economic well-being.*

> Money is always there but the pockets
> change; it is not in the same pockets after a
> change, and that is all there is to say about
> money.
> —GERTRUDE STEIN

The money supply—this has been the most obscure and one of the
most complex of economic indicators. Probably it would never have made
it from the financial page to the front page had it not been for the rise of
the monetarist school of economics in the 1970s and the adoption of
monetarist thought into federal policies by the late 1970s and early 1980s.
The chief architect of the monetarist school, Milton Friedman of the
University of Chicago, argues that the size and rate of growth of the
nation's money supply has a critical significance for the economy. The
theory, simply stated, emphasizes that the way in which the Federal Reserve tinkers with the nation's available money can either spark inflation,
slow it down, or strangle economic growth. By the time of the 1982
recession, the theory was popular enough that practically every move of
the Federal Reserve Board of Governors began to be reported, especially
as President Reagan's supply-side economists clashed with the mone-
tarists on the independent Fed. While the supply-siders were trying to
stimulate the economy through tax cuts and shifts of massive amounts of
money from social service programs to defense industries, the Fed was
holding tight on high interest rates to stop inflation and thereby making
corporate borrowing for expansion extemely difficult.

What is the money supply? It has at least two definitions, but before
explaining those, some background on the American banking system will
be helpful.

Although most people think of paper dollars and metal coins produced by the U.S. Treasury when the words "money supply" are mentioned, only about one-fourth of the total money in the United States is in
such currency form. The other three-fourths is in the form of checks
written by individuals or businesses against "demand deposits" in banks.
In other words, three-fourths of the money really is not currency at all.
Imagine that you deposit ten dollars in currency in a checking account at
a bank. The bank keeps the ten dollars in currency on hand, but is al-

lowed to "make money" by loaning out, say, forty dollars for every ten in currency you bring. The extra thirty is backed not by any existing currency, but by the bank's *promise* to convert checks into currency should the borrowers ever desire such a conversion. The system works, and works well, because few individuals or businesses want to bother changing all of their money into currency every time they make a transaction, and because they are willing to trust the promises made by banks that the checks can be converted to currency upon *demand*. It turns out to be much more efficient to pass promises around than to have to carry enormous weights of silver and gold.

Naturally, the system could be significantly abused if a bank begins promising more than it could ever hope to deliver, if, for example, your bank loans out $1 million for every ten dollars you deposit in currency. Then the promise becomes very shaky. Enter the Federal Reserve System, which regulates the amount of reserve the banks must maintain, thus controlling how much money banks can manufacture from their currency.

The Federal Reserve System has three primary methods it can use to affect the nation's money supply. It is the Fed's decisions in these areas that are closely watched by reporters. Always the goal is the same: the Fed tries to enlarge the money supply when it wants to stimulate the economy and reduce unemployment, or it tries to reduce the money supply when it is concerned about inflation. Enlarging the money supply means that banks can loan more money. Interest rates drop; the price of borrowing money cheapens. Corporate expansion occurs; more houses are bought and thus built; more autos are financed. The number of jobs increases. Shrinking the money supply has the opposite effect. Banks have to charge more for the money they have available to loan; corporate expansion slows; fewer homes are built or bought. The number of jobs declines. Naturally, in an economic system as complex as that of the United States, finely tuned tinkering is difficult, so at times the Fed may miss its mark entirely. Also, as has happened often enough in recent years, its economists may be at odds with those determining policy in the other branches of government and so various economic policies can be seeking different ends. (The Fed is a creature of Congress and its operating rules can be changed by Congress, but Congress cannot interfere with its day-to-day decisions. Neither can the president.)

The first method the Federal Reserve uses to affect the money supply is its regulation of currency reserves in banks. By demanding that banks increase those reserves, the Fed can restrict the amount of money available for loans. (For example, the Fed could require your bank to maintain twenty dollars in currency reserves for every forty dollars loaned.)

The Fed can also buy or sell government securities, such as U.S. Treasury bonds. If it wants to restrict the money supply, it sells the securities to commercial banks, thus absorbing some of the money they are making. If it wants to enlarge the money supply, it buys the securities from the banks; since the Fed's checks are not drawn against any currency reserve, it in effect is adding money to the economic system.

Finally, the third method the Fed uses to affect the supply entails changing two key interest rates that it actually controls. (Commercial banks set their own rates.) The Fed can raise or lower the federal funds rate, which is the interest rate that commercial banks charge for overnight loans to each other, and the discount rate, the amount the Fed charges banks that want to borrow from it in order to replenish their own currency reserves. Changing those rates forces commercial banks to adjust their interest charges similarly.

With that background, we can define *money supply* according to the two statistics that the Fed uses for measuring the supply. The first is the narrower of the two. It carries the rather covert sounding name of M-1 and is defined as all the currency in circulation plus all the demand deposits at commercial banks. (It does not include the currency stored in the vaults at the U.S. Treasury, at Federal Reserve Banks, or at commercial banks.) M-1 is a measure of the money that is actually in circulation and being used to buy goods and services. The second statistic, M-2, adds savings deposits to the M-1 figure.

These two statistics are the indicators of how well the Fed is succeeding at whatever strategy it happens to be pursuing.

Reporters interested in prices, unemployment, capital improvement costs, home mortgage rates, credit card interest rates, and so forth will keep an eye on all five statistics relevant to the money supply. The first three — currency reserve requirements, government security purchases or sales by the Fed, and the rate of interest charged by the Fed — give indications of the agency's strategy. (The Fed often denies having a "strategy"; often it says that it simply "follows the market demand." Such statements can be taken as so much political kowtowing to the fact that Americans do not like the idea of their government actively manipulating the economy.) The last two statistics, M-1 and M-2, measure what is happening in the economy itself as a result of Federal Reserve actions.

The seventh indicator often gets a lot of publicity but is really very limited in usefulness—the stock market averages.

Never invest your money in anything that
eats or needs repairing.
—BILLY ROSE

Appropriately, stock market averages are the last of the indicators to be discussed. They are probably the least important and least accurate, at least as indicators of how the general economy is faring, yet some attention must be paid to them simply because tradition dictates that the press ballyhoo them. Partly, the tradition has arisen because stock market averages are released daily, whereas the other statistics arrive in a more leisurely fashion. Partly, the tradition exists because many readers and viewers are assumed to own stock and thus be somewhat interested in what happened on the stock exchange.

The most widely reported average is the Dow-Jones Industrial Average, probably because it has been with us the longest—since 1884. In fact, it is the narrowest and probably the least representative of all of the averages, focusing as it does on a relatively small number of companies. Other averages, such as the Standard and Poor's composite average of 500 stocks and the New York Stock Exchange Average (NYSE), based on 1,500 stocks, are broader and more representative of marketwide changes. The Dow, however, offers more gradations; the other exchange averages are based on smaller numerical indices—in the range of 100— while the Dow ranges up to 1,000 points and beyond. Changes of ten or even twenty points on the Dow are not uncommon; such fluctuations, though practically meaningless, make better headline copy than the one or two point changes that may occur on the other averages the same day. The responsible business reporter will always include reference to the other averages, though, since they probably reflect more accurately the experience of average investors. A change of one point on the NYSE, for example, fairly closely approximates an average change of one dollar in the value of stock. The same cannot be said for a change of ten points on the Dow.

Perhaps the greatest value of stock market figures lies not in the averages that get all of the headlines, but in the changes in stock value that occur on a company-by-company basis. A business reporter does well to pay attention to the movements of stock prices of the major companies in her area. The market seems to react mostly to anticipated profits or losses, and sudden changes in the value of a company's stock can be a tipoff to the announcement of a management reshuffle, a dividend decline, or a takeover attempt by another company. Too, the value of a company's stock is an important part of its reputation and of its ability to raise the investment capital it needs to make major improvements, launch new products, and compete against other corporations. Substantial changes in the stock prices of companies you are interested in should be enough to set you off on a trip to the public relations office, the SEC 10-K, 10-Q, or 8-K file, or to a local broker.

Also, wire stories about major changes in marketwide averages should be followed by local stories on how regional corporations have fared.

RECOMMENDED RESOURCES

Among the works that a journalist interested in covering business and economics will want to read are:

Leonard Silk, *Economics in Plain English* (New York: Simon and Schuster, 1978). Silk, an economist and columnist for the *New York Times,* undertakes in this book what many might consider an impossible task: to explain economics in language that even a lay person can understand. Sometimes he succeeds; sometimes his effort can only be admired.

Louis Kohlmeier, Jr., Jon Udell, and Laird Anderson, *Reporting on Business and the Economy* (Englewood Cliffs, N.J.: Prentice-Hall, 1981). This is one of the more recent and better books on the economics beat. The book contains a good explanation of recent economic history – particularly focusing on those events that moved the business beat out of its ghetto and onto front pages – and explains the role played by various actors in the economic drama: corporate managers, government regulators, union leaders and members.

Merrill Lynch, Pierce, Fenner, and Smith, "How to Read a Financial Statement," one of the handiest aids (and free!) for reporters trying to decipher a financial statement. The book leads you step by step through a report from "Typical Manufacturing," explaining terms such as fixed assets, depreciation, profit margin, and so forth. The only shortcoming, from a journalistic standpoint, is that Typical has no problems; all is rosy.

William Ophuls, *Ecology and the Politics of Scarcity* (San Francisco: W. H. Freeman and Company, 1977), a consciousness-raising and consciousness-shaking treatment of the end of the era of abundance that is as valuable reading for business reporters as for environmental reporters.

The AFL-CIO *Manual of Corporate Investigation,* put out by that organization's Food and Beverages Trade Department, one of the best sources of learning about the paper trail that corporations leave.

Among the journalistic publications the business reporter will want to turn to regularly are *Forbes, Fortune, Business Week, The Economist,* various university economics reviews – and, of course, the *Wall Street Journal.*

EXERCISES

1. Using the business "paper trail" that exists in library reference books, create a profile of a major publicly held corporation in your area. Try to obtain — from the books only, for now — as much information as you can about company history; company management structure and divisional breakdown; background information on directors, and on linkages with other companies; sales and profits/operating profit margin history; stock issues; indebtedness; assets and liabilities; subsidiaries, if any; outlook for the corporation/recent developments; products manufactured or services offered; and dividend history and long-term trends in its stock prices.

2. Take exercise 1 another step by seeing how much information you can collect about the company from nonlibrary sources, still focusing for the time being *only* on the paper trail. Examine local court records to determine whether the company has sued or been sued recently. If so, for what? Be certain to note the names of the litigants (they could be future sources). If a regional office of the Securities and Exchange Commission is nearby, request the company's most recent two or three 10-K forms. Contact your state corporation office to see what information it has. Stop by the county assessor's and tax collector's offices to determine what real property the corporation owns and how much money the company pays in real estate taxes in your county.

3. After completing exercises 1 and 2, you certainly will have found some angle worth a story. Perhaps you want to examine the company's marketing strategy and any changes that have been made in it recently. Perhaps a new product is being brought out. Perhaps there have been virtually no changes at all: the product line, the management structure, the stock dividends have all been steady for years. In a volatile economy such as now exists in the United States, even that is news. Now contact the human sources, conduct the appropriate interviews, and write a story.

4. Collect several stories from newspapers and magazines to illustrate each of the categories of business and economics reporting: business news, personal finance information, and economic news. Discuss these in class or write a brief report. In the business news stories, did the reporter try to examine those angles of competition and strategy that are at the root of business decisions? Did the reporter write what essentially might be a press release, hyping the business or a product? If the latter, is such a story representative of the overall business coverage in the periodical where you found the story? Do any of the stories reflect attempts by reporters to localize international angles; for example, by examining the impacts of international trade on certain local businesses or on prices?

Are the economic stories written in a way that will be easily understandable by a general reader? Are the leads heavily loaded with numbers that may be hard to comprehend? Do the stories about exceptionally complicated or abstract topics start with simple and interesting leads that allow readers to grasp some concrete images before encountering the abstractions?

What kind of information do the personal finance stories convey? Are pros and cons of certain investing strategies adequately examined, for example? Are the stories such that they will be of service to readers needing to make their own decisions about retirement accounts, home mortgages, savings plans, etc.?

5. Obtain a financial statement from a local corporation. Using a basic economics text or the Merrill Lynch publication, "How to Read a Financial Report," study the statement and review it either in class or in a report. First be sure you understand the raw figures: What are the company's current assets? How are those assets distributed among cash accounts, marketable securities, inventories, and receivable accounts? How much allowance for bad debt has the company left? What are the company's fixed assets and how are they distributed among land holdings, machinery, buildings, and office equipment? How much depreciation has accumulated on those fixed assets? What are the company's current liabilities? How much did it pay in federal income taxes? What are its long-term liabilities? How much equity do the stockholders have?

From the company's income and expenditure statements, you should be able to answer these questions: What were the sales this year? How much did it cost to produce the goods the company sold? How much was netted per outstanding share?

Once you have completed the examination of the raw figures, ask yourself certain key questions: Does the company seem to be suffering substantially from bad debts? Are many creditors not paying? With what kind of profit margin is the company operating? How does it compare with other similar businesses (use the library reference works for this answer)? Does the net earning per share seem a reasonable return for the stockholders' investment?

Once you have completed your work, seek out a broker willing to give you or your class an analysis of the statement.

11 Reporting about Values and Religion

We have grasped the mystery of the atom, and rejected the Sermon on the Mount.

—OMAR BRADLEY

CONSIDER FOR A MOMENT what some might call an audacious question: do we journalists, skilled as we may be in reporting the affairs of the secular city, dare venture into reporting the events and processes of what traditionally has been considered the City of God?

The answer is obvious: of course we do. No realm of significance to human beings should be off bounds to those whose task is considered to be the description and illumination of daily life, and what is of more concern than the ongoing search for a sense of what that daily life may *mean?* The impetus of individuals and societies toward some definition of meaning says much about how they organize and operate in their day-to-day existences. However, though the other specialties described in this book are well established as beats, such is not true of the area to be examined in this chapter—that of *human values.*

A few comments about the absence may be useful. As sociologist Herbert Gans and others have pointed out, American journalism for more than a century has held out as one of the last bastions of logical positivism. That positivism gave journalists an essentially nineteenth-century philosophy that eschews theology and notions about spirit (or, as contemporary psychologists would say, "self") in favor of human behavior that can by physically observed. It insists upon a "detached observer" and believes almost blindly that the only knowledge with any validity is that which grows out of a nineteenth-century definition of science.

The positivistic philosophy has led journalists to be primarily interested in external behaviors, even while the Einsteinian revolution in physics was disproving much of the "scientific" foundation of positivism and the Freudian and humanistic revolutions in psychology were teaching us much more about the importance of the inner regions of the human psyche.

To be sure, church beats and religion beats have long existed on newspapers and some magazines, but they are narrowly defined and limited to what the late Louis Cassels, religion editor *extraordinaire* for United Press International, once described as the "grinding and clanking of ecclesiastical machinery." Such information also usually has been confined to the ghetto of the Saturday morning church page or the Sunday morning television broadcast. The beat considered in this chapter, though it may be said to include the traditional religion beat, extends beyond the factory of dogma and clerical intrigue to report about issues such as these:

• Is abortion morally acceptable? Is there a specific point at which a fetus becomes human? Should the state support abortions for welfare mothers? What values does a woman contemplating abortion confront?

• Is euthanasia justifiable? Does there come a point when life-support systems for a critically ill human being should be removed? Is it right to allow a newborn baby with severe birth defects to die? Who will have the right to decide these questions—the doctor, the family, or the state?

• Is it immoral to maintain an immense stock of nuclear weapons? Does spending for such weapons starve the poor and contribute more to causing wars than resolving conflicts? Or are such weapons necessary to propel human beings to finding other ways to settle feuds?

• Should homosexuals be guaranteed civil rights to protect them from discrimination in jobs and housing? Is a homosexual relationship as valid as a heterosexual one, a sign of healthy and perhaps even biological diversity rather than a social threat or perverse choice? What are the historical and sociological roots of the values that argue either for or against homosexuality?

• Is sex to be confined to marriage? With the advent of modern birth control methods, is "recreational sex" as legitimate an expression of human sexuality?

• Is marriage a vital or a dying institution? Is it important to the survival of the nuclear family, and is the nuclear family a critical prop of society? Or is it time to define *family* in a different manner?

• What values have been affected by the impact of industrialization? How has it affected the home? Do corporations owe employees child-care centers and paternal, as well as maternal, leaves of absence? Is the nuclear family under assault from other social trends (feminism, homosexuality, etc.) or from the economic structure that encourages mobility and transience?

• Is discrimination ever justified? What about reverse discrimination to ensure that women or blacks find more positions in schools or businesses?

• Is it moral (and legally permissible) for women to become surrogate mothers, carrying a child but after birth relinquishing it to someone else?

• Is it justifiable to use amniocentesis to determine the gender of an unborn baby and then, if that gender is not wanted by the parents, to abort the child?

• Are biologists just "doing what they should" when they splice genes and in various fashions manipulate genetic codes, moving to a day when they may be able to breed human beings with particular traits?

Each issue has received at least a little notice in the press in the last two decades, and several, such as those of genetic engineering and the accumulation of nuclear weapons, will need to be debated, investigated, and reported with much more fervor in the coming years.

Conflicts over values have certainly occurred throughout human history, but with the world still moving out of the centuries-long era in which societies existed in relative isolation and still gingerly adjusting to an unprecedented age of global economic dependence and global communications, such value conflicts can be expected to be particularly intense. Even in the United States, which has long championed pluralism, controversies tend to go more readily these days to the roots of values as the once dominant American ideology that underlay that pluralism is questioned. Americans do not as readily agree upon the presumed goodness of progress, the inherent worth of laissez faire capitalism, or the moral righteousness of the nation. Minorities do not cast off their diversity and plunge into the "melting pot" quite as uncritically; a debate about whether the government should fund bilingual and bicultural education to accommodate the growing Spanish-speaking population is not only a political exercise but a serious matter of values.

That we have arrived at a period of more substantial questioning is not really surprising. Liberal theologians, ethicists, historians such as Oswald Spengler, and poets such as T. S. Eliot and W. B. Yeats have long cautioned that the central notions that bonded Western civilization for several thousand years have been collapsing. The eminent psychologist Abraham Maslow once noted, for example, that twentieth-century human beings exist in an "interregnum between old value systems that have not worked and new ones not yet born," and he argued that these decades are "an empty period which could be borne more patiently were it not for the great and unique dangers that beset mankind." Likewise, the respected anthropologist Joseph Campbell has argued that the perfect accord that once existed in medieval thought about the nature of the universe, the canons of the social order, and the good of the individual lie shattered by the experiences and knowledge of contemporary man, and that out of the disintegrated center will rise either beneficial intelligence or, as cultures struggle to maintain forms that have comforted them for so long, horrors beyond the scale to which we have already been subjected in this century.

Is this not grist for the journalist?

To us falls the task of covering the daily expression of this "age of longing," as Maslow called it. Whatever our personal feelings and faiths, we cannot ignore the perceptions of our brightest analysts and the often confused, sometimes heroic, many times tragic struggles of ordinary people caught in the "interregnum."

So far, such struggles have been reported as adjuncts to other beats. When the debate about abortion turns into a legislative battle, it is covered by the political reporter. When the intricacies of a decision about whether to remove a Karen Anne Quinlan from life-support systems reach the judicial chambers, they are examined by a court reporter. When the neighbors' protests about a university's plan to dump wastes from genetic labs into the sewer system reach a city council, they are reported by the city hall writer.

Such reporters, however, often are better trained in covering the event and the conflict rather than in probing the fundamental questions of values that lie at the heart of each issue. Naturally, the event coverage is needed, but so is a more illuminating examination of this subject matter of values themselves, particularly their acquisition and development, their humaneness or inhumaneness, their appeal to human emotions, and their importance in human existence. What is required is a more comprehensive tying-together of the links between issues such as abortion, euthanasia, and nuclear weapons. While the in-depth research is more properly the realm of the psychologist, the philosopher, the theologian, and the anthropologist, there is no reason the journalist cannot make use of their findings to help an audience understand, for example, how people in another culture may see an issue quite differently from the way Americans see it.

Even the traditional beats need to be infused with more active grappling with value questions. How have business ethics been formed? What values are guiding the local school system? What views of life are at stake in an environmental controversy?

The assignment is challenging, for values are the internal factor that explains the external behavior. In reporting about values, journalists will confront their own beliefs directly and will need to examine closely the issue of objectivity. Notions that have been held since childhood will probably be severely challenged if the journalist is at all open to the values expressed by those in the news. As other specialists do, the values reporter also will need to study subject background, becoming familiar with different schools of thought about values, different cultural approaches, theological and psychological insights into the need for and development of such values, and philosophical reflections upon the nature of the human being.

The task for the values journalist, if it can be described simply, is not only to report in depth about the actual battles that arise because of value differences, but to help people understand, clarify, and communicate about their values. In a world still in its first generation of learning to talk globally, still trying to harmonize cultures long isolated from one another while saving what is distinct about those cultures, still trying to absorb the impact of global economics, global technology, and global science, such a task requires far more than the Saturday church page; it demands the best that journalism can produce.

Reporting about values demands remembering them first of all.

Religion is a way of walking, not a way of talking.
— WILLIAM RALPH INGE

In 1974, research biologists in the United States delivered to the nation's press a story of unusual implications, and they did so in a rather curious fashion. Rather than announcing what they were about to do, they called for the postponement of something they *had already been doing:* transplanting genetic material into bacteria so that the bacteria would act according to the "instructions" contained in the foreign genes. Before such experiments could continue, the biologists said, the risks needed to be assessed more fully; whatever benefits the new technology might have, no one was certain whether the engineered bacteria might not damage public health—or, for that matter, the health of scientists and lab technicians.

The announcement marked the media's first major encounter with the topic of genetic engineering. Biologists had long speculated about the possibilities of such willful human entrance into the affairs of life, but now they were talking about actually doing it. Science writer Rae Goodell pointed out in a 1980 *Columbia Journalism Review* article that the press initially responded conscientiously, examining not only the health and political issues involved in regulating what was becoming a rapid-growth industry, but also reporting on the ethical questions. But, she argues, by 1978 the press as a whole dropped the examination of the ethical questions and left the issue of recombinant DNA (deoxyribonucleic acid) to be covered by science writers in strictly scientific terms: Who is discovering what? What is being done? Where is it being done?

"DNA," she wrote, "was treated as a spectator sport, appropriate for public and press interest, but not involvement. . . . With the press relying almost entirely on readily available scientist-experts, much besides moderation and interpretation was missing from the typical recombinant DNA coverage. Scientist sources were inclined to narrow the issue to the question of immediate health risk, and press coverage was similarly restricted."

Often, she adds, the press did not address the value question at all; local media slept when universities or hometown industries added genetic manipulation to their activities.

The first principle of effective values, coverage then, is simply this: *Remember to raise the question.* What values are being expressed by a certain action? Are those taking the action concerned about those values? Do others disagree with their approach? Recombinant DNA, for example, raises numerous questions about biological and medical ethics as well as about the meaning of life and the limits – if there are to be any – to human control of life. Journalists do well to keep such questions on the agenda, so that the public policy debate is not narrowed simply to the concerns of the scientists or of the industry officials hoping to capitalize on the discoveries. Generally, it may be said that when journalists do not raise questions about values, it is not because the decisions being made or the issues being covered are valueless or value-free, but rather because the journalists themselves, whatever their claims to objectivity, have unconsciously accepted one set of values over another. In this case, they have adopted what political theorist William Ophuls calls the technological value: "If we can do it, then we should."

A corollary of the first principle is this: *Raise the question to all who may be affected.* It is not enough to simply let scientists and theologians debate, however critical their debate is for an intelligent decision. It is just as important to see what kinds of considerations those individuals who are struggling with their own values are bringing to bear. For example, as one psychologist discovered, although the debate about abortion has rung with rhetoric about the rights of women to control their own bodies or the rights of the fetus to live – rhetoric well covered on the evening news – individual women facing a decision to abort often make their decision much more on the basis of different values, values about which family member will be hurt, which will be pleased, which will be angry. That story should be covered, too.

For some, values are a matter of obedience. To others, they may be a matter of "feeling good." Psychologists suggest there may be several "stages of morality."

> I think if you ask people what their concept of heaven is, they would say, if they are honest, that it is a big department store, with new things every week—all the money to buy them, and maybe a little more than the neighbor.
>
> —ERICH FROMM

Are values arbitrary, based upon whatever existential role a human being wants to adopt at a certain moment? Do they flow from intellectual reflection or perhaps from a sense of universal love?

For a journalist just beginning to try to grasp what may be at the root of values, the panoply of thought about morals can be more exacerbating than helpful. There is not enough space in this book to explore the different schools of thought; that task is better left to other writers. However, it may be useful to outline one theory about values that might be at least clarify why the journalist is likely to encounter such a range of beliefs about morals.

Psychologist Lawrence Kohlberg has suggested that one's "moral IQ," so to speak, is developmental, just as are the emotions or the intellect. Children develop through various stages and, at times, individuals—or even entire societies—stop at one level. Thus, the theory would suggest, the differences in values are not so much a matter of conflicting commandments from a variety of divine beings, but more a result of individuals and cultures having reached separate levels of moral maturity.

A warning is in order before discussing Kohlberg's theory. As a psychologist, he is free to suggest a hierarchy of moral stages, each higher or more "mature" than the one before. A journalist who uses the formula to begin pigeonholing different sides, say, in an abortion controversy—pegging one side or the other as more mature—commits a grave disservice. Each of the stages can reveal something about human beings and the societies and religions they form; it is that understanding on which the journalist needs to focus, not just the opportunity for caricature.

With that in mind, consider what Kohlberg says:

Moral development occurs across three general levels: the preconventional, conventional, and postconventional. Each level breaks into two further stages. At the preconventional level, operating usually during childhood, the major concern is for the pleasurable or painful consequences of the action, not for whether the action is inherently "good" or "bad." At the conventional level of morality, the attitude of the parent, rather than the child, takes hold; the concern now is for the good of whatever immediate *group* one belongs to more than for one's own pleasure or pain. This leads one to value that which is valued by one's family, friends, classmates, Rotary Club, etc. At the postconventional level, concern shifts from the immediate group to the good of a more abstract group (the nation-state, for example) or to a notion of what is universally ethical.

By looking at the individual steps within each level, a journalist can begin to grasp some of the reasons for the existence of such widely varying values.

At the first stage of preconventional morality, the individual makes value choices out of a fear of punishment, Kohlberg says. No question is raised about whether the action is good or bad; the issue is one of obedience, and the mechanism of fear operates automatically and blindly. This is the stage of infanthood, the first step along the path to developing a moral consciousness. Being so fundamental to all of our experiences, it is also often the stage that adults will revert or adhere to. As one psychologist who interviewed the American soldiers who participated in the massacre of Vietnamese villagers at My Lai found, it is the stage that often remains operable in the military and in any organization. It is the unquestioning stage to which humans may return when confronted with a powerful authority capable of punishing them. Important for the journalist to recognize, it is not simply a stage applicable to "others"; studies of bright and supposedly mature students at Stanford and Yale universities have demonstrated that when caught in the dynamic of a group operating with a certain purpose, anyone may abandon any sense of individual moral responsibility. In one case, students administered electric shocks to people they had been told had heart problems; in another, they let themselves be turned into brutal jail guards.

Ethicist Edward Stevens, who comments upon Kohlberg's theory and extends it to a description of religions in *The Morals Game,* notes that at this first stage, "the moral life...is strictly a power game. My love (that is, my respect and obedience) of other people is strictly in proportion to the wattage of the thunderbolts that they are ready to hurl when their taboos are violated.... Religion is often used at this primitive level to back up morality with an infinite divine clout. God is not primarily a loving Father or even a lawgiver or rewarder. He is the angry, vengeful punisher. If evildoers don't get it in this life, he'll see to it that they get it in the next."

At the second stage of preconventional morality, Kohlberg describes a shift from blind obedience to an "instrumental" approach in which the goal is to minimize pain and maximize pleasure. Justice is defined in terms of fairness and reciprocity; if I share my strawberries, you had better share your peanut butter sandwich – even if I have ten crates of strawberries and you have only one peanut butter sandwich. The world exists to satisfy one's own selfish needs. One gives in order to get. As Stevens points out, philosophies constructed on this level tend to be utilitarian. Religions begin to resemble bargaining sessions in a divine marketplace: "I'll be good from now on if you. . . ."

At stage three, the first one in Kohlberg's level of conventional morality, the foundation of values becomes what *others* think is important. The aim is to help and please others, especially those capable of giving a sense of love or security. Despite pain or fear, one tries to please the groups to which one belongs; unfortunately, the demands of those groups may not be reconcilable and so one pushes toward stage four. There, contradictions can be resolved by locating the foundation of values in the more impersonal authority of the law. Duty becomes a godhead and the need to maintain order in society is seen as paramount. At the religious level, Stevens suggests, a god becomes a "supercop" and any breakdown in law is simultaneously seen as a breakdown of religion. "The laws of the nation become the laws of heaven," he comments. The loyalty tends to stop at the bounds of the nation-state.

Moving into the level of postconventional morality, a person at stage five begins to be more concerned about the *method* of arriving at societal consensus rather than the actual consensus itself. Both Ophuls and Stevens agree that such a focus is the epitome of civil religion in the United States, and perhaps in any pluralistic society. Consensus about values must rest on compromise, tolerance, and granting a "fair hearing" to all sides. If the trial is just, the verdict is just.

At the final stage described by Kohlberg, a human's moral development climaxes in a dedication to a sense of universal ethical principles. Decisions are no longer made on the basis of fear or group preference or conventionality, but rather upon the need to maintain one's self-respect by upholding principles seen as truthful. The focus for decision-making returns to the individual, but an individual far different from the fearful, blindly obedient child. This is the stage of the Gandhis, the Martin Luther Kings, the Buddhas, and the Christian saints.

Kohlberg's theory, again, should not be a formula for journalistic pigeonholing; it can help the values reporter, instead, to probe the assumptions of different groups, to explain what they share in common with others, to better sense the differences in groups and societies. For example, it can help a journalist explain the political process of "nation-building" that has been occurring in the last few decades in Africa, as governments try to shift moral loyalty from tribes (stage three) to a nation-state (stage four). The political process can also be seen as a values process, which may need to preserve the distinctiveness of the local group while creating a national consciousness and, simultaneously, joining in the increasing emphasis upon global loyalty.

Each stage in the Kohlberg theory, then, tells something about the human character; respect for each can aid in understanding the societies and cultures built upon it, as well as helping in questioning and communicating about the kinds of struggles over values that are occurring, personally or societally.

Good values reporting demands use of a variety of styles—and empathy.

> Religion is a great force—the only real motive force in the world; but you must get at a man through his own religion, not through yours.
> —GEORGE BERNARD SHAW

As do those on other beats, values reporters draw upon a variety of journalistic styles of writing in order to fully cover their subject. Sometimes the topic of values is raised in a simple interview piece, be it news or feature; other times, full-fledged profiles or news analyses are in order.

Here is an example of the latter, a news analysis of a breaking story, that of the fall 1982 massacre of Palestinian civilians in two refugee camps in Beirut. The slaughter occurred while Israeli troops occupied the city. The analysis, by David Shipler of the *New York Times,* appeared a week after the massacre became known.

JERUSALEM, Sept. 23—The Beirut massacre has plunged Israel into moral turmoil.

To many Israelis, the old foundations of right and wrong feel shaken loose. A sudden wilderness seems to have enveloped the nation. There is no voice to speak for its conscience.

"I'm afraid I don't know this country anymore," said an officer in the army reserves.

"They are destroying my country," said a woman in Jerusalem who fought to establish the state in the 1940s. . . .

With a Government that apparently does not want independent questioning [Shipler's story was written before the Israeli government agreed to an investigation], it has fallen to each individual, each circle of friends and the larger circle of the nation. Step by step the picture is being assembled as soldiers come forward and the Israeli press probes. . . .

No one suggests that Israeli troops participated in the massacre. But to a country that rose out of Hitler's death camps, the answers "We did not do it" and "We did not know" are not enough. To a people who remember that six million Jews were slaughtered as others turned their backs, the standards of behavior are more exacting, the questions more troubling. . . .

The rest of Shipler's story analyzes the actual massacre, detailing what was apparently known by Israeli army officers. The details of the *event* grow in significance once they are set in the *context* of values.

An entirely different writing style was used in a *Pacific* magazine examination of a decision by Seattle's Catholic Archbishop Raymond Hunthausen to withhold part of his federal taxes in a protest of the nuclear arms race. The archbishop's decision, made in early 1982, stirred a significant amount of local and national press coverage, most of it thrust on the novelty "specter of an archbishop fending off the IRS with a crucifix." Hunthausen was often asked why he had made his decision, but the why was never thoroughly probed until *Pacific* published an in-depth profile:

A year has now passed since Ray Hunthausen—"Dutch" as his parishioners often call him instead of "Your Excellency"—shook both religious and political officialdom, not to mention his own archdiocese, with his call for massive moral tax resistance against the nuclear arms race. It has been a year since he renamed the Trident base "the Auschwitz of Puget Sound." And it has been five months since he announced he would heed his own call and refuse to pay half of his federal income tax, thereby moving himself from the ranks of church leaders who have criticized the arms race to the cluster of priests and laymen who have decided to offer actual resistance.

This is the bishop whom Daniel Berrigan has praised as one of "the modern visionaries of our history, a bishop walking toward a new center, creating as he goes. . .a center of understanding." And this is the bishop whom others, less charitable, less impressed, less convinced have called "naive," "superficial" and "extremist."

To spend 10 minutes with Dutch Hunthausen is to be struck by the incongruity of all the notoriety. He has become a hero to those in the international peace movement. Diocesan priests return with stories about Europeans who, when told the priests are from Seattle, respond, "Ah, Hunthausen!" He refuses hundreds of invitations to speak. He receives ovations at peace gatherings. Supporters in one Seattle parish have taken to selling apple-sized, red-and-white buttons saying "I Love Hunthausen."

On the opposite side, he has been branded a grandstander by noted Catholic columnist Andrew Greeley and another writer in the diocesan newspaper has suggested the archbishop cannot distinguish between religious idealism and political reality. The Reagan administration's Navy secretary, John Lehman, himself a Catholic, accused Hunthausen of abusing his church office by speaking out against nuclear arms and labeled the archbishop's statements "ignorant and repugnant."

Yet Hunthausen is not the lean, fiery rhetorician one might expect from the controversy. His speeches pack more wallop on paper than in the delivery. The man himself more resembles a kindly, silver-haired, small-town, slightly paunchy but still muscular shopkeeper—the kind of down-home person his father was back in Anaconda, Montana. And he is far from being a media-polished counterpart to that late Catholic cheerleader for the American armed forces, Francis Cardinal Spellman, who often could be seen boarding yet another helicopter to visit yet another military base.

Hunthausen eschews pomp and praise—and publicity. In interviews, he says he dislikes the noisiness and the noisomeness that has accompanied his newly acquired celebrity status this past year. He sees himself not as a leader, but as a person simply trying to respond to developments in Catholic theology and to his best sense of what some divine being wants him to do. He drives a Volkswagen and eats at McDonald's and clings to the edge of a bus seat crowded with children on the way to a peace march like an everyday parish priest.

One is tempted to say, in fact, that the man more resembles a simple Quaker than a ritualistic archbishop. Yet the fact is indisputable: This is a Catholic archbishop who has chosen to be civilly disobedient, not because the tactic he has selected—tax resistance—will have any direct effect, except to draw attention to the issue of nuclear war, but because to him, it is the moral gesture that counts. "It counts," as Berrigan has written of Hunthausen, "no matter how received; whether it is emulated, derided, ignored, honored, condemned. . . ."

It is possible to oppose the nuclear arms race on the basis of self-survival or of secular human compassion, but those are not the only reasons that Hunthausen cites. When he explains his call for unilateral disarmament by the United States or his decision to not pay half of his taxes, he talks about "conversion," a theme that has been overlooked in media reports. . . .

The word provokes images of evangelists seeking yet more witnesses to Christ. But Hunthausen says he speaks of a different kind of "conversion," one which demands a realignment of an individual's values, away from those proffered by society— money as a measure of respect, power as a measure of success, competition as the character of most relationships, violence as the means of winning deep conflicts—to those contained in that Christian replacement of the "thou shalt nots" of the Ten Commandments with the "blessed ares" of the Sermon on the Mount. Blessed are the peacemakers, not just the peace lovers. Blessed are those who face violence with nonviolence. Blessed are those who forgive, those who desire justice for the poor, for those who are willing to suffer.

It could be a typical Sunday sermon but for the fact that Hunthausen reflects the thinking of several theologians who now argue that the community of Christians was never meant to be a majority church comfortably aligned with the values of the state, but rather a minority people actually living as witnesses to a different set of values. And they are serious about creating that community in practice. . . .

As does the Shipler analysis of the Beirut massacre, the profile of Hunthausen goes on to add a much-needed *context* of values to the specific news *event* of the archbishop's tax resistance. Hunthausen was no longer an inexplicable media freak, an individualist resisting government and seeking publicity, but rather a shy human being grappling with his role as an archbishop and with his ideals and values as a Christian.

*The more traditional "religious affairs beat"
demands excellence, a willingness to
investigate, and a dedication to probing.*

> Each religion, by the help of more or less
> myth which it takes more or less seriously,
> proposes some method of fortifying the
> human soul and enabling it to make peace
> with its destiny.
>   —GEORGE SANTAYANA

Churches are international organizations that transcend national identities and wield tremendous influence, authority, and power. Yet, as has
already been mentioned, church news has often been confined to a Saturday or Sunday morning ghetto. Whatever the personal religious faiths of
American journalists, the positivistic philosophy undergirding the definition of news has proven a problem in covering religion: the "facts" of faith
are not sensually verifiable; they concern something very old—man's
search for meaning—rather than something new, and they lead into theological controversies considered not that important. (After all, the notion
goes, theologians count the angels on the head of a pin, while scientists
discover reality.)

Yet, truly significant religious news has confronted journalists repeatedly in the past few decades. Martin Luther King's nonviolent civil
rights crusade was, first of all, based in religious feelings and religious
institutions. The emergence of the Catholic Church in Latin America as a
key representative and protector of millions of impoverished people seeking freedom and economic improvement has shaken many a government
there, as it did in Poland in the early 1980s. Mainline Christian congrega-
tions in the United States have pursued substantial, and often noisily
public, changes in theology and social action. A pope named John
launched a massive wave of reformation in the Roman Catholic ministry,
and another named John Paul II inspired crowds and confronted dictators
all over the world. The United States began shifting from its historically
dominant Protestant viewpoint to a broader acceptance of religions as
diverse as Zen Buddhism and Sufism. The era itself seemed to lay claim
to the title of the Ecumenical Century, the time when the religious tradi-
tions of East and West began to thoroughly explore and appreciate each
other, through the efforts of such people as D. T. Suzuki, Thomas Merton,
and Yogananda. As has already been noted, it was—and is—a time when
individuals searched among many churches for that "center" that Yeats
described, a period when fundamentalist churches strengthened and be-

came more vocal and when liberal churches began finding new roles for themselves.

However, although "man's never-ending quest for a confident faith to live by," as UPI's Cassels called it, may go on, reporters have sometimes tended to fall prey to the superficialities of that quest. When Pope John Paul II visited the United States in 1979, for example, many journalists focused stories on the carnival-like outpouring, even suspending objectivity to ooze about the "shimmers of magic" and the "awe-inspiring spiritual visitor." Few were able to adequately explain what those crowded to see the pope might have been looking for, and few probed the background of the theological statements the Catholic leader made while in the country.

Quality religious affairs reporting demands adherence to one, or all, of three standards. First, the reporter should strive to cover the religious event thoroughly, exploring all of its major angles just as one would any significant event. A religious-news label does not mean that the event warrants second-class reporting that overlooks investigative angles or dissolves into simplistic adulation or prejudiced derogation. Second, the event or process needs to be fitted into both its historical and theological framework. Some venturing into theology is essential and should be looked on as a writing challenge, not as a paralyzing journey. Third, when appropriate, the journalist needs to try to move beyond the externals of religious events and issues to give the audience an understanding of the *faiths* of others. The fundamental difference between organized religion, with its bricks and mortar and books of dogma, and the faith that fuels a religion or provides meaning to individuals is particularly interesting in these times when many people pull away from organized churches but seek strengthened experiences of faith.

Edward Fiske of the *New York Times* produced numerous high-quality religion stories while covering the beat for that paper, exploring angles other journalists might have overlooked. For example, in 1969 when evangelist Billy Graham was preparing to lead a crusade in New York City, Fiske refused to be satisfied with the usual "meeting coverage" approach (a speech story on day one and a color story on day two). Twelve years earlier, Graham had drawn more than two million people during a sixteen-week stay at Madison Square Garden, and even though some pundits had called it "Graham's last stand," here he was back again, stronger than ever because of his discovery of a major new ally: television. Fiske's first story was a profile of Graham in the *New York Times Magazine,* detailing Graham's theology, his relationship with established churches, his style of rhetoric, and his use of television. To make his full report even fuller, Fiske also probed the financing, sales, salaries, and mail-order network of Graham's religious organization. The background material was then reworked into the ongoing news coverage of the crusade. Fiske also examined the impact of Graham's visit on local churches and explored what happened to all those people in the audience who went down to the podium to make a "decision for Christ."

The *Times,* in short, covered Graham's descent upon the city in a way few newspapers or broadcast stations would–not just with more reporters, but with more acuteness and more interest in finding out what went on behind the scenes of the big event.

A year or so later, Fiske produced an article to which journalists, particularly those who would cover the 1980 elections and be surprised by the "sudden" political power of the evangelical movements, might have paid more attention. Traveling through the South, Fiske reported that evangelists were having to sell their tents and tone down the hell-and-brimstone: evangelism was undergoing a significant historical change because of urbanization. The preachers were moving into public auditoriums and air-conditioned churches, and they were buying more and more time on television. In short, their appeal was going not just to the rural dwellers who had been their mainstay, but, increasingly, to the suburban middle class. A decade later, in one of the most thorough reports written on the Rev. Jerry Falwell and the Moral Majority, an evangelical group that claimed to have contributed to the defeat of many liberal politicians in 1980, *New Yorker* magazine rediscovered what Fiske had reported years earlier: the evangelists had learned very effectively the techniques of broadcast and political organization.

Quality religious affairs reporting need not demand tomes or long profiles, such as that written about Billy Graham. In another story, this one limited to fifteen inches, Fiske explored the "Jesus people" phenomenon of the early 1970s, when many young people proclaimed their "rebirth" and their belief in a personal saviour and set out to preach happiness through the land. Delving into the history of such movements in the United States, Fiske produced what at the time was the rather remarkable conclusion that the "Jesus people" were not the carriers of the "hippie tradition" of the 1960s, as many reporters presumed, but were the latest heirs of a religious tradition as American–and as conservative–as apple pie and circuit riders. He compared their theology with that of the fundamentalist churches and noted their amiable relationships with many such conservative groups. In a short space, he gave readers a much clearer idea of the Jesus people's location within current events and theology than did the reporters who resorted to superficial color stories about long-haired, simple-garbed minstrels.

Meeting the third standard of quality religious affairs reporting–that of exploring the essence of a person's faith–can be even more challenging than attempting to locate a group within a theological context. The reporter confronts the apparently conflicting demands of getting inside that person's faith and communicating in words the individual might use, and of trying to remain objective. Terms such as "the Holy Spirit" and "God" may appeal to some readers but alienate others, and the reporter has to walk the line between reporting the way in which an individual sees one's personal faith and explaining that as a detached observer. The *Pacific* story about Archbishop Hunthausen, for example, refers to his use of the term *conversion*, but carefully distinguishes that from the kind of conversion of which evangelists speak – and of which many readers might think if the word was not explained.

The task of communicating what another person is experiencing or seeking for is a sensitive one. Consider the following example, written by James Wooten, again of the *New York Times*. Wooten was examining the policies of a sect called the Children of God, which demanded that its members give up their families and refuse to visit their parents. Although most of the story focused on the resultant friction such policies caused, Wooten's lead and conclusion attempted to grasp the *experience* of the members:

MINGUS, Tex. – Although the boy who calls himself Adonikum was born but 20 years ago, there is a loneliness in his eyes that is older than human history, and when he speaks, his soft words echo the accumulated desperation of the species.

"It is easy to know when you are not wanted," he said rather sadly here yesterday, as the first serious winds of the winter sliced across the barren prairie around him. "What is not so easy is to leave". . . .

Adonikum embraced himself and rubbed his hands before pronouncing what was for him a benediction to the day.

"Out there, I found everything I wanted except love, which is really what I wanted," he said. "With the Children of God, I found love, and so can anyone else who wants it. Out there I felt that love did not exist. Here it is all around me."

"Are you going home for the holidays?" he was asked.

"If my parents send the money," he said as he walked toward a great blue bus that rested stolidly on its axles, tumbleweeds bouncing off its flattened tires.

RECOMMENDED RESOURCES

A journalist who seeks to specialize in values or religious affairs reporting will want to establish a firm grounding in both Eastern and Western ethical philosophy, in anthropological studies of mythology, in contemporary theology, and in psychological theories about the acquisition and development of values.

Edward Stevens's *The Morals Game* is an excellent – though at times flippant – introduction for the layperson to the study of conflicting value theories.

Stevens categorizes different schools of thought and examines the value conflicts that arise in contemporary debates about such issues as abortion, reverse discrimination, euthanasia, the sexual revolution, war and pacifism, and the relation of the individual to the state. For the student without an adequate grounding in philosophy, this can be an easy entry point into the study of values and religions.

A study of Lawrence Kohlberg's theory of moral development is also useful, but Kohlberg should be examined in conjunction with the works of two of his students: Carol Gilligan, who argues that Kohlberg's understanding of moral development is sexist, and James Fowler, who has remodeled Kohlberg's theory to take into account the phenomenon of religious faith.

A number of psychologists and theologians have addressed the question of what, if anything, constitutes the fundamental root and dynamic of the creation of human values. Among them are Victor Frankl's *Man's Search for Meaning,* Otto Rank's *Psychology and the Soul* and *Art and Artist: Creative Urge and Personality Development,* and especially the very erudite and challenging synthesis by Ernest Becker, *The Denial of Death.* This latter book, like that of Stevens, constitutes an excellent entry point for the student concerned with the formation of values and religions.

Also useful, and enjoyable to read, is *Myths to Live By,* a 1972 collection of essays by the humorous anthropologist Joseph Campbell.

Naturally, the major works of recent theologians, such as Paul Tillich and Teilhard de Chardin, should not be overlooked.

EXERCISES

1. Collect recent stories from newspapers and magazines about genetic engineering. Do you believe the stories adequately examine questions about values, or do they concentrate primarily upon the technical, scientific, or business issues involved? Within its overall coverage of the issue over a period of months or years, has a given periodical presented a balanced examination of the value questions? Conduct similar examinations on other value issues: abortion, euthanasia, nuclear war opposition, minority rights, and lifestyles. How is your local media examining value questions?

2. Compare the religious coverage in a local newspaper with that of a specialized religious affairs periodical, such as *National Catholic Reporter.* The specialized publication's coverage will be more thorough since that is its prime focus, but what angles has the specialized publication explored that you think would have been of interest to a mass audience? How has each periodical approached the coverage of religion? Is a theological framework provided? Is the focus on the superficialities of the event? Is there a retreat from the examination of theological or historical contexts, in favor of an easier "color story" approach that describes religious figures and their audiences? What would you do differently?

3. Select one church in your area and interview the spokesman for that church about present concerns. What has been the church response to the nuclear arms race, for example? How does it minister to homosexuals in its congregation? What do its members feel about abortion? About premarital sex? Try to write a story that not only presents the results of the interview but places those opinions in the church's theological and historical context. If several classmates produce

such stories, you may also want to write a second article, comparing the approaches and theologies of several of the churches on a single issue.

4. While you are interviewing, you might as well talk to your own university officials with the same kinds of value questions. What is the role of the university in encouraging peace, for example? Should ROTC be present on the campus of the local Catholic university? What values guide biological research? What values affect the university's interaction with its local community? Would the student newspaper accept advertisements for surrogate mothers? You may not make yourself popular with such questions, but you will be raising important issues and producing valuable articles.

12 *Reporting Minority Affairs*

> The press has too long basked in a white world, looking out of it, if at all, with white men's eyes and a white perspective. That is no longer good enough.
>
> —NATIONAL ADVISORY COMMISSION ON CIVIL DISORDERS, 1968

A DECADE AND A HALF AGO, when the president's Commission on Civil Disorders issued its report after a summer of blacks rioting in American cities, its indictment of racism in the nation included a blunt declaration that every minority group already knew from experience: despite its vaunted objectivity and its commitment to fairness, the American news media had sorely neglected and greatly distorted reports about minorities in this country. The perspective of the press was—and continues to be, despite some progress—white and male.

"The media," the report said, "report and write from the standpoint of a white man's world. The ills of the ghetto, the difficulties of life there, the Negro's burning sense of grievance, are seldom conveyed. Slights and indignities are part of the Negro's daily life, and many of them come from what he now calls 'the white press'—a press that repeatedly, if unconsciously, reflects the biases, the paternalism, the indifference of white America."

That particular report chided the news media for their coverage of blacks, of course, but the years since have taught us that the words could apply equally to the media's coverage of many other minorities, several of which took to the streets in the 1970s: Chicanos, women, American Indians, gay men, and lesbian women. Each group complained—rightfully— that it had been the subject of the same kind of bias by which journalists viewed black Americans.

Largely as a result of the 1968 commission's criticisms, the press has made attempts to change. In several cities, minority affairs beats emerged during the late 1960s and early 1970s. Usually the particular thrust of the beat has depended upon the particular mix of minorities within a newspaper's or broadcast station's audience. In cities with a high black population, minority affairs usually means "black affairs"; in cities with a large Spanish-speaking population, "Chicano affairs," and so forth. Sometimes that kind of fragmentation can be helpful since it can ensure much needed coverage for a much overlooked segment of the audience; at other times it obscures the common problems that the minorities share in coping with the dominant white society.

Four kinds of minorities have tended to be discriminated against in the news columns:

• *Racial minorities,* such as blacks, American Indians, and Asian-Americans.

• *Ethnic minorities,* such as Chicanos and, in earlier decades, various European immigrant groups that had languages and cultures different from the prevailing Anglo ones.

• *Women,* who really are not a minority at all, since they constitute more than half of the American population.

• *Sexual orientation minorities,* such as gay men and lesbian women, who, according to best estimates, comprise about 10 percent of the American populace.

The bias itself shows in one of two forms: *neglect* of the minority community or *distortion* of news about that community through stereotyping. Because such neglect or distortion can show up on any beat, coverage of minority affairs is something in which every journalist—general assignment, political reporter, police writer, religion reporter—needs to have some expertise. Indeed, one of the most persistent debates about minority affairs coverage in the past decade and a half has been whether it should be a specialized beat itself, or whether it should be incorporated into other beats.

The best answer is: both. The solution to improving minority affairs coverage is not simply the creation of another ghetto, this one in the newsroom. The United States is a multi-racial, multi-ethnic, multi-affectional society and must be covered as such by reporters on all beats. At the same time, a specific minority beat is often critical if those different perspectives are going to be infused into the news coverage and if sources are going to be developed in communities that are suspicious of the "white press."

The first step in either thrust is understanding why the press has failed to cover minorities.

*The first form of press discrimination
against minorities is often neglect—neglect
of minority news, of minority aspirations,
of minority existence.*

> Shall we judge a country by the majority, or
> by the minority? By the minority, surely.
> —RALPH WALDO EMERSON

The civil disorders commission pointed out that "most newspaper articles and most television programming ignore the fact that an appreciable part of their audience is black. [For black, you can substitute "female," "Chicano," "gay."] The world that television and newspapers offer to their black audience is almost totally white, in both appearance and attitude. . . . The press acts and talks about Negroes as if Negroes do not read the newspapers or watch television, give birth, marry, die, and go to PTA meetings."

What is *not* in the news is the most insidious form of discrimination. Journalists tend to focus on the activities of white, male decision-makers or white trend-setters to the total exclusion at times of leaders or concerns of minority communities. James and Sharon Murphy, in their study of the treatment of American Indians in the media, *Let My People Know,* have pointed out that from the early years of the twentieth century until the 1960s, very little coverage of Indian affairs was carried in the white media, though that was the period of great post-defeat anguish for the natives of this nation. Similarly, a Boston-based group of gay activists, Lesbian and Gay Media Advocates, has noted in its guide to the media, *Talk Back,* that for the first half of the century the subject of homosexuality went untouched by American journalists. "The average person," the group notes, "could easily go through life without hearing anything more than an occasional oblique reference to 'inverts' or 'abnormal people.' "

Neglect can be an issue even when special sections are set aside to cover a particular community. In an analysis of the "Day" section of the *Portland Oregonian,* a section for women, the American Association of University Women found in 1974 that 62 percent of the space went to advertising, 10 percent to activities unrelated to those of Oregon women, about 8 percent to entertainment features such as comics and puzzles, and another 10 percent to advice about food, styles, and household work. Only 5 percent of the space went to *feature* articles about women (implying, the AAUW said, that were the material handled as *news,* it would never see print, much less a spot in the regular news sections of the *Oregonian*). Only 0.3 percent of the space was devoted to straight news of women's events or activities. The message, the AAUW said, was clear: women were not news.

The temptation is to pass off such neglect as the result of prejudice on the part of editors or reporters—unconscious, unintended prejudice, but prejudice nonetheless. To a certain extent, such a rationale is valid. However, a far more important reason for the neglect stems from the *structure* of American journalism—from the way in which news media have defined who they are and what journalism is about. Until that structure is altered, the neglect will probably continue. In a 1979 *Columbia Journalism Review* article entitled "The Minority Struggle for a Place in the Newsroom," Nick Kotz, a Pulitzer Prize-winning reporter who has covered the struggle for minority equality, wrote that many minority journalists feel that the words of the 1968 commission are still true today: the American press is still "shockingly backward" in its coverage of minorities.

The first structural point concerns the way in which the news media have defined who they are; specifically, who reports the news. Journalism has long been a bastion for white males and so newsrooms have not had reporters who can bring the perspectives, values, and sources needed to broaden coverage. Often editors compound the problem by demanding that minority reporters prove some sort of special allegiance to journalism; they tend to ask whether a black reporter or a female reporter can report "objectively" according to the standards of the profession. (Naturally they fail to ask whether those standards are actually objective.)

For example, a report by the Committee on Minorities of the American Society of Newspaper Editors noted that while substantial progress in integrating the newsrooms of the country had been made in the 1970s, "the prospect for ultimate success is bleak." The committee based its pessimism on the fact that blacks and Hispanics, in particular, continued to be under-represented in the nation's journalism programs, that the rate of progress in integrating newspapers had declined—even though a sustained push was being made—and that there were problems with the acceptance of minorities in the newsrooms. As of the early 1980s, about 5 percent of newspaper journalists were from racial or ethnic minorities. Few of those were in supervisory positions.

Similarly, fewer than 10 percent of the influential editorial posts on American newspapers were held by women in the early 1980s.

The statistics for openly gay journalists are even worse (no one, of course, has statistics on the number of closet gays in journalism): a 1982 *Columbia Journalism Review* article examining the coverage of news about gays pointed out that despite the existence of significant gay communities in every American city of any size, only one newspaper, the *San Francisco Chronicle,* had made any attempt to hire an openly gay reporter in order to improve its coverage. "Closeted" reporters, the article noted, are of no help since they often avoid covering gay issues because of their fear of being revealed.

Structurally, then, the American news media has been without the firsthand knowledge necessary to help it improve coverage of minorities. Its reporters live in other communities and are more likely to notice other issues. Thus, a conflict over the quality of grammar-school education in a white suburb is more likely to receive ongoing news *and* feature coverage, while a similar conflict in a Chicano barrio is lucky to receive a single feature story, if that. Too, the coverage of a Legionnaire's disease striking down white conventioneers is more likely to get sustained national play than an epidemic of AIDS (Acquired Immune Deficiency Syndrome) in the gay community, which had killed more people than Legionnaire's disease before it began to be noticed by the straight press. (AIDS, which reached epidemic proportions in 1982, began to be noticed once it started striking the nongay populace, initially through blood transfusions.)

The second reason for neglect of minority communities has not received as much attention as the first, but is just as important. Journalists define *news* in such a way that minorities are almost automatically excluded, unless they happen to riot or demonstrate. This structural definition limits coverage to that which is considered of *consequence,* or that which entails some sort of *conflict* or *unusualness.*

What is of consequence usually means what is of significance to the majority community, or what is done by people who are defined as significant. The press covers the decision-makers; the decision-makers are white and male. The press covers the community, but the community of "significance" is white. Consequence, in other words, is linked to political, social, and economic power; as such, it introduces a class definition into the supposedly objective or fair concept of news. What is of importance is what is of consequence to a particular class.

Minorities, then, enter into the news either through the routes of conflict – by protesting or threatening – or of unusualness – by virtue of "peculiar" or quaint habits. Indians are noticed by journalists when they seize federal buildings, when they seem to suffer from unusual poverty, or when they stage "quaint" ceremonies. Blacks are noticed when they burn cities, have unusually high unemployment rates, or hold Gospel rallies. Gay people are covered when a bathhouse burns down or when a few parade in drag down the streets of San Francisco.

At other times, of course, the minorities are generally neglected because they and their activities – the routine ones that, despite their routineness, would still be covered if occurring in the white community – are not perceived to be of any consequence. Also, the minority leaders do not make decisions affecting the whole community, for they do not sit in the government councils.

The only way to meet these two structural reasons for neglect is consciously and deliberately. Removing individual prejudices does not suffice; deliberate efforts to counter the effects of who is in the newsroom and how news is defined are necessary. Kotz points out, for example, what happened when *Washington Post* editor Benjamin Bradlee deliberately set out to hire minorities and improve minority coverage: city elections in Washington, D.C., a primarily black city, started being covered with "a sensitivity and bite previously absent." Similarly, when the *San Francisco Chronicle* deliberately sought to improve its coverage of the city's gay community, reporter Randy Shilts was able to produce not only news articles but major research pieces on such topics as violence against gays.

The second form of press discrimination against minorities, after neglect, has been distortion—not through ill will but simply through misunderstanding.

> A minority group has "arrived" only when it has the right to produce some fools and scoundrels without the entire group paying for it.
>
> —CARL T. ROWAN

In the 1960s blacks appeared in news columns mostly by way of police reports about suspects in this or that crime being "a Negro." If the suspect was white, that fact was not mentioned. Women made their appearance in the society pages, where the meetings of garden clubs and the organization of Welcome Wagons were often stashed. Sometimes they showed up in the regular news columns as the "petite blond wife" of a white decision-maker. American Indians commonly received mention in articles about alcoholism. Gays appeared mostly in articles about sensational "homosexual murders" or "homosexual arsons." When the murder was "heterosexual," that was never mentioned; undoubtedly, many in the audience would be appalled to learn of the number of "heterosexual murders" and "heterosexual arsons." Asians often appeared in connection with a "den" of this or that—say, a "den of gambling."

Some progress has been made in the past decade and a half. Because of protests, crime suspects are no longer identified racially, unless that seems especially important to understanding the story. Women tend to escape the irrelevant, trite descriptions (though often they now seem to be stuck with opposite ones, describing them as "businesslike" or "serious"). Gays are not normally referred to as "inverts" or "queers" anymore, as they used to be in the late 1940s and 1950s, but they may be lumped with other undesirables in descriptions of neighborhoods being "taken over by drunks, prostitutes, and homosexuals."

Progress, then, is uneven, and the American press still engages in much distortion about minority communities. Such stereotyping is the second major form of discrimination that beginning journalists need to avoid.

The media have tended to focus on minorities as fringe groups and to characterize them by their "oddities." Gays are stereotyped either as effeminate men or masculine women; all the men are portrayed as interested only in promiscuous sex ("flaunted" as publicly as possible), while the women ride motorcycles. Blacks are either grinning Uncle Toms or militant, dangerous toughs.

As black journalist Robert Maynard has pointed out, though, the media has often overlooked the normality that exists in minority groups— where people love, strive, survive, and go to PTA meetings like others— and has failed to treat the very important differences that do exist in a nonjudgmental way. "We seek portrayal of our communities as places inhabited by real people," he has said, "not pathological fragments."

Like the neglect, the distortion grows from individual ignorance about minority groups and from that structural definition of who constitutes the media and what constitutes news. A march on Washington by 100,000 gays can be easily neglected by a media that considers it of no consequence (the march *was* overlooked by most of the American media), or easily distorted by one that passes up photos of the 99,000 gays who look like your neighbor or family doctor in order to focus on the few who do not.

Distortion also grows from a reporter's selection of sources. The 1968 commission noted that many white reporters tended to stick close to the police during ghetto disturbances and report only what the police said. Understandable though that may be in a riot, it is hardly justifiable in succeeding days. Once, during the trial of a gay activist in Boston, according to Lesbian and Gay Media Activists, a reporter interviewed the district attorney; when he was approached by the activist and asked to listen, the reporter said, "I'm not talking to any homos," and walked away.

Similarly, many feminists have been suspicious of reporters who tend to want to create "leaders" whom they can then interview. The black feminist poet, Chocolate Waters, once addressed a blistering poem "To the Male Reporter from the Denver Post" attacking the journalist's preconceptions about how women ought to be gentle and content to make gradual changes.

Some of the distortion can be caught if the journalist mentally injects the name of another minority group into the copy to reveal stereotypes. Most journalists today are sensitive enough, for example, not to write that a neighborhood is being taken over by "drunks, prostitutes, and Jews." Nor would they paste up the headline, "Irish sex scandal." Why do it, then, with "drunks, prostitutes, and homosexuals" or "Homosexual scandal"? Most would not write that David Rockefeller sat "graciously behind his desk" or "delicately flipped the ashes from his cigarette" or "acted very businesslike." Why do it if the name is Patricia Rockefeller? Few would write that thousands of black men marching "without underwear" asked for their civil rights; why refer to "bra-less women" marching for their civil rights?

Some will argue that they simply describe what they see. Perhaps. If so, they see events as their culture has painted them, not as they really may be.

Neglect. Distortion. Neither has any place on *any* beat. As the commission on civil disorders said, "It is not excusable in an institution that has the mission to inform and educate the whole of our society."

One of the most controversial minority communities is that of gay men and lesbian women. Other minority groups argue for their civil rights; this one argues for its right to exist.

> The nail that sticks out is hammered down.
> —JAPANESE PROVERB

About 15 million to 25 million gay people live in the United States, according to estimates that put their numbers at about 10 percent of the total population. That means that in any large American city, say of 1 million or more people, gays constitute a sizable "city within a city" of 100,000 or more individuals.

Despite their numbers, though, gays tend to be ignored by the news media. The reasons are varied: Unlike other minorities, many gay people are "closeted" successfully and they can, if they choose, blend completely with the majority society. They do not stand out as *gay* by virtue of skin color, language, or anatomy. The shame of many is so great that they suppress their homosexual feelings, though at some cost to their own psyche. Many others acknowledge their gayness to themselves and to friends but believe they cannot afford the risks of greater openness: possibilities of losing a job, family support, or even housing. Many of those who are in journalism and are gay are afraid of being open within what is considered a very masculine and heterosexual profession; they tend to avoid pressing for coverage of gay issues.

In short, society's intolerance has been so great that, until recently, gays have been an "invisible minority," stripped of their history by scholars who refuse to include pertinent biographical facts about major historical figures or examine the substantial body of gay literature in existence; written off as a diseased fraction of the community; portrayed as child molesters and sex addicts; refused freedom of travel or of immigration by being included in the "undesirable" category; denied security clearances by a government afraid of homosexuals being blackmailed (a simple enough problem to resolve if the individuals are open about being gay).

To argue for or against homosexuality is not the point here; it is rather to treat of reality. Gay people exist in large numbers; it is not the journalist's function to be judgmental about them, but to inform and educate society. Even if homosexuality were a disease, as once argued by American psychiatrists, journalists have been much more objective in dealing with leper colonies than with gay communities. That is what the minority affairs reporter is called upon to change.

Neglect and distortion with respect to gays and lesbians take many forms:

On November 19, 1980, a man who hated homosexuals opened fire on a gay bar in New York City, killing two men and wounding six others. A few weeks later, a group of teenagers went on a "queer-bashing" spree, attacking a dozen men. The *New York Times* covered the two incidents almost as if they were just random street assaults, not seeking reactions from the city's gay community, according to Ransdell Pierson, who analyzed the coverage in a 1982 *Columbia Journalism Review* article, "Uptight on Gay News." The coverage prompted some to wonder whether the *Times* would have afforded similar treatment if eight Jews had been shot down in front of a synagogue and weeks later a gang had roamed the streets beating up Jews at random. Anti-Semitism has gotten easier to recognize, at a price of six million Jewish lives lost in Nazi concentration camps. Recognition of homophobia should not have to come at the price of more deaths.

In 1980, when more than 100,000 Cubans fled to Florida, the media for months overlooked the fact that many were gay, and that they were fleeing oppression in Cuba. The migration began in late April; not until July did a major American newspaper carry a story about the gay Cubans. At that point, the *Washington Post* noted that "as many as 20,000" gay Cubans were still in resettlement camps. Michael Massing, executive editor of the *Columbia Journalism Review,* noted that the neglect was not due to lack of awareness; many reporters on the story knew that many of the refugees were gay. "Rather," Massing wrote, "the story simply was not 'right'." Once the *Post* brought the story out of the closet, gay communities across the country responded with offers of assistance. However, follow-ups on the adjustments gay Cubans have had to make—and their difficulty in doing so—have been left mainly to the gay press.

Hiding such oppression in the closet means keeping most Americans uninformed about the difficulties gay people face.

In an especially bigoted program, CBS News in 1980 produced "Gay Power, Gay Politics," which ostensibly focused on a story largely neglected by the press: the emergence of gays as a political force in the late 1970s. The program examined the political clout wielded by gays in San Francisco. Although it opened with a disclaimer by CBS reporter Harry Reasoner that the documentary would not focus on "lifestyles or the average gay experience," practically the entire program did focus on lifestyle—on one particular part of gay lifestyle. George Crile, the producer and reporter on the program, repeatedly pulled in filmstrips and comments about the gay "tearoom trade" in park bathrooms, drag balls, and sadomasochism. The report drew complaints from gay people throughout the country, as well as from the San Francisco Board of Supervisors and the San Francisco Human Rights Commission because of what the supervisors said was a focus on "the darker practices of the gay community intended to startle viewers and to show how gays are attacking traditional values and frightening heterosexuals." The CBS report eventually drew a rebuke from the National News Council.

Repeatedly in dealing with gay people, media focus on the *sex* in *homosexual,* failing to take into account other aspects of gays' lives or to consider that gayness is not simply a matter of sex, but also of affection. Few news stories and fewer documentaries have been made examining the role of gays as parents, gays in long-lasting couples, gays and housing discrimination. Few have been written or broadcast examining not the gays as the source of a problem, but heterosexual attitudes toward gays as the problem. (Similar complaints have been made about coverage of other minorities: reporters descend upon the black community to examine "the black problem" but never go into the white community where the racism actually exists.)

In April 1981, New Orleans police arrested more than 100 gay men and women in the French Quarter, charging them with obstructing sidewalks. The local gay community responded vigorously with a protest meeting at which 700 gays attended. Two of the city's three television stations covered the meeting, which was held two days after the arrests ended. The *Times-Picayune/States-Item,* according to Pierson's *CJR* article, did not get around to covering even the arrests until five days after they had begun. "Apparently," Pierson comments, "the arrest of more than 100 men and women in a city not under martial law was not considered 'really controversial'."

In *Talk Back,* by Lesbian and Gay Media Advocates (LAGMA), several ways that media bias shows up are summarized. First, and perhaps most often, LAGMA points out, the media tend to make heavy use of the "homosexual" adjective, inevitably referring to "homosexual torture, homosexual arson, homosexual murder, homosexual rape. The group argues that the press should either use both adjectives—homosexual and heterosexual—routinely or drop the adjective altogether.

Second, stories about gay issues such as political marches tend to end up buried in the newspaper or newscast, while stories about sex scandals end up on page one. The march on Washington in October 1979, for example, got very little coverage although it drew 100,000 people; an alleged Congressional sex scandal involving claims that Congressmen were having sex with male pages drew national front page and top-of-the-broadcast spots for weeks in 1982.

Third, reporters often lack the background necessary to understand the significance of certain gay events or issues. The LAGMA points out, for example, that few journalists seem to understand that many who are in a Gay Pride march may be risking their job and family ties by identifying themselves as gay; jaded press representatives, used to marches, may tend to treat it as just another St. Patrick's Day celebration.

Fourth, gays tend to be isolated in news coverage. This criticism goes back to the debate between whether it is better to have a minority affairs beat or to infuse the other beats with an awareness of minority issues. The LAGMA argues that gays should not be confined to getting notice just in stories specifically about gays. Rather, a story about teenage sexuality should deal with *both* homosexuality and heterosexuality. A story about alcoholism among high school students might mention the specific problems of gay youths. Stories about "The Changing Church" need to take into consideration the proliferation of church groups for gay people. (Such religious groups now exist in many churches.)

Fifth, what the LAGMA calls "Hitler's opinion" is often included in stories about gays. The group notes that "a Nazi would not be required in a discussion of anti-Semitism, nor would a member of the Ku Klux Klan be called in for a discussion of civil rights for black Americans. However, it is common for members of the clergy, the psychiatric profession and right-wing groups such as Moral Majority who hold clear anti-gay opinions to be included in discussions of the civil rights of gays and lesbians."

Sixth, the media often engage in sensationalism. The LAGMA points out, for example, that during a recent fire that destroyed $6 million worth of property in San Francisco, the media quoted the fire chief as saying he feared that gay men had burned to death in "slave quarters." The chief had no substantiation for his claim, but it went into newspapers and over the airwaves unchallenged—until the media discovered that no one had been killed and there weren't any "slave quarters." However, the sensationalism had reinforced the public's distorted stereotype of gay life.

Seventh, lesbians tend to be the even more invisible part of the invisible minority. The details of gay men's sex lives are ripe for lurid reporting, but lesbians and their opinions rarely appear in print. Partly, this seems tied to the issues of racism and feminism: the news media acts as if the only homosexuals are young white males and dirty old (white) men. It tends to ignore completely females and gays of color. Even minority affairs reporters who otherwise excel at covering their particular specialty—be it the black, Chicano, or women's community—will sometimes tend to completely overlook the subject of homosexuality within that community.

Eighth, the LAGMA notes that reporters tend to select very biased words when dealing with gays. A gay bar is "crowded," while a heterosexual bar is "popular." A gay activist becomes an "avowed homosexual," which sounds much worse than "openly gay." (Think about how the connotation of "avowed heterosexual" would sound.) Similarly, some journalists balk at the use of the word *gay,* often arguing that they want to retain its use as meaning "happy." Gay activists suggest that such a reluctance may partly be based on the reporter's own discomfort with acknowledging that gay people are more than just sexual perverts. Activists argue that *gay* is used because it is less clinical than *homosexual,* which still bears the imprint of psychology and medicine, and because a minority group has the right to select is own name, rather than having to conform to one imposed by the majority society. Thus, they point out that the media should respect designations preferred by the minority groups, such as blacks rather than Negroes, Chicanos or Hispanics rather than Mexican-Americans, feminists rather than women's libbers, native Americans rather than Indians, and gay rather than homosexual.

Words also come into play when journalists write of *gay rights* rather than *gay civil rights.* Because blacks were the first major movement to demand civil rights, the term *civil rights movement* is now taken to be synonymous with that particular effort. All movements since have labored under shortened versions: *Chicano rights, Indian rights, gay rights, women's rights.* The LAGMA points out that such shortening tends to lead readers and viewers into thinking that these other minority groups are demanding some *special* rights; for example, in "Gay Power, Gay Politics," CBS narrator Crile repeatedly linked "gay rights" with what he called demands to have sex in public places. Such a link is a gross distortion. Each group has been demanding its civil rights, the ones guaranteed to other Americans. *Gay rights,* then, means protection against being refused housing or lodging because one is gay, and protection against losing a job because one is gay. Reporters do well to use the full term: *gay civil rights.*

Words such as *sexual preference* are also misleading, as is *gay lifestyle. Sexual orientation* is a more appropriate term than *sexual preference,* since most psychological studies agree that sexual and affectional orientation is established early in life, though it may be suppressed for years. Asking homosexuals if they chose to be homosexual or if they could choose to stop is similar to asking heterosexuals if they chose to be heterosexual and if they could choose to stop. *Lifestyle* implies that all gay people follow the same kind of life; the word is often used to connote days filled with caution and nights filled with reckless sexual abandon. It is as ridiculous a concept as *heterosexual lifestyle* would be.

Pierson points out in his article that many editors, sensitized to the demands of racial and ethnic minorities, still fail to see gay people as a specific minority group worthy of coverage. He quotes former *New York Times* columnist Roger Wilkins, who worked for two years as the paper's urban affairs writer, saying that the *Times* killed two columns once because they dealt with gay issues. Wilkins interpreted *urban affairs* as inclusive of all urban matters, which certainly included the one million or so gay people in New York City. The editors defined *urban affairs* as meaning only the poor and the ethnic minorities.

Pierson quotes Ben Bagdikian, the well-known press critic and former *Washington Post* ombudsman, as strongly disagreeing with the viewpoint that gay people are a fringe group undeserving of coverage: "Homosexuals," Bagdikian says, "have been treated as an inferior group in society and therefore deserve regular coverage along with other minorities such as women and blacks."

Are women a minority group? Their numbers say no. But their historical treatment says yes.

> Social science affirms that a woman's place in society marks the level of civilization.
> —ELIZABETH CADY STANTON

Women constitute more than half of the American population, but despite their numbers, they show up in perhaps 10 percent of the news and feature stories carried in the media. Historically, their concerns—

defined as food, home, and health, which are really *every* person's concerns—have been segmented from the rest of the news. Their identities have been defined only by their relationships to men (as wives, daughters, mothers, or secretaries). Their physical appearance has always been held up for comment.

Despite their status as a majority, then, women have been created very much like other minorities. They have been neglected and images of them have been distorted. As with blacks, Chicanos, or gay persons, the correction lies both with a broadened attitude that will bring women into the news columns and broadcasts at all points and with a deliberate effort to expand the definition of what constitutes news of consequence.

Jean Ward, a journalism professor and former staff writer for the *Minneapolis Tribune,* has pointed out ways in which the news media continue to stereotype women. Significantly, in a 1980 article for the *Columbia Journalism Review*—years after the start of the feminist movement—she was still able to select most her examples of sexism from the *end* of the 1970s.

First, the news media tend to assume that all people are men, until proven otherwise. Thus, doctors who are women have to be identified as such. Ditto for lawyers, business executives, coaches, and just about anyone else who is not in a "female-identified" profession, such as nursing or dental hygiene. Headlines about "women photographers," "women professors," and "women bus drivers" might have been justifiable in the late 1960s and early 1970s when women were entering jobs traditionally reserved for men, but as the years pass into the 1980s, that becomes less and less a way to point out women's gains and more a method of stigmatizing females as "something different." That a doctor may be either male or female is normal now, and reporters who need to be precise about the doctor's gender will always have to attach one of the two adjectives. Where such identification is unnecessary, forget the adjective.

The physical appearance of a woman always requires comment. Here is an example from a 1983 news story by a Seattle University student: "Sitting graciously behind her desk, [Sister Rosaleen] Trainor, who usually doesn't like to talk about herself, was able to select some characteristics she brought to the honors program. 'I have an appreciation of the uniqueness of individuals, an ability to listen,' she said modestly, her brown eyes gleaming."

Ward cites this example from a 1979 Associated Press story: "At 38, she is still a stunner, with a robust sense of humor, a throaty, husky laugh and green eyes that sparkle like gemstones."

Obviously, conflicts will arise between a feature writer's need to describe an individual's appearance and personality and the resentment by many women to being caricatured as either conforming to or defying a stereotype. Skill and sensitivity will be required of the writer in those cases where descriptions have a valid role. In any case, never describe only the *women* who appear in stories, and describe them to convey a sense of their unique personality, not to categorize them as "pert and blond" or "a mere 110 pounds under a heavy fire*man*'s uniform." Keep in mind that the purpose of personal description in journalistic stories is to convey some sense of character. Actually, physical description is often the *least* effective means of doing so; it is usually far better to describe how a person relates to other people, how they face adversity, how they choose their goals or even how they spend their money. All are far more adequate indicators of personality than simple physical description of body height and appearance.

Third, Ward points out that media still tend to use words such as *coed* to distinguish women from other groups. The *Los Angeles Times,* for example, carried a headline that said: "Reentering College: Older Women Battle to Become Coeds Again."

Women's identities tend to be defined in terms of their relationship to men. Thus, they are often subject to being described as someone's wife (sometimes their name may not even be used), or as being single or married in contexts in which men would not be so identified.

Homemaking and parenting are assumed not to be work. Ward cites this example from the *Wall Street Journal*: "The Etelsons were married in 1950, and for the first years of their marriage, Mrs. Etelson operated a cafeteria in an industrial plant. She *stopped working* between 1958 and 1961 to care for her two young daughters." The emphasis has been added.

Finally, as women enter into job markets traditionally reserved for men, many journalists succumb to the temptation to contrast female subjects to the stereotype they hold in their minds. The churchgoing, neighborly housewife is contrasted with the woman who now also acts as a corporate vice-president. Again, sensitivity is the key: would the same contrast be posed for a male? Such contrasts suggest a gee-whiz attitude especially prevalent among male reporters: "Gee-whiz, isn't it great she can do a man-sized job?"

Neglect still plays a major role in the media's treatment of women's issues. Women's conferences do not get the same kind of serious treatment as do men's, and when they are covered, debates that would be considered serious policy discussions at male-dominated meetings become "splits" or "fractures" or "catty disputes" at women's conferences.

When the Equal Rights Amendment was being considered by the Illinois state legislature, several women fasted for days trying to encourage ratification. Most of the media ignored them, in great contrast to a fast a few months earlier by male Irish terrorists. Some of the stories that were published focused more on the comments of male doctors about the effects of the fast on the women's bodies than upon the women's explanations and feelings about what they were doing.

Of course, journalistic reports often succumb to the disease of not taking women seriously, too. At the beginning of the women's movement, the term *women's libbers* was used occasionally to categorize those in the movement, even though reference to *black libbers* or *Cuban libbers* would have been unthinkable. The term continues to be used on occasion by columnists or editorialists who would never be allowed to engage in the kind of anti-Semitism or racism that would be suggested by similar demeaning references.

To cover women's news, then, a male or female reporter (being female does not automatically guarantee a sensitivity to stereotypes) needs to examine closely his or her personal stereotypes about women and to work consciously against the kind of neglect that has been the status quo. In 1975, the International Women's Year Commission suggested ten guidelines, addressed both to the structure of employment in the news media and the content of articles and broadcasts:

1. The media should strive to employ women in policymaking positions. That has been happening slowly in the past decade, but women holding influential positions still tend to be located on the smaller media (lower pay, less experience required, less prestige). The women placed in those positions should be sensitive to the changing roles that American women have begun adopting.

2. Women in the media should hold jobs at all levels and be paid equally for work of equal value. Often women performing work equivalent to that of men have been paid less.

3. The definition of *news* should be expanded so that there will be more coverage of women, and general news stories should attempt to include effects of certain action upon women. The commission noted, for example, that stories about foreign aid might note its impact on women in developing countries, and stories about public transportation might examine effects upon women's mobility and their ability to take jobs.

4. Deliberate, sustained efforts should be made to report news of women.

5. Placement of stories or broadcast reports should be based upon subject matter, not sex. Women's news should not be segregated but, rather, "treated with the same dignity, scope, and accuracy as is news of men."

6. News and feature coverage, as well as advertisements, should not use women's bodies just to add sexual interest.

7. Personal details that are irrelevant to a story, such as those referring to an individual's appearance, sex, religious, or political orientation,

should be eliminated for *both* men and women.

8. Titles should be minimized, but when they are used, an individual should be able to choose whether to be referred to as Ms., Miss, or Mrs.

9. Gender references should be avoided as much as possible, so that words such as *firefighters* substitute for *firemen, mail carriers* for *mailmen, police* or *patrol officers* for *policemen.*

10. Women's organizations and activities should receive the same respect as those of men. *Women's libbers* is a derogatory term, for example, as is *black libbers* or *Palestinian libbers.* Jokes should not be made at the expense of any group.

A journalist seeking ways to avoid sexist language would do well to consult a book such as *The Handbook of Nonsexist Writing,* by Casey Miller and Kate Swift. They offer countless examples of both the subtle and not-so-subtle forms of sexist language as well as ways of correcting the language.

One final note is in order about the effect of sexism in the media. Journalists are now being challenged to look at the *reverse* effects of the kinds of images that have been created of women by the media, and to do so by looking at the kinds of images that have been created of men. Segregating women's activities has also enclosed men within half a world. Men are defined as being interested in politics, business, and sports – and not in cooking (unless it be barbequing), personal health, fashion, or emotions. Indeed, the media have tended to support an image of the man as an unsmiling Marlboro cowboy – tough, decisive, logical, self-confident – by often demeaning those who did not live up to the image. When Sen. Edmund Muskie, running for president, once cried at the end of a particularly long campaign day, during which a conservative newspaper publisher had attacked Muskie's wife in an especially virulent editorial, the press immediately raised questions about his suitability for the presidency, arguing that he had shown weakness. On another occasion, when a group of 100 or so men gathered to discuss their feelings about their jobs, their sexuality, and their upbringing as boys, a woman reporter for the *Seattle Weekly* blistered them as "wimps" who probably could not wash their own clothes.

News, of course, is often defined by masculine values. The choice of a few male union leaders to call a strike of teachers is news because it entails conflict and battle (presumed to be male traits) while the day-to-day education of students by female elementary school teachers, entailing the kinds of inner tensions and excitements that constitute growth (a female value), is not news.

Guidelines adopted by the McGraw-Hill Book Company for treating men and women in its books contain valuable suggestions for journalists who tend to approach either reporting or writing in a manner that reinforces stereotypes:

> Members of both sexes should be represented as whole human beings with *human* strengths and weaknesses, not masculine or feminine ones. Women and girls should be shown as having the same abilities, interests, and ambitions as men and boys. Characteristics that have been praised in females—such as gentleness, compassion and sensitivity—should also be praised in males.
>
> Like men and boys, women and girls should be portrayed as independent, active, strong, courageous, competent, decisive, persistent, serious-minded, and successful. They should appear as logical thinkers, problem solvers and decision makers. They should be shown as interested in their work, pursuing a variety of career goals, and both deserving of and receiving public recognition for their accomplishments.
>
> Sometimes men should be shown as quiet and passive, or fearful and indecisive, or illogical and immature. Similarly, women should sometimes be shown as tough, aggressive, and insensitive. Stereotypes of the logical male and the emotional, subjective female are to be avoided. . . .

Covering racial and ethnic groups remains the core of most minority affairs reporting.

> It is always the minorities that hold the key of progress; it is always through those who are unafraid to be different that advance comes to human society.
> —RAYMOND B. FOSDICK

Traditionally, to speak of minority affairs coverage has been to speak of the treatment of racial and ethnic groups, most especially blacks, Hispanics, Asian-Americans, and native Americans. The National Commission on Civil Disorders (also known as the Kerner Commission, after Otto Kerner, who chaired it) delivered the most succinct statement on the media's coverage of such minorities. In 1982 a major study on the status of such minorities in newsrooms and in news coverage reiterated what the Kerner Commission had said fourteen years before: journalists have a professional responsibility to cease looking at the world through a "white man's" perspective.

The 1982 study, conducted by the American Society of Newspaper Editors (ASNE) in conjunction with the Medill School of Journalism at Northwestern University, also arrived at the bleak conclusion that the passage of fourteen years since the Kerner Commission report had not really changed much. Despite some gains in the numbers of minorities employed in newsrooms, the yearly percentage of gain actually seemed to be slowing. Blacks and Hispanics especially were under-represented in college-level journalism programs, and numerous editors saw no reason — no "professional imperative"—to seek out minority reporters. That, the report said, was unfortunate because the improvement of minority coverage seemed to best occur when minority reporters were included on news staffs.

Fourteen years after the Kerner Commission report, William Jones, managing editor of the *Chicago Tribune,* told the preparers of the ASNE report that his newspaper's coverage of the black community was "nowhere near adequate." Acel Moore, associate editor of the *Philadelphia Inquirer,* commented that if he were asked whether his newspaper covered blacks adequately, the answer would be "an unequivocable no." A reporter for the *San Diego Union* said that that city's large Hispanic community and its news were "unknown territory to editors, and they really don't want anything to do with it."

Though a nation composed of many racial and ethnic minorities, the United States and American society has often equivocated in its attitudes. The image of the country as a giant "melting pot" into which separate groups will be plunged and homogenized remains strong, so that differences are distrusted. In *Racial Oppression in America,* sociologist Robert Blauner has argued that a strong "assimilationist bias" pervades the work of many American academics and Americans themselves. Minorities, which may initially be seen as competitors by the dominant groups, are supposed to find a way to accommodate themselves to American society and then be assimilated. Many a journalist goes into stories with such an approach, perhaps examining ways in which illegal Hispanic immigrants supposedly take jobs away from whites, or the manner in which a ghetto-ized minority community is assumed to be able to assimilate itself.

For example, though the initial waves of refugees arriving from Indochina or from Cuba in the 1970s and 1980s received heavy coverage, once those groups passed a certain stage in which they were assumed to be accommodating themselves to American society, coverage faded. The refugees were assumed to have entered into the long period of assimilation, not newsworthy in itself.

It is the "assimilationist bias" that leads journalists into that first form of discrimination: neglect. A reporter who assumes that a minority group is being assimilated thereby also tends to assume that no special coverage of that minority is needed.

The reporter also tends to assume that there is only a single possible viewpoint on news, and that once minorities have been sufficiently assimilated, they will be covered automatically, just as whites are. To engage in any special coverage, then — to suggest that special efforts to cover the news of minority communities need to be made, or to argue that a journalist might be professionally required to seek out a "black perspective" – appears artificial and contrived. The ASNE report, for example, quotes one editor who explains that no effort has been made to recruit minorities because "the purpose of a small town newspaper is to inform readers and to serve the community, not to embark on social engineering."

Certainly some of the controversies that arise today, such as disputes about whether schools in areas with large Hispanic populations should provide bilingual and bicultural programs, are fights rooted in the question of whether and how much minorities should assimilate. American society has tended to be most comfortable when cultural differences can be reduced to tourist attractions: when Indian ceremonies become powwows open to the public, Irish sentiments are restricted to St. Patrick's Day marches, and Hispanics hold Cinco de Mayo celebrations.

The first step for a journalist, then, particularly an Anglo one, may be reflecting upon ways to challenge what may be an assimilationist bias. Did the last story about welfare cuts take a particular look at effects upon the Indochinese, or did it report "average" figures? Do stories about the purchase of new elongated buses to serve the suburbs with high-speed, freeway transit runs also take note of what kind of buses are being placed on the inner-city routes? Are the food pages oriented only toward the eating customs of an Anglo middle class?

The reality is that although many minorities do assimilate, many do not do so to the degree that America's dominant groups like to assume. Also, many assimilate only at a cost of great suffering physically and psychologically. Most of this goes completely untreated by a news media, which may be part of the harm. Certainly the forcible attempts made to assimilate native Americans cost that group many, many lives, not only during the conquest of the tribes but in the following decades when federal policy severed children from their families to send them to distant boarding schools and encouraged men and women to move away from the reservations. As James and Sharon Murphy point out in *Let My People Know*, "during that long period of Indian anguish and tribulation (which lasted almost sixty years) little coverage of Indian affairs or events was provided by white newspapers."

Similarly, blacks have not been assimilated successfully into American society. Unemployment and underemployment among blacks always runs substantially higher than among whites. Pay is lower. Perspectives are far different.

At times – especially in the 1960s, for example – American society has confronted this reality that certain groups do not assimilate and has responded with the notion that such assimilation stalls because of the prejudice of individuals in the dominant groups. Blauner argues that such a theory is as simplistic as the assimilationist bias and that those who hold such a preconception—including journalists—end up seeing only a distorted and crabbed view of reality.

In an attempt to explain why racism persists even as laws are passed to ensure equality and opinion surveys show declines in racial prejudice and stereotyped thinking in past decades, Blauner writes that "prejudiced attitudes are not the essence of racism." "Racism," he argues, "is institutionalized. The processes that maintain domination—control of whites over nonwhites—are built into the major social institutions." For example, conventional procedures may exclude all but those who have successfully mastered the elements of Anglo language and culture. Journalism departments in universities may attract few blacks and Hispanics not because the instructors and administrators are prejudiced, but because the news media has not covered those communities. Thus interest among blacks and Hispanics in working in journalism has not been stimulated much; then too, blacks and Hispanics do not hold to the "white perspective" dominant in newsrooms.

A journalist, then, who adopts assimilationist and prejudice theories may totally overlook stories of vital importance to minority communities as well as the reason for doing such stories. Minority coverage demands serious questioning of customs and structures that perpetuate racism, and it demands that journalists avoid the attitude of one editor quoted in the ASNE study. Explaining why he made no effort to recruit minorities, the editor said, "I do not think I should. I have never persecuted a Negro. Neither has anyone in my family. I feel no guilt."

Far better that journalists adopt the attitude expressed by Larry Green, a bureau chief for the *Los Angeles Times,* in the same study: "We have to, in our reporting, tell people that these [minority] issues are not issues of color or race but they are issues of the community. We all share one small patch of ground."

Clearly, reporting with understanding includes a professional imperative not only to go into the minority communities to report their news, but to go into the dominant communiity and reveal those structures that continue to perpetuate racism, sexism, homophobia—biases of all kinds that interfere with the struggle by different peoples for respect and acceptance.

EXERCISES

1. Often the best source for information about a minority community is that community's own press. Seek out a nearby minority press and examine the issues covered. Does a black press exist? A feminist press? A gay press? Are the issues they are covering getting exposure on mainstream publications and broadcast

outlets of your region? (If no such press exists in your area, find out why. Examine a *national* minority publication for blacks, Hispanics, native Americans, gay men and lesbian women, etc.)

2. Invite some of the journalists who work for a minority press to speak to your class, or interview them individually. What are their perspectives on journalism? Do they see themselves trying to accomplish the same goals as the larger publications and broadcast stations? Often you may find that they have more of a community-building notion of journalism, similar in concept to that common in Third World countries and different from the kind of adversarial notions held by journalists in the mainstream press. What kinds of issues have they covered? How do they view coverage of the same issues by the dominant news media?

3. Journalism departments have been criticized as being training grounds for elites who write for elites. Examine your own department. How many minorities are represented? What is the thrust of the courses? Carry the examination further and explore what your university is doing to offset structural racism or sexism. What positions do blacks and women hold, for example? Does the recruiting office recruit in primarily minority high schools as much as in white high schools? Is information about black history, women's history, gay history, etc., available on campus? In what form is it available—incorporated into regular classes or covered in special classes? Interview minorities in your area to find out how they feel about the educational resources available. You may choose either to discuss your findings in class or to publish them in your student or local press.

4. Find a minority reporter, or an acquaintance who is a member of a minority group, who will allow you to accompany them on some of their rounds. If you are a member of a minority group yourself, find a member of a different minority group to accompany. Being such a spectator may be uncomfortable for you and for others, but journalists can only hope to broaden their perspectives by experience as well as by reflection. Go to a gay men's bar; go also to a more nurturing type of gay gathering, such as a counseling group or a potluck. Similarly, go to the black neighborhoods, the Asian neighborhoods, the native American gatherings—not to ogle as if they are people different from yourself, but to break down any stereotypes you might have. Remember: Anglos are not the only people with stereotypes. Often one minority group has just as many stereotypes about another as the dominant society has.

5. Get a copy of the May/June 1980 *Columbia Journalism Review* and take the "Check out your sexism" quiz prepared by Jean Ward. It contains a number of excerpts from stories that reveal sexist presumptions.

6. Check the census to see what percentages of minority groups live in your region, then conduct a content analysis of the local press. How many minority issues are covered? How many times do minority group members get mentioned? Does the coverage seem reasonable in light of the size of the groups?

7. Interview reporters and editors of the mainstream press in your region. Have they made efforts to hire minority reporters or increase minority coverage? Do they feel any need to do so? Do they think that news is "colorless" or "sexless" and so should be equally appealing to all groups?

Index